READING AMERICA

A VOLUME IN THE SERIES
Studies in Print Culture and the History of the Book

Edited by
GREG BARNHISEL
ROBERT A. GROSS
JOAN SHELLEY RUBIN
MICHAEL WINSHIP

Reading America

*Citizenship, Democracy,
and Cold War Literature*

KRISTIN L. MATTHEWS

University of Massachusetts Press
Amherst & Boston

Copyright © 2016 by University of Massachusetts Press
All rights reserved
Printed in the United States of America

ISBN 978-1-62534-235-5 (paper); 234-8 (hardcover)

Designed by Jack Harrison
Set in Adobe Garamond Pro with Century Schoolbook display

Cover design by Sally Nichols
Front cover graphic from a 1963 National Library Week poster

Library of Congress Cataloging-in-Publication Data
Names: Matthews, Kristin L., 1973– author.
Title: Reading America : citizenship, democracy, and Cold War literature / Kristin L. Matthews.
Other titles: Citizenship, democracy, and Cold War literature
Description: Amherst : University of Massachusetts Press, 2016. | Series: Print culture and the history of the book | Includes bibliographical references and index.
Identifiers: LCCN 2016031023 | ISBN 9781625342355 (pbk. : alk. paper) | ISBN 9781625342348 (hardcover : alk. paper)
Subjects: LCSH: American literature—20th century—History and criticism. | Books and reading—Social aspects—United States—History—20th century. | Literature and society—United States—History—20th century. | Cold War in literature. | Politics and literature. | Identity (Psychology) in literature. | Citizenship in literature. | Democracy in literature.
Classification: LCC PS3613.A8488 R43 2016 | DDC 810.9/0054—dc23
LC record available at https://lccn.loc.gov/2016031023

British Library Cataloguing-in-Publication Data
A catalog record for this book is available from the British Library.

For my family

Contents

Preface ix

Introduction: "There Is Much to Be Gained by Our Reading" 1

1. America Reads: Literacy and Cold War Nationalism 10

2. Reading for Character, Community, and Country: J. D. Salinger's *The Catcher in the Rye* 32

3. Reading to Outmaneuver: Ralph Ellison's *Invisible Man* and African American Literacy in Cold War America 53

4. Reading against the Machine: Oedipa Maas and the Quest for Democracy in Thomas Pynchon's *The Crying of Lot 49* 80

5. Metafiction and Radical Democracy: Getting at the Heart of John Barth's *Lost in the Funhouse* 106

6. Confronting Difference, Confronting Difficulty: Culture Wars, Canon Wars, and Maxine Hong Kingston's *The Woman Warrior* 131

Conclusion: "Reading Makes a Country Great" 154

Notes 161

Index 197

Preface

The seed of this book was planted in the Midwest. I grew up in the shadow of the Wisconsin state capitol and the University of Wisconsin at Madison, where I heard tales of Senator Robert "Fighting Bob" La Follete, Senator Joseph McCarthy, and the student protests of the 1960s and 1970s. My school librarian taught me about Wisconsin's storied commitment to education, libraries, and literacy and about how great writers such as Lorraine Hansberry, Eudora Welty, Jean Toomer, and Saul Bellow had attended "our university" just down the road. My parents had also attended the University of Wisconsin, embracing its motto about light, knowledge, and public service and turning our home into a house of learning. I read books at an alarming rate, making frequent trips to my small but determined public library branch. I loved reading and felt it to be part of my heritage and duty as a Wisconsin Badger. The more I read, the more I became interested in what, how, and why others read.

It seems clichéd that a person who has been reading for longer than she can remember should write a book about this pastime, but at some point my enthusiasm for reading turned to an interest in the relationship between reading and citizenship during the Cold War. Although reading and democracy have been fused since before America's founding, the injunction to be a good reader, and therefore a good citizen, took on different dimensions after the victories and upheavals of World War II. I know many scholars have explored reading's role in U.S. Cold War foreign policy, but few have looked at how reading influenced and was shaped by what was happening on the home front. Thus, in this book I have chosen to map out the ways in which postwar Americans from across the political spectrum—"great works" proponents, New Critics, New York intellectuals, civil rights leaders, student radicals, postmodern theorists, feminists, neoconservatives, and others—valorized particular texts and promoted particular interpretive methods as they worked to make their vision of America a reality.

The seed planted in my youth took root and grew when I returned to the University of Wisconsin at Madison to work with Thomas Schaub, Nellie McKay, Paul Boyer, Stanley Kutler, James Danky, and Louise Robbins—scholars whose archives and archival knowledge opened me to new ways of thinking about Cold War literature, reading, print culture, and citizenship. I immersed myself in the university's excellent library system, finding more than I needed at Memorial Library and the Library and Information Sciences Library as well as at the Wisconsin State Historical Society. My work on this book came to fruition at Brigham Young University, where I have benefited from the Harold B. Lee Library and Special Collections as well as from the generous conference and research support extended by the College of Humanities and the English department. Because of this support, I have been able to develop my theories on Cold War reading and citizenship at various symposia and conferences, including the national meetings of the Modern Language Association, the American Studies Association, the Reception Study Society, the American Culture Association, and the International Society for the Study of Narrative. The resulting feedback has helped me to focus my research and to publish various articles related to it. A portion of chapter 4 appeared in "A Mad Proposition in Postwar America," *Journal of American Culture* 30, no. 2 (2007), and is used here with permission of John Wiley and Sons. Likewise, a version of chapter 5 was published as "A Paranoid's Guide to Reading America: Reading Reading in Thomas Pynchon's *The Crying of Lot 49*," *Arizona Quarterly* 68, no. 2 (2012), and appears here by permission of the Regents of the University of Arizona.

Perhaps even more important are the human resources—scholars, mentors, and colleagues—who have inspired, informed, motivated, and challenged various parts of this project, reading draft after draft and helping me to become a better scholar, thinker, and person. My book would not exist without Thomas Schaub, a gentleman and a scholar, who has been my most rigorous reader and my most constant supporter. My gratitude also goes to Jacques Lezra, David Fleming, Louise Robbins, James Danky, and the late Paul Boyer and Nellie McKay for their direction and feedback during the book's earliest stages. I am grateful, too, to Walter Benn Michaels and Jennifer Ashton, who read an early version of the introduction, posed hard questions, and pushed me in the right direction.

Throughout my academic career I have been fortunate to be surrounded by some of the greatest minds of my generation. Without them, this book would not have happened. Thanks go to Michael LeMahieu, Steven Belletto, Matthew Stratton, Elizabeth Rivlin, Janine Tobeck, Mitchum Huehls, John Tiedemann, Jack Opel, Elizabeth Miller, Matthew Hussey, Thomas Crofts, Kimberly Rostan, Sara Hosey, and the rest of my Madison crew for pushing me intellectually, supporting me emotionally, and always having a killer karaoke song on the ready. Upon arriving in the mountains of the West, I found yet another supportive group of scholars. I am indebted to Phillip Snyder, Frank Christianson, Robert Colson, Peter Leman, Edward Cutler, Elise Silva, Rachel Ligairi, Riley Lorimer-Reznik, and James David Fife for reading chapter drafts and offering transformative questions and suggestions. In addition, thanks go to my colleagues Dennis Perry, Matthew Ancell, Steven Tuttle, Brandie Siegfried, Julianne Newmark Engberg, George Handley, and Dean John Rosenberg for their unflagging encouragement and support. Even when I doubted myself and this project, they did not.

I've also had the opportunity to learn from and with great scholars of book history, print culture, and reception studies. In addition to those already mentioned, my thanks go to Catherine Turner, Greg Barnhisel, Erin Smith, and Trysh Travis. I am grateful for their work, for their feedback on my work, for the lively conversations we've had at conferences, and for their tutelage as I have entered the wonderful world of book history.

This book would not be what it is without the guidance of Brian Halley. I cannot imagine working with a more careful, thoughtful, and patient editor. Thanks also to the anonymous readers of this manuscript: this is a better book because of your rigorous reading and generous feedback.

To my friends in Madison and Provo and around the globe, thank you for the food, the conversation, the "getting Kristin out of the house and away from the laptop" interventions, and the constant belief that I could be not just a reader but also a writer of books. To my Provo family, the Ashes, and my Salt Lake family, the Johnsons, thank you for your love and faith. To Kimberly Johnson, thank you for being my sister, my cheerleader, my rational voice, and my friend. To my parents, thank you for reading to me even when you didn't want to and for never doubting my abilities. To my stepparents, thank you for being patient and generous with this absent-minded professor you've inherited. To my grandparents, both here and gone—Neale Hoeft, Joyce Hoeft, Wendell Matthews, Shirley Matthews, and Janet Sayer Hoeft—thank you for being readers and for encouraging me to read. To my sisters, thank you for being my constant in this world. You remind me about what is really important in this life, and you keep me humble even as you buoy me. Finally, to Connor, Parker, Oliver, and Greta, may you always love books and know that I love you.

READING AMERICA

Introduction

"There Is Much to Be Gained by Our Reading"

In September 1951, the U.S. Department of Agriculture sponsored a conference to address a purported national reading crisis.[1] The participants represented a cross-section of American citizenry: renowned educators, prominent politicians, leading publishers, concerned homemakers, rural and urban librarians, and farmers. Linking potential increases in agricultural production to improved reading capacity, the federal organizers asserted a causal relationship between the intellectual fruits of reading and the literal fruits of one's labor. Throughout the conference, participants celebrated reading as both an American product and a means to produce a better America.

Two years later, the conference organizers published *The Wonderful World of Books*. The driving faith behind this much-heralded text was best articulated by Mrs. Charles W. Slater in her chapter "I Belong to a Discussion Group," where she claimed that reading would cultivate the American spirit and make it grow. Representing the average American homemaker and farmwife, Mrs. Slater testified that "we need to show the world that democracy can work and that spiritual integrity does pay, and if we don't do this, our Christian civilization may soon be doomed. . . . Trial and error may take us in the wrong direction, so there is much to be gained by our reading—reading the right things—and by the exchange of ideas."[2] By attesting to the power of "reading the right things" and its ability to fortify America's citizens, she verbalized what would become a cultural leitmotif of the 1950s. Indeed, the whole of *The Wonderful World of Books* affirmed that good reading would teach, guide, and enlighten the population about how to do their democratic duty. At the same time, its contributors placed great emphasis on how and why someone reads, suggesting that reading methods were just as important as content in terms of literacy's power to form citizens and preserve democracy.

By investing reading with the power to spread democracy and fortify America, *The Wonderful World of Books* helped forward an unprecedented national reading endeavor. The collection's contributors linked reading and democracy, as did many other Cold War reading advocates, including *Time* magazine's editor, Carl Solberg. In "You, Citizen-Reader in a Democracy," he offered a multi-pronged argument for why reading was central to the idea and civic health of America. First, it prepared an individual American "to speak his informed and considered opinion" in day-to-day happenings and "whenever he votes in elections." Second, it helped Americans understand their national government and "the global size, nowadays, of its responsibilities." Third, it allowed Americans to "see the wider meaning of what our eyes have told us" about "how differently people live" in America and elsewhere. Ultimately, Solberg claimed, "a good citizen is a good reader"—that is, an informed person is "an alert member of the American democracy."[3]

The scope of this ambitious national project is revealed in the broad and varied chapters of *The Wonderful World of Books*. By detailing specific programs and literacy efforts targeting foreign readers, young readers, adult readers, returning readers, rural readers, librarians, writers, and publishers, the book was able to address both real and ideal citizen-readers. Section titles such as "Books Are Friends," "Books Look Upward," "Reading More Effectively," "City and Country," "Reading for Citizens," "Toward Wider Horizons," "Libraries Are For You," and "Books for Everyone" mapped out plans for a version of manifest destiny, one that would extend reading throughout the nation and into the four corners of the globe—a mission that supported Cold War America's aim to spread democracy throughout the planet. Participants celebrated books because they introduced readers to a new world, but they also saw books as a way to understand and win the Cold War. According to the conference and the text's contributors, books offered a solution to the myriad perceived threats (both foreign and domestic) associated with the era's geopolitics. Calling the book a labor of love and patriotic duty—"the responsibility for it rests on us as citizens"—the authors worked to guide Americans towards personal and national stability.[4]

They were not alone: "reading" was the watchword on nearly everyone's lips during the Cold War, and a postwar cultural fascination with and commitment to reading defined America and Americanness during the era. As the afterglow of World War II faded, the reality of the changed world caused both policymakers and average Americans considerable uncertainty and concern. The perceived threat of global communism, the shifting gender codes triggered by the nation's many "Rosie the Riveters," the refusal of African American veterans to accept Jim Crow America, the rise of a new middle class, the increased rates of postwar immigration, and an upsurge of juvenile delinquency all challenged postwar hopes for easy stability and tranquility. Significantly, reading was proposed as a panacea that could bring about national and international peace. From the schoolhouse, to the White House, to the publishing house, people promoted reading as both the fruit and the mechanism for spreading democracy. As I show in this book, they saw it as a method of socializing and acculturating immigrants and foreign visitors, a means of narrativizing and actualizing national unity, and a central way to define and defend America.[5]

In the immediate postwar period, scores of books by reading experts and amateurs alike flooded the American marketplace, most of them attempts to develop good citizen-readers and fortify democracy at home and abroad. Yet the link between reading and democracy was neither new nor unique to Cold War America, and it was rooted in a revered part of U.S. history. Even before the nation formally existed, religious, political, and cultural leaders had identified reading as an activity that could constitute and secure America. Puritan leader Cotton Mather wrote *Bonifacius* (1710) in part to stress reading's importance to national strength and personal salvation. Benjamin Franklin similarly underscored the importance of literacy in his *Autobiography*, claiming that his American Subscription Library had "improv'd the general Conversation of the Americans, made the common Tradesman & Farmers as intelligent as most Gentlemen from other Countries, and perhaps have contributed in some degree to the Stand so generally made throughout the Colonies in Defense of their Privileges." Founding father John Adams also linked literacy and democracy, claiming that "Liberty cannot be preserved without a general knowledge among the people, who have a right . . . and a desire to know." In 1859, Abraham Lincoln, then a senator from Illinois, said, "A capacity, and taste, for reading, gives access to whatever has already been discovered by others. It is the key, or one of the keys, to the already solved problems. And not only so. It gives a relish, and facility, for successfully pursuing the [yet] unsolved ones." Likewise, a significant piece of WWII propaganda quotes President Franklin D. Roosevelt as saying, "Books cannot be killed by fire. People die, but books never die. No man and no force can put thought in a concentration camp forever. No man and no force can take from the world the books that embody man's eternal fight against tyranny. In this war, we know, books are weapons." As Benedict Anderson details in *Imagined Communities*, since the early eighteenth century, the Americas have pioneered nation formation with their use of print-capitalism to create a "new consciousness" and republican identity from a diverse body of peoples.[6]

Cold War reading initiatives and rhetorics drew from this lettered history and cultural inheritance. Proponents saw reading as the mechanism by which individuals and the nation might once again negotiate political and social uncertainty and come out victorious. Yet postwar America differed from previous periods; now its uncertainty was wedded to seemingly unlimited power. Thus, in *Books, Young People, and Reading Guidance,* Geneva Hanna and Mariana McAllister reminded teachers and young readers that America's position is one of "freedom accompanied with great responsibility." Senator Lister Hill made a similar observation: "Freedom carries its own responsibility, perhaps a heavier one than if freedom were absent."[7] The United States emerged from World War II as a global force and world leader, and with that new position came an even greater urgency to cultivate an informed and intelligent citizenry. To those in positions of political and social power, the idea of America and American ideas were central to securing the confidence of allies abroad and preventing the spread of global communism. Never before had the United States faced such geopolitical responsibility and possibility, and never before had the stakes of reading well seemed higher.

The national and international scope of Cold War America's reading endeavors, the improved mechanics of mass printing and dissemination, a greatly expanded reading audience, and the unprecedented diversity of stakeholders also differentiated the era's reading push. No longer were reading advocates limited to a single political party, economic class, or intellectual faction. Instead, they represented all facets of the nation's political, economic, social, and educational spectrums. While some efforts, such as *The Wonderful World of Books,* were coordinated, most were independent but overlapping actions that tapped into a common cultural concern; and together they created a discursive network of sorts. The national turn toward reading was evidenced in texts and initiatives forwarded by both anti-Communists and Communists, both highbrow intellectuals and comic-book purveyors, both college educators and do-it-yourself gurus, both white supremacists and civil rights workers, both traditionalists and feminists, both conservatives and radicals. All looked to reading as a way through which a young but powerful nation could embrace, magnify, and perfect its national ideals. To promote and preserve democracy in this new "cold" world, reading guides and political texts attempted to define an American tradition of letters, cultivate a current reading public, and engender lifetime learning.

As a term, *Cold War* is simultaneously historical, political, ideological, and romantic. At its most basic level, it is a historical marker, designating a particular period in America's history: 1945–1991. This temporal definition frames the second, more ideologically driven and commonly invoked definition: the geopolitical tension between the United States and the Soviet Union that dominated foreign policy and America's cultural imagination during the latter half of the twentieth century. The nation's comprehensive campaign to promote democracy and prevent the spread of international communism took place on rhetorical battlegrounds and in very real locales such as Korea, Cuba, and Vietnam. These battles were intimately tied to a third definition of Cold War: the struggle in postwar America to delineate *the good American*. Often characterized as a war of words, the Cold War triggered a scramble among stakeholders to compose the "best" story and thus attract allies, strengthen borders, and defeat the enemy. The United States and the Soviet Union battled to narrate their political ideologies in ways that demonstrated how each system of government—democracy or communism—could best serve the citizen-reader. A "winning" articulation of political philosophy or national values would capture the most readers and help win the war.

More recently, scholars of Cold War studies have begun to address the domestic skirmishes involved in defining nation, self, and other during the tempestuous era. Like Steven Belletto, Julia Mickenberg, Leerom Medovoi, Christina Klein, and Mary Dudziak, I, too, have moved beyond the theories of containment culture that dominated Cold War studies in the 1990s to examine the multifaceted definitional struggles of the period.[8] More than a binary us-them struggle, Cold War politics involved inter- and intragroup efforts to answer questions such as, What does it mean to be American? What are exceptionally American values? Who qualifies as an American? What is the meaning of *nation*? What does citizenship require? What are the demands and rewards of political participation? These and other questions haunted the sociopolitical landscape of postwar America, suggesting that the nation was not only struggling to define democracy in the face of communism but also engaging in a complicated internal battle to frame the terms of citizenship and nationhood amid a changing set of political, social, and economic realities.

Reading took on multiple meanings and functions as it played its complex part in Cold War America's definitional struggles. On one level, the term invoked the physical and cognitive processes involved in interpreting print, and postwar calls for better reading addressed citizens' ability to understand literature and other written materials. On a second level, as anti-Communists, civil rights activists, student radicals, feminists, neoconservatives, and others sought to attain or maintain power, their political discourses about reading used, reused, and reframed the language of literacy. Each group hoped that good readers would be able to shape and promote its particular definition of democracy. Indeed, the private act of reading was publicized as the key to national security and success. On a third level, reading was a social act that stabilized or destabilized conventional social structures established by economics, race, gender, or geography. Reading proponents touted literacy as both a springboard to improved social status and a mechanism for preserving conventional sociality. Citizen-readers were instructed to turn their interpretive gaze inward to read themselves and analyze how they did or did not fit into particular cultural narratives, therein revealing a psychological dimension to literacy. Thus, the multiple valences of reading reflected, engaged, and perpetuated the era's anxieties about national security, class mobility, racial integration, mass culture, middle-class consumerism, shifting gender roles, and Americans' evolving relationship to Judeo-Christian values. All of these concerns affected national efforts to unite the home front and "bring to peoples abroad a true concept of America as a champion of democracy."[9]

It seems that nearly everyone was talking about reading during the Cold War. Yet to see literature as merely an object or a weapon is to overlook how writers themselves envisioned and represented reading's role in postwar America. As literacy experts, political pundits, and social theorists were focusing on the personal and national benefits of reading literature, touchstone literary texts were also exploring it as an individual and sociopolitical act. Cold War literature is riddled with examples of characters who are reading books, talking about books, or using literacy as a political act. These texts demonstrate a self-consciousness about reading that goes beyond simple thematics or characterization. Rather, they demonstrate how the cognitive, political, social, and psychological mechanics of literacy worked to corroborate, complicate, or challenge the ideological and institutional foundations of Cold War democracy. Many texts saw literacy and democracy as inextricably linked, claimed that "free thought" is an American heritage, and suggested that the country would "find its way to a human path" by reading.[10] Other texts identified a more problematic dimension in the link between literacy and nationalism, noting that literature could be used to exclude or constrain certain people and populations. Whether it echoed, contested, or revised definitions or assumptions, Cold War literature used the concept of reading to examine ideas of self, nation, and other and therein compose an ideal of America and Americanness.

In many Cold War texts, literacy and literature represent democracy and freedom in its best form. Whether it is Richard Wright's introduction to "new realms of feeling" or the incurable "reading fever" that Saul Bellow's title character experiences in *The Adventures of Augie March,* Cold War literature self-consciously addresses the ways in which reading frees the individual and exposes him to new worlds of possibility. At the same time, American literature of the era underscores reading's social function, highlighting the way in which it promotes a sense of responsibility in its citizen-reader. Both minority and majority writers saw literacy as an act that authorizes individuals to make, shape, or change their societies. For example, the title story in Philip Roth's *Goodbye, Columbus* wrestles with the role that reading and book access play in social advancement and change. J. D. Salinger's *The Catcher in the Rye* invokes reading as an act that can maintain order and provide stability, an analogue of the Museum of Natural History through which the protagonist Holden Caulfield wanders. Like *Catcher*, Ray Bradbury's *Fahrenheit 451* suggests that reading can "restore" the world, helping people become interested in more than themselves and combating the "paste pudding norm" perpetuated in mass culture. Similar arguments appear in the writings of postwar New York intellectuals such as Dwight MacDonald, Bernard Rosenberg, and Clement Greenberg.[11]

Such calls for social responsibility are echoed in more overtly revolutionary texts that equate "socially responsible role[s]" with challenging and transforming American culture's status quo. Thus, *The Autobiography of Malcolm X* argues that the author reads "to help the black man." Norman Mailer's *Armies of the Night* teaches readers how to recognize the military industrial complex's "totalitarian" narratives, which work to eliminate multiplicity and dull individuals' sense of possibility, thereby depriving them of the authority to create their own narratives. Kurt Vonnegut's *Slaughterhouse Five* works to correct the fact that "people [can't] read well enough anymore to turn print into exciting situations in their skulls" and connect to others.[12]

Reading also played a significant role in the formal strategies and experimentations of the Cold War period. As Marshall McLuhan infamously wrote, "the medium is the message." In the course of discussing the social and political import of reading, writers thematized it through formal choices that demand particular types of reading and readership. Some texts, such as John Barth's *Lost in the Funhouse*, aggressively seek out "the reader! You, dogged, uninsultable, print-oriented bastard, it's you I'm addressing." Others, such as Joan Didion's *Democracy*, explicitly incorporate the reader in the process of authoring the text: "you tell me." Bellow's *Augie March* and Ralph Ellison's *The Invisible Man* use modified forms of the picaresque (with its cyclical, or boomerang, structure) to present readers with a pattern and demand they suss out the meaning in what Gertrude Stein once called "repetition with a difference." *The Catcher in the Rye* uses repetitions such as Holden's verbal tics to make readers attend to the veracity of his utterances and interrogate his mode of reading the world. Thomas Pynchon's *The Crying of Lot 49* and Joseph Heller's *Catch-22* construct paranoia-inducing labyrinths of allusions and circuit-blowing catalogues of characters who seduce readers into their ranks. Like Oedipa Maas or John Yossarian, readers begin performing interpretive detective work to find some "transcendent meaning" in a world where "there [is] no way of really knowing anything."[13] In all of these texts, form works to extend greater authority and access to readers, therein attempting to democratize not just what but how people read.

These textual efforts to train readers are similar to those used by the literacy experts, book clubs, culture guides, and government officials who promoted reading during the Cold War. Of course, methods changed as postwar America's political and social climate changed, yet all were concerned with democratizing reading and reading for democracy. Furthermore, readers of postwar fiction were doubly dosed with reading imperatives as they increasingly read about reading in self-conscious and deliberate ways. Thus, these texts are primers that not only teach us about reading's ever-evolving modes but also school us about the shifting sociopolitical ethics of literacy in postwar America. One cannot fully understand the era's literature until one reads it within the context of the reading project of which it was a part.

In this book, I draw from the fields of book history, Cold War studies, library studies, and literary studies to map the continuities and conflicts of these various texts, taking care to identify how form and content operate to theorize reading's larger import in America's story and the story that is America. Although I could easily have catalogued multiple examples, I have chosen to cite a selection of major works, many of which were best sellers or were adopted by schools or significant national organizations.

Chapter 1 establishes the context, demonstrating that a perfect storm of educational, economic, social, and political factors brought reading to the fore during the era. In chapter 2, I consider J. D. Salinger's *The Catcher in the Rye* alongside Cold War reading guides as a way to examine reading's function immediately after World War II. I begin chapter 3 by briefly tracing the history and mythos of African American literacy; I then read Ralph Ellison's *Invisible Man* in the context of postwar civil rights and how activists interrogated and used reading in their struggle.

In chapter 4, I discuss the links between Thomas Pynchon's *The Crying of Lot 49* and emerging radical political and literary theories and argue that the novel represents an important transitional time in postwar American ideas about reading. Chapter 5 examines John Barth's *Lost in the Funhouse* alongside radical student writings and contemporary literary theories, demonstrating that all were part of a larger, dynamic, radical search to redefine interpretive processes and allow individuals increased authority and social connection. Chapter 6 puts Maxine Hong Kingston's *The Woman Warrior* into conversation with feminist and multiculturalist attempts to extend reading's democratizing function in the 1970s and 1980s. I conclude with an examination of reading in post-9/11 America.

In many ways, the struggle to define America and the battle to determine who gets to define it and how lie at the core of our nation's version of democracy. As we continue to work through how we understand ourselves as individuals and citizens, we are practicing democracy's give and take. Thus, reading about reading in Cold War America not only gives us greater insight into the workings of that unique period but also speaks to the larger narrative of reading and writing "America."

1
America Reads
Literacy and Cold War Nationalism

"Consider our country's size and the global size, nowadays, of its responsibilities," invited Carl Solberg in his essay "You, Citizen-Reader in a Democracy." Underscoring the nation's old and new duties in the wake of World War II, he stressed that reading well, widely, and "more self-consciously" was "a way to enlarge our awareness of the national community in which we share" and the larger world of which Cold War Americans were a part. Solberg noted the importance of reading books that "don't just pump information into us" but "provoke us, to think out subjects for ourselves," and he called on Americans to "*Read!* Read a great deal. Read with an open, inquiring mind. Read something about many subjects. . . . Read different kinds of books." By doing so, he asserted, one could become "an alert member of the American democracy," a citizen who could help determine "where our nation goes from here." Like many public figures in the immediate postwar period, Solberg expressed both enthusiasm and nervous uncertainty about the nation's current and future path as an international power. He asked, "Are we in fact prepared?" and wondered whether or not the world would see America as worthy of such "responsibilities."[1] Never voiced but always implied was the threat of what might happen if Americans did not do their duty and read: political immaturity, national insecurity, and global chaos.

Solberg, like many of his contemporaries, saw reading as a way in which Americans could prepare themselves to become responsible citizens of a global superpower. His essay advances what became a predominant postwar discourse and theory of reading: that reading particular texts in the right way could train Americans to understand, practice, defend, and spread democracy across the globe. At their root, Cold War reading initiatives linked America's national security with the nation's ability to author and read itself. While illiteracy was the ostensible foe, the actual enemy was any narrative perceived to threaten particular ideas of Americanness.

On the Cold War's rhetorical battlefront, self-definition was key. Just as the Declaration of Independence was a rhetorical act of self-naming that constituted both the idea and the nation-state of America, postwar acts of self-definition worked to establish the borders of the nation-state and its ideology, including deciding who was a citizen, an ally, or an enemy. According to this logic, outside definitions of America and democracy were attacks on the nation and its way of life. Thus, self-definition was both a weapon against America's detractors and the principle or idea that the Cold War nation-state needed to protect. Because reading shaped and advanced particular ideas of Americanness, it was a key to winning or losing the Cold War.

Reading for Democracy

In the years immediately after World War II, Americans struggled to understand their nation's new position of seemingly unlimited power. Having just won the largest military victory in modern history, the United States found itself in a position of global authority that "brought, along with a sense of power, bewilderment and confusion." These perplexities exacerbated what the scholar and critic Howard Mumford Jones saw as a "deep-seated anxiety to comprehend the responsibility of our culture in the world." Like Jones, many politicians, social thinkers, journalists, and scholars worried about how the international community perceived America and Americans. As the journalist Raymond Daniell wrote, "We are an unknown quantity."[2]

In particular, Cold War Americans worried that the United States lacked cultural and international respect. Pieces such as Daniell's 1947 *New York Times* article, "What the Europeans Think of Us," warned that the country's perceived cultural deficit was a drag on postwar foreign relations: "We have not done a very effective job of explaining ourselves and our motives to Europe." Consequently, "opinion is divided on whether America is a nation of sentimental altruists or of sinister predatory imperialists." Daniell expressed great concern about "America's role as a world power" and its poor job at communicating "what kind of people we really are." Noting that Europeans tended to stereotype Americans as smug, hypocritical, brash, and brutish, he wrote, "There is something wrong with a country, the majority of whose citizens seem to prefer swing music to Beethoven and Bach, don't know the difference between the uses of burgundy and port, but on the whole prefer whiskey with their meals." Daniell concluded that America's national security would suffer because the peoples of the world would not take a nation composed of such citizens seriously as a global leader. As a corrective, he proposed greater use of U.S. Information Centers, better education for G.I.s, and a program that would post visiting dignitaries in strategic European locations to win over "the people." The take-home message was that reading and cultural education would save America's reputation and its interests abroad. Daniell's report and others like it signaled a heightened self-consciousness and the necessity of a self-image that would correspond with the country's new international role.[3]

Exacerbating these concerns was the uncertain nature of America's new enemy. The clearly delineated enemies and battlegrounds of World War II had been replaced by a less easily definable foe—global communism. As the historian Tom Engelhardt has noted, communism was particularly troubling because "it was never fully identified with or contained within any single ethnic or racial community." Neither was there an "obvious rule-of-thumb for isolating Communists by dress, customs, language, or religion; nor, like Japanese-Americans during World War II, could they be rounded up and incarcerated by look." The incompatibility of former epistemological systems, which were based on definite markers that could be identified and classified, with the current political conflict, which was grounded in beliefs and ideological "truths," created great anxiety. George Kennan's infamous "Long Telegram" underscored this shift, warning that the Communist enemy was unlike any other and advising the United States to overhaul its foreign policy, military strategies, and understanding of global alliances if it hoped to defend democracy and its national borders from the encroaching "specter."[4]

The uncertainty generated by the Communist "threat" was compounded by changes in America's social structure at the beginning of the Cold War. With waves of new immigrants, platoons of returning G.I.s, and a burgeoning middle class, the home front was anything but stable. Conventional conceptions of gender, race, and class were eroding the definitions of American and America that had seemed so solid during the war. Although the 1950s are often stereotyped as a golden age of stability or an ominous culture of surveillance, they were actually a period of significant aesthetic, cultural, and social change. Popular narratives that privilege *Leave It to Beaver* conformity or *Crucible*-like containment gloss over the complexity and diversity of this transitional time and its influence on the revolutionary 1960s. The image of white, middle-class, hetero-normative malaise does not correspond to the realities of women or the working class or to racial, ethnic, and sexual minorities, all of whom were challenging the people in power and demanding the right to define themselves as citizens. Their agitations caused great social, cultural, and political variability; Cold War America was marked by "an ambivalence of hope and dread, with which we perceive the explosive forces of change in our society."[5]

Facing instability at home and abroad, political and cultural leaders repeatedly suggested one particular solution: reading. Tapping into familiar American narratives of literacy and freedom, they proposed that reading would combat contemporary "tensions and anxieties" while offering a "new system of controls," ensuring that "personal drives may be expressed in socially desirable fashion, while the well-being of society is promoted." Politicians, educators, and writers recognized that America needed to be able to "'read' the world." Thus, political and social leaders advertised reading's liberating and democratizing potential abroad in efforts to prevent the spread of communism and promoted it as a means of shoring up national defense at home. Columbia University's Ruth Strang argued, "It is in part through reading that decisions of national and international importance are made, sustained, and implemented. . . . [B]etter education is the key to better democracy." This and other postwar reading guides avowed that "good" reading not only provides "ideas useful in our bedeviled condition, but tells us where it is that we live, whence we have come, and what we must now attend to."[6]

Reading advocates repeatedly asserted that "an informed citizenry is basic to a healthy democratic community, and books play an indispensable role in the continuous process of education." Organizations such as the Rockefeller Foundation called for improved reading education because "among the tasks that have increased most frighteningly in complexity is the task of the ordinary citizen who wishes to discharge his civic responsibility intelligently." The Parent-Teacher Association's 1952 manual declared, "Only as Americans are educated can they remain free. A well-informed citizenry is dependent on reading. Books, a universal medium of education, in the schools and out, can help to keep our children free."[7] In a Cold War world, reading was what made Americans "civilize[ed]," "rational," "worthy, happy citizen[s]," and an overall "useful citizenry."[8] The promotion of reading as a civic duty took both prescriptive and proscriptive forms, advocating the "best books" and cautioning citizens about "dangerous" ones that could harm their intellect, psyche, and nation. All of the reading guides offered a warning, either explicitly or implicitly: bad books and reading habits could strike a blow at democracy and undermine America's strength and stability.

To prevent bad books from winning, authorities and reading experts of all stripes emphasized the importance of both what and how Americans should read. The most frequently consulted and best-selling reading guides were written and published by those in positions of cultural power—for instance, by prominent academics such as Mortimer J. Adler, Howard Mumford Jones, and Robert Hutchins; public intellectuals such as Leslie Fiedler, Jacques Barzun, August Heckscher, Frank Jennings, and Clifton Fadiman; and established associations such the American Library Association, the American

Book Publisher's Council, and the National Book Committee. Likewise, political texts on postwar democracy often adopted the language of literacy to educate their readers. Authors of such texts included government figures such as J. Edgar Hoover, Joseph McCarthy, and Robert Stripling as well as professional anti-Communists such as W. Cleon Skousen, Anthony Bouscaren, and the American Legion. These individuals and organizations occupied positions across the political spectrum. Nevertheless, all appealed to ideas and ideals of Americanness in their calls to read, all claimed to be operating in the name of peace, stability, and freedom; and all believed they were operating in the best interest of the nation and its citizen-readers. These stakeholders believed that their books linked reading "to life, liberty, and the pursuit of happiness."[9]

Anyone with even a small stake in reading put out a reading list or guide in the postwar period. The American Library Association, the American Book Publisher's Council, the National Book Committee, and the U.S. Office of Education all developed programs, created reading lists, and adopted a wide range of texts to help citizens attain global literacy. Literary journals, popular magazines, radio shows, reading programs, libraries, academics, and public intellectuals published reading guides. Like Adler's *How to Read a Book* and Fadiman's *The Lifetime Reading Plan*, most of the guides drew from the classics of western literature (works by Homer, Virgil, Dante, Shakespeare, Chaucer, Milton, Pope, and so on) and the so-called "best" of America's own literature. By implying that America was the logical inheritor of the western tradition, the list makers canonized a particular body of American letters and authorized new myths for the Cold War period. They saw American literature as the logical extension and reflection of western civilization's progress, and they forwarded myths of American exceptionalism by celebrating the nation's literature. They praised citizen-readers for adopting the best of the past, rejecting the failures of other cultures, and creating a new story worthy of the country's grand scale. They suggested that democracy was both the culmination of centuries of ideas and the future of great new ideas and that America's duty was to spread and defend these particular narratives.

On the international front, the U.S. government used reading as both a weapon of war and a token of peace. Cold War scholars such as Greg Barnhisel, Amanda Laugesen, Martin Manning, John Hench, Frances Stoner Saunders, Kenneth Osgood, and Nicholas Cull have published significant work on the ways in which the American Library Association, the Council for Books in Wartime, the U.S. Information Agency, the Information Center Service, the Congress for Cultural Freedom, the Franklin Book Programs, and others waged a cultural war abroad. Their goal was to show the Europeans "who we really are," win support from cultural leaders and opinion makers in friendly nations, and convert curious or hostile nations to the American way.[10] As Senator Lister Hill, author of the 1951 Library Service and G.I. bills, argued, "the printed word in its various forms is one of the principal means of interpreting the United States and its democratic principles to the rest of the world."[11]

The U.S. Information Agency's mission statement aligned with Senator Hill's claim. The agency explained that its aim was "to bring to peoples abroad a true concept of America as a champion of democracy—with its inherent concepts of individual freedom" via "selections that most truly represent the United States and that are felt to be of greatest value to certain countries." Distributed materials included anti-Communist pamphlets, "informational" texts about the Communist movement, pro-democracy fiction, and even the Sears, Roebuck catalog, all of which "matched the political and economic interests of the United States." As Amy Laugesen contends, the criteria for agency book selection revealed the stories it was selling: anti-communism, pro-American consumerism and commercialism, and American benevolence in international organizations. This Department of State project was an ambitious undertaking in foreign relations; between July 1950 and February 1953, the agency had reportedly "presented to organizations, libraries, and persons abroad more than 2,350,000 copies of American books," and by 1953 U.S. Information Centers were operating in more than sixty countries.[12]

Altruistic claims about spreading democracy were complicated by the other strategic political aims of U.S. book distribution abroad: establishing American ideological and military power while opening up new commercial markets for cooperating book publishers. Despite his efforts to communicate a democratizing aim to America's Information Center programs, Senator Hill was also describing a prescriptive literacy project, one that would allow the government to control the way in which the world was "interpreting" the United States and what it represented. In Hill's scenario, the "printed word" would not itself be open to interpretation. Thus, while disparaging Communists for disseminating propaganda, the U.S. Information Agency was performing a similar function. It was teaching non-Americans how to desire democracy and its idealized trappings: profitable cities, idyllic agrarian communities, efficient industry, and opportunity for all. Books were tools for creating and selling the American dream internationally and for preventing communism from gaining a foothold in those markets. In his bestseller *Teacher in America* (1945), the educator and public intellectual Jacques Barzun rightly pegged America's many global literacy programs as elements of what he called an "adopt our nationally advertised brand and avert chaos" campaign. He dismissed as naïve or blatantly misleading those "who want Kitty Smith from Indiana to be sent to Germany, armed with Muzzey's *American History*, to undo Hitler's work" and argued that "it is impossible to 'teach' democracy, or citizenship . . . [for] they occur as by-products" of living in a democratic nation.[13] Other observers echoed Barzun, noting that, too often, the democratizing ideal of reading rubbed up against less savory realities that advocates did not or would not acknowledge.

As Cold War reading programs swiftly advanced into friendly and hostile territories abroad, anxiety about the quality of America's reading and readership wracked the home front. In the words of Spider-Man, a well-known character in the era's much-disparaged comic-book medium, "with great power comes great responsibility"; and many cultural figures worried about how the world was perceiving American readers and what sort of example the nation should offer up to its gaze.[14] What if the model being sold abroad was failing at home? How would that failure affect American democracy's geopolitical credibility? A February 1950 Gallup poll revealed that "the United States has the lowest proportion of book readers of any major democracy . . . with only one adult in five reading books." Pedagogues, politicians, and parents cited such poll results as they fretted over America's alleged mediocre readership, claiming it was the "surest sign of [the] nation's lack of maturity and civilizatory progress."[15]

Reading proponents feared that non-readers would be less likely to understand and participate in the democratic process and more likely to be duped or radicalized by Communist propaganda, and sometimes people with a political or economic stake in reading initiatives manipulated and exacerbated this anxiety. For example, Rudolf Flesch, whose *Why Johnny Can't Read—and What You Can Do About It* (1955) alleged that traditional reading primers were putting America and its children at a disadvantage, warned that the word recognition method was "gradually destroying democracy in this country" and that "the American Dream . . . [was] beginning to vanish in a country where the public schools [were] falling down on the job." The solution, he argued, was to adopt his phonetics program to stave off national catastrophe. While many educators dismissed Flesch's scare tactics and were skeptical of his research methods, the disquiet it and similar texts provoked had great staying power, drawing the public's focus onto what and how students were reading and creating an industry of Chicken Little literacy experts.[16]

Even established thinkers such as the distinguished English professor Arthur S. Trace, Jr., tapped into postwar fears to win converts to his educational program. His *What Ivan Knows That Johnny Doesn't* (1961) was a comparative study of American and Soviet school materials. Trace concluded that American children were woefully behind Soviet children when it came to education and warned that "this unwillingness to permit children to work hard in school can do as much to bring about the destruction of the free world as any weapon in the Communist arsenal." Of course, the Soviets' launch of

FIGURE 1. The cover of Rudolf Flesch's phonics text, first published in 1955. Reprinted by permission of Hachette Book Group.

Sputnik had much to do with his fervor. As Louis Menand noted in his 2002 *New Yorker* article on Dr. Seuss and Cold War reading politics, parents at the beginning of the era demonstrated a "general fear that American children were growing up in a dumbed-down culture." This belief that was "crystallized by the launching of Sputnik," validated their anxieties about America's inferior intellectual capacity. Soon after the satellite made its first orbit, the librarian and professor Ralph E. Ellsworth noted, "It is certainly fashionable today—especially in the post-Sputnik days—to lament over the poor backgrounds and learning behavior of the college graduate." The educator, editor, and book reviewer Frank Jennings pointed out that, until "the first Sputnik beeped across our private heavens, only professional complainers dared to compare American education unfavorably with that of other countries." Post-Sputnik, however, "a Pandora's box of complaints was kicked open, [and] the bins of our dirty educational linen were exposed to public view."[17] Reading had become yet another front on which battles must be waged for the sake of freedom, democracy, and America's children. Long before John F. Kennedy voiced his concern about a missile gap, educators, politicians, and publishers were claiming that a dangerous reading gap existed between the United States and the Soviet Union—a gap that had the potential to destroy the world as Americans knew it.

Reading was "weaponized" through the efforts of government, industry, and university experts, who combined to create a sort of reading industrial complex. The passage of the 1958 National Defense Education Act channeled money into education programs that were "important to our defense." By means of an amendment to "Title III: Strengthening Instruction in Critical Subjects," the act extended its existing program to include English, reading, and civics, allotting an extra $20 million for "library resource and reference books, maps, globes, projectors, [and] specialized devices for use in teaching reading." Reading, like math and science, was viewed as a valuable skill, and newly established reading centers in universities across the country performed a significant number of studies as the Cold War progressed. Between 1957 and 1968, 257 national reading-research projects—including Cornell University's Reading-Study Center, the University of Chicago's Laboratory School, and the University of Florida's Reading Laboratory and Clinic—received more than $12 million in support. Everywhere, academic institutions were committing faculty and funds to the study of reading.[18]

Studies such as Project Literacy, coordinated by Harry Levin of Cornell in conjunction with the federal government succeeded in shifting reading from "'little science' to 'big science.'"[19] As in the social sciences, reading studies began to include stimulus-response models, field- or cognitive-learning theory models, and linguistic models. Rutgers University researcher John J.

Geyer counted at least forty-eight distinct reading models in existence by 1970. This research push drew flocks of students to new graduate reading programs, which, by the early 1970s, numbered at least two hundred. Not only did the increase in reading research lead to the publication of research-backed reading lists, but journals such as *Reading Research Quarterly, Reading Forum, The Reading Teacher,* and *Journal of the Reading Specialist* gained greater recognition and readership.[20]

While the focus on reading was intended to open new worlds of ideas and skills to readers at home and abroad, it sometimes also became an instrument of violence, compelling Americans to read in specific ways and thereby forwarding a form of compulsory and narrow nationalism that challenged reading's democratic nature. For instance, Senator Joseph McCarthy, whose name is synonymous with Cold War anti-communism, used fear of illiteracy to rally his troops, warning parents that Communists were poised "to infiltrate the educational system of this country and control school and college publications."[21] Because he and his allies saw reading education as a dangerous conduit for communism, they launched a preemptive strike, appropriating literacy education for their anti-Communist attack.

In his confessional bestseller *Witness* (1952), the repentant ex-Communist Whittaker Chambers wrote, "In the war between capitalism and Communism, books are weapons, and, like all serviceable weapons, loaded." Following the 1940 Alien Registration Act (later known as the Smith Act), perceptions of guilt were more often based on an "organization's literature, rather than on its activities." In this new ideological war, ideas, texts, and language itself were suspect. Because the government struggled to produce material evidence of seditious activities, subscribing to the *Daily Worker,* owning a copy of *The Communist Manifesto,* or reading subversive material (the definition of which perpetually changed) became grounds for arrest and arraignment. In many cases against suspected Communists, literature was the only evidence entered into trial. It was common "during the 1940s and 1950s, [for] the prosecutors, investigators, and others who needed to make a case against the Communist party and its members . . . to rely on indirect, often literary, evidence." What and how a person read determined his or her fate in the prosecution and persecution of suspected Communists and social agitators.[22]

Accordingly, anti-Communists provided Americans with scores of how-to books claiming to teach good Americans how to "read" Communists and communism. Some of these proscriptive texts were written by top government officials, such as FBI Director J. Edgar Hoover, whose *Masters of Deceit* promised that learning how to read and interpret the "facts of communism" would help Americans "open our eyes, inform ourselves, and work together" to "keep our country free."[23] Texts like his advertised themselves as "primers" of anti-Communist activity, written to teach the reader how to "free [themselves] from this [Communist] influence and to develop independent judgment" through "persistent training of one's mind." These texts linked protecting one's freedom and independence to correctly reading what Robert Stripling of the House Committee on Un-American Activities called the "A.B.C.'s of the Case vs. Communism" in his book *The Red Plot against America*.[24]

A good example of such anti-Communist primers is W. Cleon Skousen's overnight sensation, *The Naked Communist*, which claimed to be a library of Communist philosophy for anti-Communist readers and went through nine printings in less than three years. Taking a page from the *Reader's Digest* approach, Skousen offered his readers "a distillation of more than one hundred books and treatises—many of them written by Communist authors," abridged and simplified for widespread reading comprehension.[25] In general, reading Communist literature was considered "dangerous" and "suspect," but Skousen presented the texts in an "acceptable" format, excerpting, paraphrasing, glossing, and using communism's words against itself in hopes of educating readers. What anti-Communist primers like Hoover's, Stripling's, and Skousen's taught was that no one was safe from either the menace or patriots' efforts to root out dangerous or suspect behavior. Many anti-Communists wanted specifically anti-Communist schools and were disgruntled because these primers were their only option. Thus, many of the publications assumed overtly educational forms, tones, and purposes. The best-selling *What We Must Know about Communism* (1958) was even written by actual educators, the well-respected liberal professors Harry and Bonaro Overstreet. It warned that inattentive reading could lead to domestic and foreign disaster and offered definitions, examples, rhetorical examinations, review questions, reading lists, and a checklist of anti-Communist activities so that citizens could protect themselves from Communist arguments that preyed on unschooled minds.[26] The Overstreets' primer and others like it promised that reading such books would equip individuals to fight the good fight, protect their country, and enjoy the rewards of living in the free world. This promise was echoed throughout Cold War America. Citizens were taught that there were right and wrong ways, reasons, and books to read and that their choices could have both personal and national consequences for good or ill. If they chose wisely, they could improve their station in life, strengthen their community, and spread democracy. If they chose poorly, they could lose everything they held dear: freedom, status, and America itself. Thus, reading became a metonym for American ideals even as it was deployed as a weapon in service of those ideals.

"A Heroic Age for the Printed Word"

The reach and impact of Cold War America's commitment to reading cannot be overstated; as the editors of the fifth volume of *A History of the Book in America* crowed, "the last half of the twentieth century . . . was a heroic age for the printed word." A host of structural, ideological, and demographic changes had made the period the most literate and reading-focused in American history. First, the Cold War reading efforts benefited from the book infrastructure already created by the Council for Books in Wartime. Formed in 1942, the council had both a public and a less well known purpose: to help the war effort and to revitalize the ailing publishing industry. Comprised of leading publishers, editors, critics, and educators, it anchored its deliberations, programs, and publicity in the ideas of President Franklin D. Roosevelt: "In our country's first year of war, we have seen the growing power of books as weapons. Through books we have appraised our enemies and discovered our allies. We have learned something of American valor in battle. We have, above all, come to understand better the kind of war we must fight and the kind of peace we must establish." As Trysh Travis and John B. Hench have demonstrated, during its short existence the council blitzed the United States and its allies with programs designed to cultivate life-long readers sympathetic to democracy and America.[27] Its "Words at War" radio adaptations of books, its library events and celebrations, its recommended reading lists, and its short films strove to arm America's citizens with a love of reading and democracy, preparing them to engage with both the physical world and the world of ideas. By the end of the war, Americans were used to hearing about books, seeing advertisements about them, attending lectures about them, and equating reading with civic duty. Consequently, they were also primed for a postwar reading push.

The council is best remembered for its Armed Services Editions (ASEs)—pocket-sized, mass-produced, paperback editions of high- and middlebrow books sent to American troops on the battlefront, in Veterans Administration hospitals, and in prisoner-of-war camps. According to John Jamieson's official history, more than 1,324 ASE titles were printed, and 122,951,031 volumes were delivered to troops during the program's three years of operation. The *Saturday Review of Literature* gave the council an award for the project, declaring that the books "have become part of soldiers' regular equipment" and citing an air force lieutenant, who remarked that "fellows are delving into some fine literature which they might never have done otherwise were it not for you. It has certainly put good literature on a democratic (small 'd') level that it has never enjoyed before."[28] The Council for Books in Wartime and literary publications such as the *Saturday Evening Post* repeatedly printed

FIGURE 2. A poster originally published by the U.S. Office of War Information, 1942.

anecdotes about soldiers who were reading in "non–ivory tower conditions": trenches, beaches, foxholes, and ships awaiting the D-Day invasion.[29] These publications repeatedly stressed that the troops were "reading far more books than such a cross-section of American men [had] ever read before. Some are reading books for the first time since childhood." ASEs were "as Popular as Pin-Up Girls," *Senior Scholastic* noted in 1944. As one private wrote to the *Saturday Review of Literature,* "on the ship, everywhere one looked, one saw soldiers eagerly devouring these books."[30] The letters and anecdotes shared by the council repeatedly celebrated the ASEs for boosting troop morale, exposing new readers to good literature, and elevating America's readerly taste.

If we base an evaluation on sheer numbers alone, the Council for Books in Wartime was extremely successful in its goal of putting books into the hands of readers who could then return to the United States and benefit from the G.I. Bill and other postwar education and reading measures. But the council also wanted to influence the peacetime book and leisure market, and their efforts to set up a war-era printing and distribution infrastructure later helped participating publishers expand their postwar business. Self-serving press releases often warned publishers, librarians, educators, and editors that it was their duty to keep Americans reading after the war; otherwise, wartime sacrifices would be for naught. Private John L. Van Der Voort's oft-cited letter to the *Saturday Review of Literature* reminded publishers that "the American soldier is becoming an avid reader through force of circumstances. Let the publishers keep him so after the war. . . . Let them not drive him back to the intellectual stagnation of the pulps and slick magazines." *Publishers Weekly* advertised, "[The G.I.s] are the readers who are now coming back into every American community so that the list of titles is worth the careful study of all the book trade and the librarians."[31] Certain themes recurred in such admonitions: reading is democratic; reading is a civic duty; reading is an American tradition; a reader's taste should be elevated for reasons of national well-being; reading has a socially normative influence; publishers, librarians, and invested citizens should work to protect America's citizen-readers and facilitate their assimilation into postwar culture. By waging a battle at home for new markets, elevated reading, and a cultured nation, council members helped the cause while helping themselves.

Cold War reading programs benefited from the fact that more Americans than ever before now had access to books. The Servicemen's Readjustment Act of 1944 (commonly known as the G.I. Bill) transformed the traditional locus of lettered learning—the university—by subsidizing tuition and housing so that veterans might attend postsecondary institutions. Consequently, education was no longer reserved for the privileged few but extended to working- and middle-class men—"the masses." As the legendary publisher

Jason Epstein noted, "it is obvious that the GI Bill was a glorious attempt to fulfill the promise of American democracy." College enrollment in the United States increased by 78 percent between 1940 and 1950, and "by the time the program expired in 1956, 2.8 million veterans had used it to attend college." The number of women and minorities enrolling in college continued to increase in the immediate postwar period, while adult education programs grew in popularity and number as colleges, libraries, community associations, and corporate trainers rushed to meet the national hunger for learning and skill acquisition. These programs responded to Alvin Johnson's legendary call in *The Public Library—A People's University* (1938): "the crux of the adult educational problem is concerned with the civic and cultural development of the individual. It is obvious that a democratic civilization can maintain itself and make progress only through a wide diffusion of sound ideas, political, social, and cultural."[32]

Meeting this unprecedented influx of students was a mode of literary criticism and pedagogy that strove to open up literature in new ways to new readers. What came to be known as New Criticism began in the 1920s and 1930s, with the work of a diverse group that included John Crowe Ransom, Alan Tate, Robert Penn Warren, René Wellek, and later Cleanth Brooks. Immediately after the war, however, it was part of a larger national move to democratize reading; push back against the dehumanization of war, mass industry, and rampant consumerism; fend off lazy reading that would make people susceptible to totalitarianism; and thereby shore up democracy.[33] The New Critics challenged modes of literary criticism that had privileged biography, historical facts, philological mapping, and psychological moralizing over textual examination, arguing that those interpretive modes were elitist, abstract, and rigid and that they denied readers texts and texts readers. Declaring their independence from the "blight" of previous readerly schools, New Critics claimed that literary study was not only "a distinctive subject and teachable method" but also a democratic one. As Brooks later said, "we didn't demand as much library or technical or historical work as other teachers might have at the time." Instead, New Critics invited readers to look at the art itself. Ransom called poetry itself "a democratic state" because it invited all readers to engage with it. Returning veterans and first-generation college students didn't need to be experts in Latin or Greek, or trained archivists, or owners of a vast number of arcane texts to find meaning in a poem or a piece of prose.[34] They just needed the work itself and their active minds.

For citizen-readers who were war-weary and exhausted by the era's many changes and challenges, this mode of interpretation also offered them hope of a better world. Even though the postwar climate was troubled, they could find order, unity, and community in texts and close reading. At the same time,

New Criticism taught readers how to identify and sometimes reconcile themselves to the existence of ambiguity, paradox, tension, and other aspects of epistemological and ontological uncertainty. By learning about and through complexity, students might "recover the denser and more refractory original world which we know loosely through our perceptions and memories." Thus, while "offer[ing] a form of knowledge which was different [from] the abstract forms of scientific positivism . . . [and] was a creative process" and demanding that readers be active participants in making meaning, New Criticism worked to train them to navigate uncertainty and unknowability without succumbing to nihilism or existentialist despair. By the late 1950s, New Criticism as a practice had become largely rote, prescriptive, and uniform, and it has since been mischaracterized and maligned by many literary critics and theorists as always having been so in both theory and practice. But in early Cold War America, it was "a humanistic criticism . . . that relie[d] upon common sense and shared values in interpreting literary works as aesthetic achievements which speak to us about familiar human concerns."[35]

Outside of the university, programs to educate, acculturate, and assimilate at-risk populations into the American way multiplied, promoting reading's liberatory possibilities while forwarding particular ideas about citizenship. These programs were not wholly new but built on the tradition of reading uplift as practiced by Quakers, Progressives, Sunday School leaders, and others. Working-class readers encountered scores of how-to-read books unabashedly aimed at instructing the "common" Joe.[36] Cornelius Hirschberg's self-consciously Ben Franklinesque text, *The Priceless Gift* (1960), promised farmers, factory workers, and day laborers that they could rise above their station if they would just open a book. Some reading guides and programs focused on minority readers and recent immigrants as populations who needed help establishing themselves as profitable citizens. In the foreword to *Books for Adult Beginners* (1954), the editor Viola Wallace declared that the American Library Association's adult literacy program would provide immigrants with opportunity, success, and security. She identified the reading guide's purpose as "literacy, Americanization, and citizenship classes" and equated literacy with learning the language of "Americanism" and its "faith, aspirations, and ideals" as defined by the texts selected for this course of study. The guide's reading list provided models of "good" Americans—those "immigrants whose fine contributions have enriched the land of their adoption."[37]

The 1950s also saw the rise of organizations that targeted girls and boys with gender-specific texts to attract them to books and distract them from the growing juvenile delinquency problem.[38] Teenagers had more time and money than ever to read, and libraries tried to capture their attention with reading campaigns. New publications such as *Classics Illustrated* attempted to capitalize on the comics craze, and *Mad Magazine* regularly printed satires of the classics, cultural primers, and book clubs for its rabid readership.

In the Cold War era, public libraries offered Americans the greatest variety of reading materials ever recorded. As Louise S. Robbins and Julia L. Mickenberg have demonstrated, librarians' roles had changed during World War II: from being guardians of taste and morals, they became advocates for intellectual freedom.[39] After the war, in response to government and public calls for censorship of dangerous books, the American Library Association published "The Freedom to Read" statement, which contended that "books are among our greatest instruments of freedom" and that readers should be able "to choose freely from a variety of offerings." To expedite such choice, the association recommended that libraries eschew their earlier formal and informal policies promoting moral policing and instead work to adopt all kinds of books for all kinds of readers. It further recommended that libraries hire extra staff to help patrons develop reading lists suited to their interests and needs. Many postwar American librarians wrestled with intense outside censorship attempts and their own inclinations to censor particular readings and readers, reactions that highlight the paradox within Cold War reading initiatives. Even so, many ultimately concluded, like Wisconsin librarian Karen Kreuger, that "the rights guaranteed in the First Amendment are guaranteed to all, not just those that can afford to buy their books and newspapers and magazines, or those who hold generally accepted ideas or beliefs. The public library is the great equalizer—all ideas free to all."[40]

The desire to unify Americans through free access to ideas prompted a flurry of programs working to put good books into the hands of nontraditional readers. For instance, as Christine Pawley details in her 2010 study *Reading Places,* Wisconsin's Door-Kewaunee County Regional Library strove to extend library service and reading opportunities to rural populations, citing "a vision of print and reading as essential to the exercise of democracy, as well as a desire to widen educational opportunities for local children, especially those growing up on hardscrabble farms where books and magazines were rare." Despite early opposition and problems, the service's trial run provided participating counties with "a vastly improved library system."

> Local libraries not only cooperated in selecting, purchasing, and cataloging materials, but also provided public services—including reference, readers' advisory, and children's story-telling—that urban residents might take for granted, but which rural residents rarely, if ever, enjoyed. The regular bookmobile service also offered a range of choice in reading materials that the region's farm families had never previously encountered. Overall, library circulation figures soared to two-and-a-half times their previous level. Over

90 per cent of grade-school children in the rural schools made use of the bookmobile service, and their reading scores improved beyond expectation.

Access, choice, and community formation were just a few of the positive by-products of this and other national reading initiatives; and in 1956, Congress passed the Library Services Act, "designed originally to funnel funds to rural areas without real libraries," and eventually "sending millions of dollars to both research and public libraries throughout the nation."[41] By opening book access to underserved populations, these programs attempted to practice the American ideals of freedom, equality, and equal protection celebrated in their best books.

In the "consumer republic" that was Cold War America, book buying became easier than it ever had been, and quickly it also became a status symbol for the rising classes.[42] World War II and the Council for Books in Wartime helped to modernize American publishing, a change that subsequently affected who patronized bookstores, where bookstores were located, and how bookstores organized and advertised. The publishing initiatives known as the Overseas, Armed Services, and Transatlantic Editions modernized mass printing and cultivated new populations of readers. Following Penguin and Pocket Books' lead, Anchor, Random House, Knopf, and other publishers started producing quality paperbacks that gave readers access to writers previously available "only in expensive hardcover editions." Paperbacks extended classic reprints and eventually offered new titles to an increasingly diverse reading public, helping to democratize and popularize literature while increasing sales "from roughly $14 million in 1947 to $67 million in 1959"—that is, from 95 million texts in 1947 to 270 million in 1952.[43] An increase in good-quality, lower-priced hardbacks and better-quality paperbacks forced traditional booksellers to reorganize and systematize their shelves to make their stores more friendly to readers and browsers. New bookstore chains such as Waldenbooks and B. Dalton thrived after the war, with Waldenbooks stocking fifty-nine stores by 1969. Most were in the new shopping malls and centers that were springing up in the proliferating suburbs, and book shopping became associated with plentiful parking, welcoming interiors, and non-intimidating displays.[44]

No longer solely the domain of elite urban intellectuals, bookstores increasingly catered to the middle and lower classes, signaling a class revolution in reading unlike any since the rise of the novel in the eighteenth century. Thanks to prewar labor reforms and the wartime boom, Americans were seeing shorter workdays, an increase in the minimum wage, and a greater number of better-paying jobs. Compared with previous generations, the rising working class had more money and more free time; and the special issue of *Life* magazine titled "The Good Life" gleefully details how "zestful Americans enjoy their new leisure" and concludes that leisure time leads to "a better civilization."[45] Pictures of famous people gardening, golfing, cooking, and reading graced the full-color pages. Not only did the average American have more time to go to the library and check out books to read for pleasure, but many Americans now had enough disposable income to build their own libraries—both the physical space in their split-level homes and the books needed to fill it.

In reputable newspapers, literary journals, and popular magazines, advertisers shrewdly directed their marketing toward the political and social status that reading could confer. Despite disdaining the low-quality pulps, many publishers adopted the pulps' marketing strategies, placing books in supermarkets, newsstands, and drugstores to target new populations and increase reader access. Mail-order sales were also on the rise, and publishing houses worked to replicate the prewar success of companies such as Book of the Month Club. By focusing on readers rather than authors, Book of the Month Club had challenged traditional publishing methods and reaped great financial rewards. The club's cofounder, Harry Scherman, "believed many more people could be persuaded to become book readers if they were given better access to books as well as to the kind of advice that would explain not the particulars of a book's content but how it would address readers' interests, desires, or needs." Book of the Month's direct-mail orders had helped individuals who lived outside urban centers and in communities without libraries get the latest releases, and after the war other publishers took notice. The best-selling American magazine of the mid-twentieth century, *Reader's Digest*, threw its hat into the book-publishing ring in 1950, offering condensed versions of books to readers through direct mail four times a year. *Reader's Digest* subsequently published its own original nonfiction hardback books, operating with the "basic purpose . . . to deliver information as engagingly as possible without diluting it."[46] In marketing these books, advertisers attempted to sell values central to Cold War American capitalist ideology: individualism, choice, and easy free-market abundance.

Advertisers were not the only ones selling nicely packaged American values. The hundreds of reading programs that flourished in the postwar period also sold the promise of freedom and growth through reading education. Encouraged by organizations such as the established Great Books Program and community programs developed by local bookstores, libraries, parish councils, and civic organizations, book clubs began forming everywhere. Like Ben Franklin's Junto, New York City's Phoenix Society, Europe's eighteenth-century bluestocking salons, and other precedents, these postwar reading groups promised intellectual growth, social advancement, moral uplift, and

FIGURE 3. An April 1952 advertisement in the *New York Times* for the Book of the Month Club.

community. What distinguished them was their scale and systematization, and the most famous exemplar was probably the Great Books Program. Founded in 1947 by the University of Chicago's Mortimer J. Adler and Robert Hutchins, the program became an enormous success in the 1950s.[47] Joan Shelley Rubin notes that, by 1948, it already had more than 80,000 members, and it continued to flourish during the Cold War as Americans sought "not simply a means of self-improvement but also an opportunity to join the community of the well-read." Embracing the belief that great books provide a liberal education, the object of which "is the excellence of man as man and man as citizen," the program distributed reading lists and discussion questions to any interested reader or book group. Its supporters believed that it constituted "democracy in action," allowing "the wisdom of the ages . . . [to] becom[e] the common property of Americans." Fifteen years after founding the program, Hutchins declared, "The books should speak for themselves, and the reader should decide for himself," for "these books are the means of understanding our society and ourselves."[48]

Detractors contended that such programs, with their set reading lists, preformulated questions, and institutionally approved moderators, encouraged group think rather than independent discovery. They claimed that the programs were a form of public coercion, inducing participants to read in the "right" way. Moreover, for many Americans, the desire to be accepted by and into "the community of the well-read" turned reading into yet another avenue of what Vance Packard called "status seeking" for the rising classes. He and others believed that reading's liberating powers were being sacrificed to the gods of social acceptability.[49] Still, book clubs such as the Chat-an-Hour Social and Cultural Club, which offered African American readers a chance to discuss "not only literature but also a wide range of topics related to African American identity and contemporary race relations," challenged the prescriptive trend and generated their own community.[50] Depending on who determined the aims and terms, reading groups in the Cold War era could constrain community, create community, or do both at once.

The marriage of structural capacity and cultural need produced a reading boom in Cold War America. Never before had so many Americans from so many different walks of life owned or read books. Books were in increasingly busy libraries, they were delivered to rural regions, they were in drugstores, they were in working-class and minority neighborhoods, they were on the radio, they were reviewed in the papers, they were discussed in popular magazines, and they were adapted into comics. Books were in millions of homes, and Americans of all stripes had access to reading's democratizing potential. The promise of knowledge's power seemed to be within the grasp of citizen-readers who previously had been denied it. Advertisements, reviews, and book discussions promised success and advancement to those willing to read. The promise of peace also seemed to be bound up in books. As the playwright Arthur Miller said when called before the House Committee on Un-American Activities in 1956, "we are living in a time when there is great uncertainty in this country. . . . [Y]ou just pick up a book-review section and you will see everybody selling books on peace of mind, because there isn't any."[51]

"Peace of mind" was what books of all kinds ultimately offered to Americans searching for stability during this time of great change. Yet lurking in peace's shadow were concerns about who, what, how, and why people read, and they haunted American reading culture throughout the Cold War. For many reading advocates, merely reading for pleasure was not enough. Reading was a duty and a responsibility, the proper performance of which was key to protecting one's kin and country from America's enemies. Indeed, Erich Fromm warned that "in spite of the fact that everybody reads the daily paper religiously, there is an absence of understanding of the meaning of political events which is truly frightening," in part "because our intelligence helps us to produce weapons which our reason is not capable of controlling." In the "bomb's early light" of an atomic America facing off against totalitarianism, the inability to read, interpret, comprehend, and communicate "the meaning of political events" loomed ominously over national security.[52]

Thus, anxiety that America wasn't reading enough, correctly, or for the right reasons was almost always at the fore of any reading guide, list, program, or lecture. In fact, the educators Sam Duker and Thomas P. Nally argued in 1956 that the glut of reading experts and guides was itself creating a "hysterical mass." In a similar vein, Frank Jennings saw reading as "the proverbial touchstone for anxiety and hysteria . . . in recent years."[53] This "anxiety and hysteria," so often invoked by Cold War reading proponents, went beyond the fear that Johnny couldn't read to signal a larger national concern about citizenship and nationhood in postwar America.

2

Reading for Character, Community, and Country

J. D. Salinger's *The Catcher in the Rye*

A famous moment in J. D. Salinger's 1951 novel *The Catcher in the Rye* illuminates central Cold War concerns about reading's effects on individual and national character. The protagonist, Holden Caulfield, rests on a grade school's steps and notices some graffiti:

> I saw something that drove me crazy. Somebody'd written "Fuck you" on the wall. It drove me damn near crazy. I thought how Phoebe and all the other kids would see it, and how they'd wonder what it meant, and then some dirty kid would tell them . . . and how they'd all *think* about it and maybe even *worry* about it for a couple of days. I kept wanting to kill whoever'd written it. I figured it was some perverty bum that'd sneaked in the school late at night to take a leak or something and then wrote it on the wall.[1]

Holden's concern about how the phrase will affect the children at his sister's school evokes multiple internal responses: visceral—he wants to "puke"; psychological—he fears that kids will "*think* about it"; moral—he's anxious that children will "*worry* about it for a couple of days," as he is worrying; and classist—he's convinced that the offender must be a "perverty bum that'd sneaked in the school late at night to take a leak or something." Ultimately, his greatest worry is not that these immature readers will see the words and be sickened but that, like the "dirty kid" who explicates the text, they will be excited and corrupted.

Like the legions of censorship advocates who have opposed *Catcher* simply because it includes the phrase "Fuck you," Holden apparently believes in the mimetic function of reading—that words on the page trigger actions that lead to, in this instance, the degradation of character.[2] In both the novel and the story surrounding it, fear about the reception of language and its power to transform immature readers generates a response that often borders on violence. Holden imagines meting out vigilante justice: "I kept picturing myself catching him at it, and how I'd smash his head on the stone steps till he was good and goddam dead and bloody" (201). Similarly, anti-*Catcher* censors have claimed that Salinger and his protagonist are "perverty bums," have accused them of violating America and its children, and have threatened them with various forms of "justice" for causing filthy "words [to be] implanted" in young readers' minds.[3] Those who decry the novel may find it ironic that Holden himself is a censor who wants to control what is written and read in order to prevent the transmission of smut and its presumed effect on intellect and innocence.

The intersections among reading, maturity, and postwar character in *Catcher* illuminate the importance of reading to Cold War nationalism and invite us to rethink its categorization as a novel of rebellion. In fact, it thematizes the theories and practices of the era's reading advocates, who were trying to cultivate greater political and cultural maturity in Cold War Americans. While the phrase "you are what you read" may seem clichéd to a twenty-first-century audience versed in America's book and cultural history, the truism carried real ideological, sociopolitical, and geopolitical weight in the early days of the Cold War. Reading advocates and experts believed that what, how, and why a person read influenced character and personality, a vital consideration in an uncertain age. They warned that books of questionable morality created social unrest and damaged America's international reputation, and they called for more "sound" and "upstanding" texts to affirm the nation's values and democratic stability. They also advocated methods that taught individuals how to read closely, wrestle with ambiguity, engage uncertainty, and create a sense of wholeness from many disparate parts. This combination of materials, methods, and intention would give citizen-readers the tools they needed to create "the mature, functioning democracy that the United States is supposed to be."[4]

Holden's relationship to mainstream American values is complicated. Yes, he does act out in ways that resonate with the Cold War period's many tracts about juvenile delinquency.[5] Like the 1960s student radicals who idolized him, he rebels against and questions those institutions and individuals who control "the game" and deny power to all but the "hot shots" (8).[6] At the same time, his critiques of mass culture, conspicuous consumption, and status obsession resonate with much postwar liberalism.[7] Holden's reading practices, cultural preferences, and social biases demonstrate that he has absorbed the established and establishment discourses about reading, citizenship, democracy, and nation found in countless works of postwar criticism. Like Cleanth Brooks, who believed "that modern society was sick" and isolating, that it "lacked any shared set of values through which [individuals] could relate to one another," Holden sees loss everywhere in his world and turns to literature to find "a diagnosis of its problems."[8]

Many scholars have studied *Catcher* in a Cold War context. For instance, Alan Nadel discusses how the rhetoric of McCarthyism infiltrates Holden's speech. Leerom Medovoi considers how the novel's critical reception played a role in constructing a youth culture and a liberal politics of global consumption. Pamela Steinle investigates *Catcher*'s censorship battles, and Abigail Cheever highlights concerns about phoniness, uniformity, and individualism in postwar America.[9] In contrast, I focus on the function of reading *in* Salinger's text, with the goal of demonstrating both the centrality of literacy in the novel's narrative and character development and the significant ways in which the book reflects literature's complicated relationship to and influence on Cold War America's reading push. Holden's efforts to understand himself and others are shaped by his training in how, what, and why people should read; his reading practices and philosophy reflect national narratives seeking to define the good American. Thus, reading reading in *The Catcher in the Rye* expands our understanding of not only Holden's search for stability, order, and what he calls *niceness* but also reading's role in the early Cold War imagination.

Reading America's Character

Like Holden, many postwar Americans were engaged in identifying and erasing anything that interfered with the development of good character and a healthy democracy. This concern about the nation's perceived immaturity is reflected in a swath of best-selling books published in the late 1940s and 1950s that articulated America's commitment to grow up and into its global role. Henry Steele Commager's *The American Mind* (1950), David Riesman's *The Lonely Crowd* (1950) and *Faces in the Crowd* (1952), C. Wright Mills's *White Collar* (1951), David Potter's *People of Plenty* (1954), Louis Hartz's *The Liberal Tradition in America* (1954), Erich Fromm's *The Sane Society* (1955), William Whyte, Jr.'s, *The Organization Man* (1956), Eric F. Goldman's *The Crucial Decade: America, 1945–1955* (1956), and Vance Packard's *The Status Seekers* (1959) all tackled the country's character problem, identifying influences on and threats to good character and reflecting on the individual and national ramifications of de-emphasizing traditional Judeo-Christian values. As the historian Warren Susman has noted, the terms often used to define character tend to reflect stereotypically American values: "*citizenship, duty, democracy, work, building, golden deeds, outdoor life, conquest, honor, reputation, morals, manners, integrity,* and above all, *manhood.*" Although he locates these values firmly in the nineteenth century, they reemerged after World War II in claims that "persons with good character make a society good" and in celebrations of good character as a cultural, political, social, and moral constant—a rock that could weather political, economic, and social uncertainty or change.[10]

Postwar concerns about character were exacerbated by the ubiquitous cult of personality that had taken off in the early part of the twentieth century. Correspondence courses, how-to books, standardized tests, and radio programs taught ambitious Americans how to get the "girl" or the man, land the desired job or contract, and "win friends and influence people." The cult of personality capitalized on the seismic social shifts of the early twentieth century and became a lucrative hook for advertisers, statisticians, and pop psychologists. Among them was Erving Goffman, whose popular sociological study, *The Presentation of Self in Everyday Life* (1959), examined and advocated social flexibility and performativity as a way of achieving economic and social success. Contending that all persons are inherently performers, he offered research-based advice on how to maximize "impression management." The key was to teach people to be "concerned with maintaining the impression that they are living up to the many standards by which they and their products [including themselves] are being judged."[11] In other words, morality was a performance rather than a core ethic, and it was contingent on what various audiences wanted.

Although this focus on personality sold well on the mass market, postwar theorists of all political stripes became increasingly skeptical. On the left, C. Wright Mills argued that it was turning the individual into a commodity "shaped" by the desires of others, whether they be employers, customers, or a peer group. He called such learned behaviors a "mask" that rendered individuals "anonymous," made sincerity "a detriment," and substituted lies for feelings. Mills concluded that those who privileged personality had become "generalized" and "self-alienated," therein contributing to the "all-pervasive distrust" that characterized the era. The psychologist Erich Fromm similarly decried the "personality market" and "personality package" for eschewing the concrete and replacing meaningful interactions with artificiality. Asserting that this artificiality rendered democracy a charade because individual will no longer existed, he warned that America was "marching toward barbarism."[12]

Occupying a more centrist position, William Whyte, Jr., saw the focus on personality as externally driven by "the organization" and "reward[ing] the conformist, the pedestrian, the unimaginative." Targeting personality tests in particular—which he called "tests of conformity"—Whyte expressed concern that people were trying to "fit" into a perceived idea of normality and desirability, ultimately making themselves "the victims of one another's façades." On the political right, Senator McCarthy argued that Communists were the ultimate masters of personality: pretenders who could tailor their behavior and appearance to impersonate "good American[s]" while secretly working to corrupt democracy. Likewise, FBI Director Hoover described the "communist man" as that "mechanical puppet, whom they can train to do as the Party desires," and feared that Americans without solid characters could be easily manipulated by authoritarian powers. The implication in these critiques is that personality masks one's "true self," or character.[13] Whether they called it "status seeking," "fellow traveling," or being "outer-directed" or "phony," postwar thinkers spoke with trepidation about personality's malleability, instability, seeming conformity, and potential uniformity.

Personality's threat to character undergirded many concerns about the nation's perceived cultural inferiority to Europe. According to the historian Henry Steele Commager, it "was by no means clear" "that the American mind was more mature in the mid-twentieth than in the mid-nineteenth or even the mid-eighteenth century." Thus, as observers pondered the nation's readiness to assume the mantle of global leader, they spent much time examining American culture and cultural consumption. Taking reading as a unit of measurement, many found its related materials, methods, and distribution mechanisms to be risky and immature. The University of Chicago sociologist Edward Shils bemoaned, "Our fellow countrymen are not readers. This lamentable fact has been documented by some sample surveys in various countries which have shown that at any given time the United States is fairly far down on the list of the literate countries as compared with the Scandinavian or the Low Countries or even England, which is, with respect to most of its population, not a land of great readers." William Gray and Bernice Rogers, also at the University of Chicago, concluded in their study *Maturity in Reading* "that the number of highly mature readers is small and that a large proportion of the population is relatively immature in reading. Such statements indicate the magnitude of the adult reading problem which this country faces."[14]

Many intellectuals and social critics argued that American letters themselves had yet to grow up. Leslie Fiedler accused authors of "cultural naïveté" and of latching onto "a style, a subject and tone, usually anchored in their adolescent experience—and these they repeat compulsively, like a songbird his single tune."[15] Despite the vastly improved publishing and distribution infrastructures and processes developed during the war, some still saw book distribution as a problem. Leonard Shatzkin, the vice president of the publisher Crowell Collier, wrote, "Like it or not, education, cultural achievement, and the printed word have not had the prestige in the United States that they have had in Europe."[16] When measured against the culture and character of its allies, America's appeared to be dangerously juvenile.

Professing faith in literacy's power to "determine the shape of our nation and the character of our people," books such as *The Wonderful World of Books, Reading for Life, This Is Reading, Reading in an Age of Mass Communication, Making Better Readers, That All May Learn to Read, How to Read a Book, Promoting Personal and Social Development through Reading, Promoting Growth toward Maturity in Interpreting What Is Read,* and *Maturity in Reading* worked to cultivate cultural maturity in America's citizen-readers.[17] These texts contended that reading was a primary means of effecting "social growth"; as the University of Chicago's president, Robert Hutchins, declared, "books are the means of understanding our society and ourselves. They contain the great ideas that dominate us without our knowing it," allowing us to attain the "wisdom" that begets good character. Similarly, Jacques Barzun wrote that "the man with the moral fervor of patriotism is likely to be the man with the moral fervor of scholarship; in both cases, the student sees himself as owing a duty to something greater than himself." Implicit in such claims was a warning about what might happen if Americans did not embrace the "moral fervor of scholarship" and a larger fear that the nation's current and future challenges were "rooted in our own inadequacy as truly moral human beings, in the lack of devotion and integrity of character."[18]

Behind such beliefs was the age-old assumption that reading is mimetic, yet they were prompted by issues that were unique to the nation's current political position and needs. Like Holden Caulfield, many Cold War reading advocates were driven by the concern that immature readers could get their hands on "bad books" that would taint them and turn them into poor citizens or, worse, into dangerous social beings—delinquents, Communists, or initiates into the cult of personality. These advocates believed that a text's themes could either uplift or pervert. Characters could model well adjusted or pathological behavior. A book's affect could promote connection or alienation.

Similarly, how one read could either fortify or destroy character. Bad reading habits included skimming, Evelyn Wood's trendy speed reading, reading for plot, reading for titillation, or reading for useful talking points to display at one's next social gathering. As Paul Lazarsfeld and Robert Merton argued, "large numbers of people have acquired what might be termed 'formal literacy,' that is to say, a capacity to read, to grasp crude and superficial meanings, and a correlative incapacity for full understanding of what they read. There has developed, in short, a marked gap between literacy and comprehension. People read more but understand less."[19] Many expressed concern that such degraded reading skills would lead to poor comprehension, easy persuadability, and a lack of personal integrity. Conversely, good reading habits—such as reading slowly, rereading for comprehension, reading to identify formal patterns and order, wrestling with ambiguities and complex concepts—would prepare an individual to engage in higher-order thinking, make decisions for herself, identify connections in her world, and see herself as part of something bigger.

It was no coincidence that New Criticism cemented itself as the predominant mode of reading and criticism at this time. Calling for close and "careful reading," the New Critics pushed back against superficial textual engagement, the commodification of literature, the scientification of interpretation, and the critical impulse to reduce literature to author biography, historical facts, affective excess, or political puppetry. Instead, they saw literature as a site of creative struggle for understanding and focused on the ways in which linguistic forms demanded a new "mode of cognition" that put author, text, and reader into conversation. New Critics examined how formal devices such as irony and ambiguity begat tension without resolution and how language itself struggled against control. They privileged texts that pushed readers to "work *hard* and read *hard*."[20] Both theorists and teachers saw New Criticism as a weapon against totalizing ideologies and a means of training individuals to interpret their world responsibly while battling modern America's alienating effects.

These various postwar concerns about America's immature readership and character were central to and typified by the controversies that beset *The Catcher in the Rye*. As Pamela Steinle has shown, the threat of communism, shifting social structures, and media accessibility in the years after World War II contributed to critics' anxieties and charges about *The Catcher in the Rye*. Among its many would-be censors, the fear that "you are what you read" drove their criticisms of the novel. For instance, in 1954, the National Council of Juvenile Court Judges proclaimed, "There is a growing realization that such foul publications, through their distribution to children and youth and their extensive encouragement to read them, contribute to the breakdown of the moral sense in children which today is causing an increase in juvenile delinquency." In a letter to the Marin County District Board of Trustees, a concerned parent named Kristen Keefe said, "The mind of a child is an unchalked slate," and argued that allowing students to read *Catcher* would inscribe "bad" ideas and create "bad" children. In recounting the objections of New Mexico parents, a school secretary named Justine Pas noted that many "were dead set against that book being available; . . . I think that it was the language—that reading that type of book would make their children that type, that that kind of stuff was all right."[21]

As they battled to ban *Catcher* from libraries and classrooms, people often employed words such as "brainwashing," "training," and "implanting," claiming that the book's language was dangerous because "what you take in you will give out."[22] They argued that banning the book would protect young readers' character and healthy development. Yet even though they were legitimately concerned about the well-being of children in an uncertain era, their means often devolved into forms of totalizing control similar to the so-called Communist strategies they were decrying. At the same time, while educators and librarians staunchly defended readers' right to have access to books such as *Catcher*, their arguments about the texts' transformative power relied on similar assumptions about reading's mimetic function and a desire to strengthen American character through good reading habits. To create healthy, mature, upstanding Americans, one needed give them good books that would help them adjust to the "expectations of the adult world" and "instill . . . ideals of courage, loyalty, perseverance and a sense of personal responsibility toward God, country, and mankind."[23]

It is not surprising, then, that critics were drawn to Salinger's best-selling novel as evidence of America's mature culture and good character—or its lack thereof. Rejecting it as "smut," as a childish author's juvenile pap, or as a work with no claims to "serious fiction," some defensively attempted to establish themselves as mature readers via their critique of Salinger's text.[24] Meanwhile, others announced, "There never has been a more 'American' novel"; it has "recreated in twentieth century terms that simultaneous sense of character and society of the great nineteenth century realists"; it "fits into a major tradition of American literature, what might be called the effort to define the Good American."[25] They promoted *Catcher* as a new and exciting text within a newly mature American literary tradition. In short, whether praised or scorned, no other American novel of the era received so much scholarly attention. Ironically, much recent scholarship focuses primarily on this reception narrative, thus privileging the use-value of *Catcher* over the thing itself. That is, contemporary critics flirt with replicating the commodification and alienation against which Holden Caulfield battled. Looking at reading *in* and not just *of* Salinger's novel illuminates its complex and at times ironic contribution to the cultural debate over postwar character.

"Catching" Cold War Character

Initial readings of *The Catcher in the Rye* tend to focus on Holden's actions in New York, using them to argue that he is an antihero who challenges the dominant culture through acts of juvenile delinquency.[26] Holden has dropped or been kicked out of multiple prep schools because of his laziness. He tells lies and uses mild profanity. His social interactions often border on or incite violence: he goads Ackley, fights with Stradlater, and is punched by Maurice.

He phones a call girl and invites a prostitute to come to his hotel. He is a performer and a ham. Although he has a code of honor (phoniness being the worst of all crimes), his actions seem to challenge Cold War ideas about good morals and good character.

Yet many readers fail to recognize that Holden's behavior is rooted in a nostalgia for and romanticization of traditional values.[27] Like many mid-century social and literary critics, he is reacting to what he sees as the loss of American ideals and the corruption of character. In this way, he mirrors many of his New Critical counterparts, who saw the world as "complex," "discordant," and "fail[ing] to reveal or bring about a satisfying order" and consequently turned to reading because "the order we need *is* available in literature."[28] Like many postwar thinkers on both the right and left, Holden reacts to the "excesses and abstractions of the capitalist will to power" and to how the "market has destroyed the possibility of genuine individualism and community."[29] Within the seeming disorder of his life, he is a self-appointed harbinger of character and moral fortitude. His actions criticize mass culture and honor reading as a way to restore and preserve values such as loyalty, honor, integrity, and innocence.

Throughout *Catcher*, Holden alludes to various novels to establish his readerly credentials and thus his authority on character—for instance, with his opening-line reference to Charles Dickens's *David Copperfield*: "If you really want to hear about it, the first thing you'll probably want to know is where I was born, and what my lousy childhood was like, and how my parents were occupied and all before they had me, and all that David Copperfield kind of crap, but I don't feel like going into it, if you want to know the truth" (1). *David Copperfield* is a touchstone text in Cold War reading guides such as *America Reads: Good Times Through Literature* (1951), used to help readers learn to interpret structure, images, foreshadowing, and character as well as serve as a model for the types of choices and behaviors that lead to good character.[30] Not only does Holden's reference reveal his exposure to the novel and its didactic function, but it also allows him to position his own autobiography within and against the book's narrative tradition. His approach is similar to Fadiman's in his "biblio-autobiography," *Reading I've Liked* (1943), which models good reading for others by way of a self-reflexive introduction detailing his own development into a good reader and citizen.

Holden reveals that his library includes a broad range of canonical texts, including works by Ernest Hemingway, Isak Dinesen, Somerset Maugham, Thomas Hardy, and William Shakespeare, not to mention *Beowulf* and other "classics." His reading list mirrors those compiled and published by leading reading advocates of the postwar period (see chapter 1) and, with the exception of Ring Lardner's work, reflects what he has been taught in his English classes.[31] Although he flunks out of school, he is a good reader because he has internalized what he has been taught. Various literary allusions crop up in his discourse, such as *Gatsby*-isms ("Ace" and "Old Sport" [141]), or references to *Hamlet* (he calls Ackley "a real prince . . . a gentleman and a scholar" [47]). While versed in popular fiction, he admits that those texts do not pack the same aesthetic and intellectual punch: "I read a lot of war books and mysteries and all, but they don't knock me out too much." Yet he claims, "I'm quite illiterate," a statement that seemingly undermines the authority that he has been working to establish. At the same time, the statement can also be read as a marker of his readerly maturity: while he is well read for his age, he recognizes that his experience is still limited. Like a postwar Socrates, he understands that the more one reads, the more one realizes one has not read anything—a failing he hopes to correct by "read[ing] a lot" (18).

Holden's reading methods also demonstrate his critical training. He does not read to accumulate historical factoids, translate arcane words, or understand author biography but to determine how various formal components work independently and as a whole. In his modern-day Sherlock Holmes hat, he is both a detective who reads to make sense of the complexities, tensions, and ambiguities in a text and a hunter who, like other postwar literary critics, wields "formalism as a weapon."[32] He is a self-directed reader, creating meanings as he wrestles with a work's texture. He approaches his books responsibly, reading and rereading them like any critic worth his mettle. For instance, "[I] sat down and started reading that book *Out of Africa*. I'd read it already, but I wanted to read certain parts over again" (19). In this way, he demonstrates a type of reading that Ransom advocates in *The New Criticism* (1941); his rereading provides "unification of multiplicity"—a sense of stability made possible by a unified understanding of multiple ideas. The approach also matches the more popular recommendations of writers such as Fadiman: "All of us have read books that we have not finished yet, books perhaps unfinishable, books so subtle and multileveled as to reveal themselves newly with each rereading. . . . Such books do not surrender themselves at once but are like the most desirable of women, difficult in the beginning but, once won, durable in their appeal."

Leaving the sexist analogy aside, we see Fadiman associating good reading (both material and practice) with pursuing books that do not yield meaning easily or on the first read but that will continue to educate and enlighten with multiple readings, therein creating a more "durable" understanding and character. Like Harrison Smith's review of *Catcher* for the *Saturday Review*, Holden embraces a reading philosophy and methodology that demands a book be "read thoughtfully and more than once."[33]

Holden's literary detective work moves him to seek out further dialogue, an approach that postwar reading experts said would help develop intellectual skills, refine character, and build intellectual community. Holden hankers after texts that "when you're all done reading it, you wish the author that wrote it was a terrific friend of yours and you could call him up on the phone whenever you felt like it" (18). Yet even as this desire seems to validate more popular reading engagements, his reading behaviors extend New Critical practice to its logical conclusion. Like Ransom, Tate, Warren, and Brooks, who saw New Critical methods as ways to challenge aspects of modern culture that alienate individuals and obstruct true community, Holden uses reading to connect with others and bridge the gaps forged by postwar mass consumer culture. Thus, his training leads him to texts whose parts promote formal unities (not uniformities), communicate transcendent values, and thereby work to create mature and informed readerly communities.

In *The Liberal Tradition in America* (1954), Louis Hartz claimed that Cold War America lacked the depth of European thought, culture, and politics; but Holden's reading habits suggest the contrary—or that he's no average American. In fact, his understanding of authenticity versus phoniness depends on what he sees as a text's depth and resistance to simplistic or transparent meaning making. Like Emily Dickinson, whose poetry Holden's brother Allie deems "the best" (140), he values literature that tells the truth but, in Dickinson's words, "tell[s] it slant." Her poem claims that truth in its full glory is "too bright" and will "blind" us. For his part, Holden holds that a seemingly transparent text blinds, dulls, and insults the reader's intellect. Works such as Hemingway's *A Farewell to Arms,* he argues, appeal to immature readers like his sometime girlfriend Sally Hayes and his brother D.B. because they seem easy, require little erudition and exploration, rely on affective response, and can be packaged into socially useful quotations. Holden believes that art requires mindful engagement; it should not just be consumed.[34] He appreciates complexity and "digression," seemingly resisting pressure to "*uni*fy and *simpl*ify all the time" (185). In this, too, he is like Fadiman, who organized his book's "casual commentary in the form of some confessions—and digressions—of an incurable reader." Holden's narrative is told at a slant as he digresses and leaves ambiguities unresolved; nonetheless, he ultimately creates a unified and ordered truth, for each digression informs the story's organizing principle—his reading of himself and others.[35] Because he does not find order in his life, he attempts to create it in his narrative. As both reader and author, he seeks an order that recognizes but ultimately absorbs digression into its pursuit of cohesion and stability.

As a mature citizen-reader, Holden translates his methodology from the page to the people and institutions around him. He is a vigilant social reader, continually analyzing how people, places, and things do or do not fit his vision of a unified and "peaceful" America (204). In his search for order and community, he perpetually returns to what he considers an ideal American text: New York City's Museum of Natural History. Holden reads and analyzes the museum's plot, narrative, and formal structures just as he would a "best" book in order to see how its parts operate individually and as a whole. He claims, "I knew that whole museum routine like a book"; and like good books, the museum bears multiple readings. It allows digression, self-guided tours, and repetition—"sometimes we looked at the animals and sometimes we looked at the stuff the Indians had made in ancient times" (119). It invites readers to examine how its parts—cement floor, "nice" security guards, various exhibits—operate together to produce meanings and a whole understanding, and its structure encourages an intimate intellectual engagement with its various characters. Speaking in familiar terms of Columbus, Ferdinand, Isabella, and the Native Americans who are "rubbing sticks together to make a fire, and a squaw weaving a blanket," Holden sees them as individuals and as elements of a larger multifaceted narrative (121).

Like the critics who read *Catcher* as a lesson in transcendent values, Holden reads the Museum of Natural History as a lesson in creating and preserving good character. Indeed, its very purpose is conservative: it is a repository of cultural artifacts preserved and held so that generations may view and enjoy them. Holden tells us that, once a year, teachers and docents lead students through the museum to educate them on the finer points of America and its narrative of expansion and development. The museum is a tool that invests students with American character: it teaches them about exploration and courage (Columbus), industry (weaving and fishing), innovation (fire building), domesticity (squaw), family, and nation—values central to postwar liberal narratives of Americanness. By reading and interpreting the museum's narrative, visitors are unified in the imagined whole that is America.[36] Holden recalls that "the best thing" about the museum "was that everything always stayed right where it was. Nobody'd move. You could go there a hundred thousand times. . . . Nobody'd be different" (121). Subject neither to foreign influence nor to domestic uncertainty, the preeminence of America's narrative is preserved in this building for all to see. Holden's critical sensibility celebrates this constant structure: he "get[s] very happy" just thinking about it (119–120).

It is because Holden reverences the museum as an ideal American text that he is so upset by the "Fuck you" he finds "written with a red crayon or something, right under the glass part of the wall, under the stones." The violation of the museum's purity horrifies him: "you can't ever find a place that's nice and peaceful, because there isn't any. You may *think* there is, but once you get there, when you're not looking, somebody'll sneak up and write 'Fuck you' right under your nose" (204). Peace and niceness are violated by those who, like the "perverty bum" near Phoebe's school, come from outside to deface what is ordered and unified (201). Like the postwar Americans who were implicitly or explicitly fighting the red conspiracy to destroy the American way, Holden is distressed by cultural transients whose red words challenge and modify his idealized order.

In his search for stability, peace, and niceness, Holden creates a museum-like character taxonomy that groups populations according to American values. Practicing the type of social classification that John Higham details in "Cult of the 'American Consensus'" (1959), he uses "the concept of national character" to theorize class, organize history, and categorize the present.[37] Holden equates goodness with order, transcendence, purity, and complexity and links badness to chaos, mutability, profanity, and superficiality. Ultimately, however, it is reading ability that determines character and status in his schema: he believes that good characters read good books that make them good characters.

Illustrating this tautological principle is Holden's childhood sweetheart, Jane Gallagher. He fondly recalls that she "was always reading, and she read very good books. She read a lot of poetry and all. She was the only one, outside of my family, that I ever showed Allie's baseball mitt to, with all the poems written on it. . . . She was interested in that kind of stuff" (77). During an era when verse is still king, Jane's interest in "that kind of stuff" sets her apart in Holden's mind. Thus, he is furious to learn that Stradlater, his oversexed roommate, is going on a date with Jane. He knows that Stradlater wants to strip her of her complexity and reduce her to a sex object instead of appreciatively reading the various parts of her character, from her "big damn Doberman pinscher," to her "[dance] practice about two hours every day," to her much-discussed checkers strategy (31–32). Holden believes he knows Jane because he has read her *as* a character—"I knew her like a book"—and has found her to be mature and good (76).

Likewise, Holden ranks his younger sister Phoebe high because she is a good reader. Phoebe is the artist-in-residence at the Caulfields' Manhattan apartment, writing incessantly and littering her room with "a bunch of notebooks. She has about five thousand notebooks. You never saw a kid with so many notebooks" (160). Phoebe is able to quote poetry verbatim, even correcting Holden: " 'If a body *meet* a body coming through the rye'! . . . It's a poem. By Robert *Burns*" (173). As with the young title character in Salinger's short story "Teddy," her reading ability extends beyond actual text to her heightened perceptiveness about people and situations.[38] Phoebe's ability to correctly read Holden, family circumstances, and more conventional texts sets her above the other people he encounters in his wanderings. Significantly, his difficulty in separating her reading skills from her character demonstrates his conflation of the two: someone who is a good reader cannot help but be "so damn *nice*" (213). That niceness reinforces conventional attributes of Cold War character: loyalty, honesty, industry, and faith in American institutions (like schools) to train and produce good people.

Despite his admiration for Jane and Phoebe, Holden sees his younger brother Allie as the ideal reader and character. Allie has already died of leukemia when the novel begins, yet he remains a concrete presence in the novel. Holden regularly speaks to him and compares most people against him.[39] Allie "was two years younger than I was, but he was about fifty times as intelligent. He was terrifically intelligent . . . But it wasn't just that he was the most intelligent member in the family. He was also the nicest, in lots of ways." Once again, Holden links goodness to intellect. A superior student and nice person, Allie never "got mad very easily" and always supported his brother (38). Holden describes him as sensitive, loyal, and good, an essential part of what Holden sees as a lost, ideal world that values character and community.

If Allie represents the ideal reader and good American, then his baseball mitt represents a golden age of America and American letters. When pressured to write a descriptive composition for his roommate, Holden writes about Allie's mitt because "it was a very descriptive subject. It really was. . . . The thing that was descriptive about it, though, was that he had poems written all over the fingers and the pocket and everywhere. In green ink. He wrote them on it so that he'd have something to read when he was in the field and nobody was up at bat" (38). Yet what, as a text, does the mitt describe? Allie? Holden? America? Literature? More than a surface covered with poems, the mitt serves as a metonym for America, which Allie has inscribed with the good reading he extols. As Philip Roth's extravagantly titled baseball satire *The Great American Novel* (1973) suggests, "America's pastime" was a symbol of stability, power, citizenship, and democracy in the 1940s and 1950s. Families attended games together. Disparate populations united to cheer on their team. Many players came from working-class or immigrant backgrounds, and by succeeding in the sport they seemed to embody the American dream.[40]

Many aspects of the sport—clean play, individual work, and sacrifice for the team—became synonymous with American character. As the baseball historian Richard Skolnik writes, it "was offered to the public both as entertainment and as a barometer of American society." His lofty rhetoric is typical of those writing on or about baseball: the game "could be anointed guardian of traditions and repository of values considered fundamental to the culture, [and] could serve as the gateway to an idealized past." He highlights the values fostered by baseball—innocence, integrity, hard work, patriotism, honesty, and so on—all integral to postwar notions of American character. Even the book's title, *Baseball and the Pursuit of Innocence,* points toward the game's symbolic function as a representation of all that was, is, and could be good about America and American character.[41]

Allie's baseball mitt, this symbol of America and Americana, is covered with poetry, refiguring the definition of citizenship in terms of readership. Whereas Holden reads British, Danish, Germanic, and American texts, Allie and his mitt are devoted to an American readership and tradition. The poems on the "fingers and pocket and everywhere" saturate the mitt with text, anthologize great works, and construct a canon of American literature (38). They also serve as a defense of that literature. For instance, when asked who is a better war poet, Emily Dickinson or Rupert Brooke, Allie retrieves his mitt and argues for Dickinson (140). Because we know that Allie's goodness, niceness, and maturity stem from his reading, this defense has two significant implications: first, that American letters themselves are mature; and, second, that American literature is a vehicle for good character.

In contrast to the ordered, idyllic, and perceptive American readers represented by Allie's mitt, poor readers, in Holden's view, are driven by the cult of personality's promises of social acceptance and status. They are a symptom of individual and social failings. He criticizes the herd mentality of mass consumerism, deeming it detrimental to the construction of individual and national character and asserting that the massification of good books leads to what Harvard professor Reuben Brower (and Aldous Huxley before him) has called the "age of the New Stupid." Poor readers focus on cultivating a profitable personality rather than constructing a cultured character and consequently float, anchorless, in a sea of information. As the critic and editor Bernard Rosenberg claims, "there can be no doubt that the mass media present a major threat to man's autonomy. . . . No art form, no body of knowledge, no system of ethics is strong enough to withstand vulgarization." By connecting mass culture with injury to self, he also forecasts the demise of art, ethics, law, and, ultimately, democracy. Brooks similarly bemoans the "vulgarizations" of criticism and good reading "in the gossipy Book-of-the-Month Club bulletins, and in the columns of the *Saturday Review of Literature."* Holden critiques common "dopes" such as Stradlater, who "are very mean. Guys that never read books. Guys that are very boring" (123). He derides "the guys that belong to the Book-of-the-*Month* Club," who are unable to take part in intelligent conversation because they are too busy "stick[ing] together" (131). He points out "intelligent" people who allow popular taste to dictate not only their consumerism but also their literary choice and interpretation (105).[42]

Sally Hayes typifies those whom Holden blames for ruining good reading and character. She is attractive and popular, a representation of the immature yet fashionable postwar readers known as culture vultures. She typifies the personality-driven, status-seeking reader whom critics such as Barzun bemoaned, one who "buys the Five-Foot Shelf not to read—for it is hard work—but to dazzle their friends."[43] Holden admits, "I used to think she was quite intelligent, in my stupidity. The reason I did was because she knew quite a lot about the theater and plays and literature and all that stuff. If somebody knows quite a lot about those things, it takes you quite a while to find out whether they're really stupid or not" (105). He revises his opinion after witnessing how she uses reading.[44] For instance, during intermission at a matinee performance by famed actors Alfred and Lynn Fontaine Lunt, she uses her reading knowledge to facilitate circulating with "phonies," "rubbering and raving" about the performance and flirting with a "phony Andover bastard" who had used a "snobby," "Ivy league [voice]." As Lane Coutell does in Salinger's 1955 story "Franny," Sally reads to win friends and influence people.[45] Her sentimental, social "slobbering" commodifies reading and makes Holden decide that he "sort of hate[s]" her (126–128).

At one point Holden imagines Sally "out with the Lunts and all somewhere, and that Andover jerk. All of them swimming around in a goddam pot of tea and saying sophisticated stuff to each other and being charming and phony" (151). His vision suggests that the act of reading is not an end in itself; what people gain from it and how they use that knowledge determine their character and status. Although Sally, the "Andover jerk," and the actors could be considered distinguished and cultivated, Holden condemns them as vulgar because they commodify art in order to have charming, sophisticated conversation points at tea. Later in the novel, when Sally is faced with ambiguity, tension, or difficulty, she cannot comprehend them. As Holden states in a Prufrockian moment, "You don't see what I mean at all" (133).

Most disappointing to Holden is his older brother D.B., who represents good readers gone bad. Although he once idolized D.B. as an excellent reader and short-story writer, D.B.'s work as a Hollywood screenwriter has dropped him in Holden's estimation. Holden equates screenwriting with a lack of integrity, commitment, and loyalty to art. He sees the profession as subject to the whims of a fickle crowd and thus a betrayal of more stable values, and his views echo critiques such as Dwight Macdonald's: "Mass Culture is not an art form but a manufactured commodity, it tends always downward, toward cheapness—and so standardization—of production."[46] Holden is shocked that D.B. recommends Hemingway's *A Farewell to Arms*: "It had this guy in it named Lieutenant Henry that was supposed to be a nice guy and all. I don't see how D.B. could hate the Army and war and all so much and still like a phony like that" (141).[47] As a reader, a writer, and a veteran, D.B. is supposed to be able to distinguish a good war novel from a bad one, yet his literary sensibility is geared toward a popular taste that values the sentimental and the romantic. In response, Holden, who distrusts sentiment as form of vulgarity, labels both D.B. and Hemingway as common and relegates them to a lower stratum of his social structure.

Yet sometimes Holden himself uncritically internalizes what he reads and thus demonstrates the dangers of bad reading. At one point in the novel, the already tired and upset boy confesses, "This damn [magazine] article I started reading made me feel almost worse. It was all about hormones. It described how you should look, your face and eyes and all, if your hormones were in good shape, and I didn't look that way at all. I looked exactly like the guy in the article with lousy hormones. So I started getting worried about my hormones." He then turns to "this other article about how you can tell if you have cancer or not" and convinces himself that he does. The fact that Holden becomes consumed by what he reads both illustrates and reinforces his beliefs about reading's power and the dangers of certain literature. Not only do these articles make him feel "almost worse," but the death sentence they deliver makes him act irrationally—he laughs hysterically, mutters to himself, and runs into traffic. Bad literature destabilizes his good character and makes him a potential danger to himself and others (195–199).

Holden's obsession with his physical and psychological health seems to validate his belief in the infectious qualities of bad books, and such a focus on the language of exposure and fatality is common in Cold War rhetorics of character, maturity, and reading. In *The American Adam* (1955), R. W. B. Lewis famously writes of the era as "an age of containment; we huddle together and shore up defenses; both our literature and our public conduct suggest that exposure to experience is certain to be fatal." Erich Fromm similarly bemoaned that, "instead of giving us the best of past and present literature and music, these media of communication, supplemented by advertising, fill the minds of men with the cheapest trash"—minds that are "thus poisoned" and threatened with insanity.[48]

These ideas apply not only to Holden's hypochondrial suggestibility but also to criticism of *Catcher* itself. In a review for the *Christian Science Monitor*, T. Morris Longstreth writes, "Fortunately, there cannot be many of him [Holden] yet. But one fears that a book like this given wide circulation may multiply his kind—as too easily happens when immorality and perversion are recounted by writers of talent whose work is countenanced in the name of art or good intention."[49] The reviewer's attempt to prevent readers from being exposed to "perversion" brings us back to Holden's own attempt to erase the "Fuck you" from the grade-school wall. Both Holden and Longstreth see reading as contagious and identify immaturity, immorality, and perversion as infections that risk damaging the character of American readership.

In truth, however, Holden is striving to create and preserve a lost ideal of American character, and his wanderings in and among texts may be read as his efforts to recover this ideal. Although he has read widely, it is the American authors Ring Lardner and F. Scott Fitzgerald who "kill" him (18, 141). Allie's mitt invokes both a storied American tradition and a secure future. Phoebe stars as Benedict Arnold, "practically the biggest part," in a school play titled *A Christmas Pageant for Americans*. Like Dickens's Scrooge, Arnold's character learns to embrace good American values with the aid of ghostly visitors who show him that he's "ashamed and everything. You know. For betraying [his] country and everything" (162). Although this scene can be read as a satire of postwar patriotism and pageantry, the play's espousal of loyalty and honesty works to echo Holden's own values. In fact, Holden depicts D.B. as an Arnold of sorts, a man who has abandoned his talent and his American character for less noble and worthy purposes—the kind of man who dates "this English babe that's in this new picture he's writing, . . . pretty affected, but very good looking," and buys "a Jaguar. One of those little English jobs that can do around two hundred miles an hour. It cost him damn near four thousand bucks. He's got a lot of dough, now. He didn't *use* to" (213, 1).

In the end, it is not Phoebe's Benedict Arnold but Allie's ghost who represents the American spirit that Holden needs to survive. Allie's absence is an oppressive force in the novel, not unlike Seymour Glass, who haunts all of Salinger's later fiction.[50] Holden seems to need Allie's ghost in order to *be*: "Every time I'd get to the end of a block I'd make believe I was talking to my brother Allie. I'd say to him, 'Allie, don't let me disappear. Allie, don't let me disappear. Allie, don't let me disappear. Please, Allie.' And then when I'd reach the other side of the street without disappearing, I'd *thank* him" (198). Like the ghost of Hamlet's father, Allie's specter commands his brother's attention. He drives Holden's frustrated desire for cultural order, stability, and moral transcendence and prompts him to compose his narrative while he is institutionalized. That narrative becomes a concrete record and presence, an act that prevents Holden from disappearing. By gesturing toward connection with his readers and asking for their sympathy, he attempts to bring them into his world, his system, and his aesthetic.[51]

Reflecting on Allie and the values he represents lets Holden construct his own character in the form of this text. Allie is the perfect past—untainted and protected from the buffetings of personality. But Allie needs to be dead so that Holden can be the "catcher"—the one who protects others from the dangers of the Cold War world. Without his brother's death, Holden would not have the mitt; he would not have the ideal toward which he strives; he would not have the pastoral image of poetic fields. As the spirit of America, Allie represents order, loyalty, integrity, and, most significantly, sacrifice. Yet his absence suggests that taste and character may be as ephemeral and uncatchable as a ghost. While Allie, as pure text, cannot be influenced or corrupted by current trends, he is also only an idea and a memory that can fade or change. Recollection necessarily involves reordering, reshaping, and reprioritizing those things being "collected." Thus, because Allie's character is subject to time, place, individual desire, and personal taste, it is also a form of malleable, unstable personality. Despite his best efforts, Holden learns that there is no constancy and comes to recognize that character, whether individual or national, is always subject to change. Yet even as this recognition prompts his breakdown and institutionalization, it signals his attempt to come to terms with these uncertainties (213). Like the postwar American moment of which he is a part, his future is ambiguous and uncertain.

Caught

On 19 January 2013, National Public Radio (NPR) aired a segment on *All Things Considered* titled "New Reading Standards Aim to Prep Kids for College—but at What Cost?" Driving the segment was the question of whether or not changes to the national reading core would improve or damage the fitness of American youth for college, future employment, and overall life success. Significantly, NPR used Salinger's protagonist to remind listeners that reading is a political and politicized issue:

> Once upon a time, in a long-ago world of high school reading on a hilltop far, far away, Holden Caulfield was perhaps the epitome of angst, a young man suddenly an outcast in a world he thought he knew. J. D. Salinger's anti-hero was about to enter a perilous journey of self-discovery. . . . Today, down from the hilltop, high school English teachers may identify with Holden because reading scores for American students have dropped precipitously. How much? David Coleman, president of the College Board, says it's alarming.

As the segment's word choice makes clear, the epic dimension of this issue cannot be overlooked: the language of questing—"outcast," "perilous journey," "self-discovery," "precipitous[ness]"—itself speaks to a tradition of *Catcher* criticism initiated by Ihab Hassan's touchstone essay, "The Idea of Adolescence in American Fiction" (1958).[52]

After this introduction, the segment continues to tread familiar ground, calling Holden an "anti-hero" and associating him with angst and rebellion. It refers to English teachers who oppose the new Common Core standards (which require 70 percent of high school reading to be nonfiction) the new Holden Caulfields, thus suggesting they are the new American rebels.[53] In fact, these teachers *do* resemble Holden, but not for the reasons the piece implies. Rather than "sticking it to the Man," they are conservationists working to retain and protect the classics and their students from new, less literary requirements. Like Holden, they resist change and prefer to maintain an older set of standards. Although they express concern about lower reading scores, they are wary of curricular changes that privilege test results over exposure to the literary canon.

Just two days earlier, NPR's *Talk of the Nation* had featured Kevin Smokler's book *Practical Classics* (2013), advertised as a reading guide for adult readers turned off by literature in high school. Once again, the interview's lead-in referred to Salinger's protagonist: "Back in high school, we started to read grown-up books whether we wanted to or not. English teachers assigned us to explore the lives of Holden Caulfield, Huckleberry Finn, and Jay Gatsby . . . and most of us stashed the paperbacks into [a] cardboard box somewhere after we graduated, never to be opened again."

During the interview, Smokler cited both Fadiman's *The Lifetime Reading Plan* and Harold Bloom's more recent *How to Read and Why* as his models. His aim, he said, was to reintroduce people to the classics, offering guidance on how to "redefine our relationship" to them and value "great books" and "great literature." His discussion of *Catcher* is the longest in the collection and is framed as a defense, complete with a defensive tone. Fighting against teenage reviewers on Amazon.com, who have dismissed Holden as out of touch and irrelevant, Smokler counters that the character was sexy and cutting edge in 1951—a *Risky Business* figure for the postwar generation.[54]

This argument falls a bit flat. In 1951, the prematurely gray-haired teenager (9) was just as much of an old man as he was in 2013, at least in terms of his sociocultural and political values. Smokler declares that the intended audience of his *Catcher* essay includes parents, neighbors, and older siblings, a signal that he himself may have subconsciously accepted Holden's cultural old age. In fact, perhaps the very reason that Smokler appreciates Holden better as an adult reader than he did as a teenager is because the character does not fit easily into the young antihero box.[55]

Holden is a preserver of culture and a standard bearer for American taste, value, and standards, yet commentators and critics continue to see him as a rebel. In a way they use Holden as Holden uses Allie: to confirm their presence and position. Perhaps thinking of him as a rebel and an antihero helps them feel like young rebels themselves. A person cannot be the Man if he or she still reads and speaks like a boy. But as a reader, Holden himself wants to be the Man—the catcher—even as he challenges the institutions that govern him. Recognizing this conflict is one way to understand his struggle to read himself into the postwar landscape. Indeed, such a reading of *Catcher* demonstrates how Cold War concerns inflected a discourse that has seemed to so many readers the very model of literary dissent. Even as Holden struggles against cultural politics that limit the range of socially acceptable behaviors, he employs reading strategies that reinforce those politics. Even as he rejects organized religion, formal education, and other conservative institutions, his reading aesthetic emulates their values: order, purity, innocence, loyalty, security, transcendence. Even as *Catcher* offers a radical critique of consumer culture and the postwar commodification of reading, the author participated in and took advantage of that culture: the novel was a 1951 Book of the Month Club selection. Even as Salinger positioned himself as an intellectual and social rebel with a delinquent past, his literary works embrace established and establishment values, both moral and cultural. By investigating reading in *The Catcher in the Rye,* we see that it is both a novel of dissent and a product of its time. As much as Holden and his creator complain about the system, they cannot separate themselves from it. They are, despite themselves, good Americans.

3

Reading to Outmaneuver

Ralph Ellison's *Invisible Man* and
African American Literacy
in Cold War America

Perhaps the longest tradition in African American letters is the one linking literacy to freedom. Slave narratives by Frederick Douglass, Harriet Jacobs, and Olaudah Equiano exemplify "pregeneric myths," which the scholar Robert Stepto defines as "shared stories or myths that not only exist prior to literary form, but eventually shape the forms that comprise a given culture's literary canon." For him and many other literary scholars, "the primary pregeneric myth for Afro-America is the quest for freedom and literacy."[1] The two have been coupled so often in scholarship on African American letters that their connection has supplanted almost all other readings.[2]

Such scholarship has focused primarily on slave narratives, laws restricting slave access to reading, and exemplary figures such as Douglass who defied these laws and stole the power to read. More recently, however, several scholars have extended the concept of literacy beyond the temporal, geographic, and formal bounds of southern slave narratives and culture to expand our understanding of the many ways in which African Americans have read, written, and authored America.[3] Since the earliest days of the Republic, literacy has been part of African American community building, religious practice, social activism, civic engagement, and educational uplift, helping the people prepare for the full rights of citizenship and thereafter contribute to the nation.

Even so, there is a marked shift in how African American writers, educators, and political leaders framed literacy after World War II. Like the many African American soldiers who returned home and refused to accept Jim Crow as American, their contemporaries on the home front began to question the various power structures dictating access to and definitions of reading. As Mary Dudziak demonstrates in her paradigm-shifting *Cold War Civil Rights* (2000), the Cold War itself made America's racial politics a critical battlefield in the geopolitical struggle between democracy and communism, thus amplifying all stories pertaining to America's racial struggle.[4] Instead of reading literacy solely as an access point into full citizenship, many of the era's African Americans questioned the politics and ideology undergirding reading initiatives and contested the ways in which those initiatives maintained a racial status quo.

During the 1950s, there was a range of thought in African American letters about what constituted good reading and good readers. Many commentators—for instance, those writing in the *Journal of Negro Education*—adopted positions that were strikingly similar to or consonant with mainstream Cold War reading discourses. They merely noted that America's ideals would be fulfilled once African Americans were able to participate in and contribute to the nation and its security. Other postwar African Americans redefined literacy, challenging the given definitions of good readership and English, questioning who may define what it means to be literate, and rejecting the assumption that literacy is a benefit bestowed by whites. These writers and thinkers from across the political spectrum refused to accept literacy as either a universal or a neutral practice but saw it as what most literacy scholars of the past thirty years have finally recognized: a social construction that powerbrokers sometimes wield as a weapon to exclude and disenfranchise others.

Literacy does not exist in a vacuum but is part of specific historical moments, sociopolitical contexts, and cultural dynamics.[5] As an examination of 1950s educational texts, popular periodicals, political speeches, book reviews, library journals, and fiction will demonstrate, postwar African Americans were engaged in a complex and changing conversation about reading's potential to bind or free individuals. Their reading practices developed in the shadow of Jim Crow laws, discriminatory library practices, and segregated educational facilities. Yet they also emerged from the progressive efforts of individuals and communities to craft lyceums, reading groups, traveling libraries, and other initiatives. Whether denied, attained, questioned, or challenged, literacy has remained essential to these citizens.[6]

In their texts, African American authors explore a range of positions on reading's role in black communities. Some works, such as James Baldwin's *Go Tell It on the Mountain* (1953) and Lorraine Hansberry's *A Raisin in the Sun* (1959), depict reading as the route to transcending the limitations of one's status—albeit one that comes at great cost. Others texts, in a variation on the Douglass theme, depict it as a radical awakening—for instance, Richard Wright's *Black Boy* (1945), *The Autobiography of Malcolm X* (1965), and Eldridge Cleaver's *Soul on Ice* (1968). Still others represent literacy as a weapon wielded by dominant powers to control, exclude, or erase blackness; Toni Morrison takes this tack in her first novel, *The Bluest Eye* (1970), and again in a later work, *Song of Solomon* (1977). As they work to unpack the complex history and role of literacy in African American lives, these twentieth-century writers rely on books to construct themselves as individuals, community members, and citizens.[7]

In *Invisible Man* (1952), Ralph Ellison examines the complex politics of reading and citizenship in the world of midcentury African Americans.[8] Like his peers, he explores the relationship between reading and power, demonstrating how such power might be used to liberate or control and how wresting reading from oppressive institutions might offer new sociopolitical possibilities. Most literary scholars see the novel's central character as an orator—a speaker, a rabble rouser, a crafter of words.[9] But most have failed to recognize that the invisible man is primarily a *reader* (albeit a poor one) and that his reading practices shape his speeches as well as the novel's plot, aesthetic, and politics.[10] Over the course of the novel, what, how, where, and why he reads illustrate the various literacy practices and contests shaping the midcentury moment. Like *Go Tell It on the Mountain, The Bluest Eye, Black Boy,* and the essays in Addison Gayle, Jr.'s, *The Black Aesthetic,* Ellison's novel questions the terms—literal and figurative—and costs of entrance into America's social and political life as a citizen-reader.[11] As it wrestles with the central tenets of Cold War reading initiatives, *Invisible Man* considers how to read itself into a cultural tradition that still relies on language and literacy to exclude African Americans and questions whether it even wants to be included in such a tradition. The novel and its protagonist seek a mode of reading that outmaneuvers oppressive institutions and literacy prescriptions and allows for imagination, collaboration, self-determination, and new consciousness.

Reading Black

Perhaps the best-known story of African American literacy is the tale of its denial. To the many people forcibly transported from Africa to the American South, language was yet another thing stolen from them; indeed, "slave descendants are the only U.S. citizens who were unable to bring their heritage language with them to these shores." As part of this "literacy blockade," southern states passed laws forbidding slaves from reading and whites from teaching slaves how to read. Those who were caught reading were fined, beaten, imprisoned, or killed. Jim Crow laws extended these prohibitions after Reconstruction. In the South's burgeoning industrial economy, "maintaining a high illiteracy rate within the black population suited the interests of capitalists" because "workers who could read would only cause trouble." Thus, "the pattern of public education which eventually emerged in the South was suited to keep the Negro in practically the same status he had occupied before the War for freedom had been won." Jim Crow also impeded library access. In addition to outright exclusion, segregated library practices included limiting black patrons to books by mail, traveling libraries, library stations, back-room library access, inferior county branches, and so on. All of these obstructions functioned as instruments of social control to keep black Americans illiterate and therefore "in their place."[12]

Yet the people in southern black communities continually found ways to read. Some churches did teach slaves, although their instruction was largely "confined . . . to encoding and decoding, mostly reading the Bible." Negro periodicals such as *Freedom's Journal,* the *Colored American,* and the *Appeal*— David Walker's explosive pro-literacy and pro-suffrage tract—found their way into slave hands, and both their forms and their content bore witness to reading's "ability to contest white racism."[13] This understanding spurred a range of revolutionary literacy practices in the mid- and late nineteenth century. As the Civil War raged, Negro troops convinced Union soldiers, commanders, and civilians to teach them how to read so they might be prepared "for their future lives as citizens and self-dependent free men and heads of families." Despite the risk of extreme violence, the Freedman's Education program in North Carolina formed in 1865 to help newly freed men learn to read. In 1898, black Alabamians formed the state's first library. These efforts continued in the early twentieth century. In the 1920s, Kathryn M. Johnson drove her Ford coupe more than 25,000 miles in only two and a half years to sell books to text-hungry southern black communities.[14] The wildly successful Faith Cabin Library program helped African American participants finance, build, organize, and run more than one hundred community libraries in the South.[15] Communities such those on the Carolinas' remote sea islands founded programs that taught reading as a way to enhance citizenship and everyday living.[16]

Free blacks in the North also developed a transformative set of literacy practices, including reading rooms, lecture societies, and publishing houses. As early as 1770, African Americans were organizing aid societies that eventually addressed "the urgency of creating their own opportunities to become readers and institute systems through which to exchange and produce literature." Philadelphia's Colored Reading Society, New York's Phoenix Society, the Boston Literary and Historical Association, the Bethel Historical and Literary Association, and many other literary societies were "places of refuge for the self-improvement of their members" and "acts of resistance to the hostile racial climate that made the United States an uncomfortable and unequal place for all black Americans, regardless of their social or economic condition." These groups offered members access to books and the world of ideas in hopes of prompting the "many Negroes who could read to read further, and those who were unable to read to learn to read." By the time the Civil War broke out, northern African Americans had set up more than fifty libraries and "debating and reading-room societies," driven by the belief in "literacy as social action" and a way for black Americans to "voice their demands for full citizenship and equal participation in the life of the nation." An important part of these efforts were the numerous African American publications (among them *Freedom's Journal*, the *Colored American*, the *Weekly Anglo-African*, the *Anglo-African Magazine*, the *Afric-American Quarterly Repository*, and the *North Star*) that supplied materials to help African Americans prepare for citizenship, organize the masses, and defeat racial prejudice.[17]

In the face of persistent opposition, African American literacy practices continued to develop during the twentieth century. As it did for earlier generations, an abiding faith in reading's ability to facilitate self-improvement and racial uplift and fulfill the promise of America's founding documents sustained those who were struggling. In 1933, the journalist, historian, and activist Carter G. Woodson expressed his hope that Americans would use education "to help the Negro rather than exploit him," enabling him to become "proud of his past by approaching it scientifically himself and giving his own story to the world" rather than perpetuating an educational system that "has been worked out in conformity to the needs of those who have enslaved and oppressed weaker peoples." Likewise, in a 1936 article in the *Journal of Negro Education,* Dorothy Porter celebrated the work of literary societies to help black citizens "improve their mental and moral condition" and assist their youth to prepare to participate in the workings of the nation—a common theme in the magazine. A belief in uplift and progress motivated much of the rhetoric in educational, literary, and print media circles in the early twentieth century. Equally important was the faith that reading helped a person become a "credit to the race." Thinkers such as J. Saunders Redding saw African American journals such as the *Crisis* as necessary "for the expression of all sorts of ideas that r[u]n counter to the notion of Negro inferiority"; for "transformation" of themselves, their community, and the nation; and as a context for "creating for themselves a new freedom."[18]

Like other Americans, African Americans made great sacrifices during

FIGURE 4. A poster originally published by the Works Progress Administration's War Services, New York City, circa 1941–1943.

World War II, enlisting to serve in the armed forces, working in factories, and dealing with the everyday struggles of wartime living. Participation in the war "altered black aspirations and increased political and economic opportunity."[19] Yet after it ended, black servicemen and women returned to Jim Crow laws, job discrimination, restrictive housing covenants, and the daily indignities of racial prejudice. The rights they had defended abroad were denied to them at home. As a result, midcentury African Americans became more active, organized, and radicalized, "creating for themselves a new freedom" by revisiting the founding documents as texts, interpreting them for themselves, and identifying the disjuncture between the spirit of the texts and their application in American life. Chas. H. Thompson, a Howard University professor and the founder of the *Journal of Negro Education,* acknowledged that the "Negro as a citizen is presumed to enjoy all of the rights, duties and privileges of any other citizen." Yet "as an actual fact, . . . nowhere in this country does he enjoy such privileges to the same extent as native born white citizens." Still, Thompson said, he worked and hoped for "a democratic social order" in which black youth's political, social, and educational "lot will be more tolerable than their parents'."[20] In their criticisms of slavery, segregation, and the continued oppression of black people, many educators, librarians, community leaders, and reading guides asserted that segregating schools and libraries was a "direct challenge to the American democratic ideal," turned a "deaf ear to Jefferson," and was "unconstitutional." They and their allies vociferously pointed out the difference between what America's founding documents claimed and the lived reality of black citizens.[21] Like Ellison, they identified "the conflicts within the human heart which arose when the sacred principles of the Constitution and the Bill of Rights clashed with the practical exigencies of human greed and fear, hate and love," and demanded a reconciliation of profession and practice.[22]

In such a climate, it is not surprising that many midcentury African Americans had a complicated relationship with Cold War America's reading discourse. While they embraced its faith in good reading and good citizenship, they also recognized that the definitions of both ideals were controlled by authorities who often sought to disempower nonwhites. African Americans saw these ideals as a means through which they could create for themselves an equitable and free world—an empowering and necessary act, given that white institutions had, more often than not, impeded this work. Emphasizing that "literacy and education" constitute the "path to a 'rightful place' of full citizenship," African American educators advocated improving reading and writing programs at all educational and community levels. Ambrose Caliver, the first African American assistant to the commissioner in the U.S. Office of Education, focused his research and work on black illiteracy, calling it "a blight on the Nation." He advocated increased research, funding, teacher training, and federal support to improve literacy rates and attitudes toward education in African American communities, ultimately hoping to improve "peace and harmony" and "human relations" globally. Howard University's assistant dean of liberal arts, Carroll Miller, proclaimed that "in a democracy it is essential that the citizenship potential of each individual shall be developed and the maximum contribution of each realized" for the good of the nation and the world, and he saw literature and reading as central to that quest.[23]

Other advocates wrote that "good literature" would "strengthen the growth of democracy" in schools, libraries, homes, and daily life. They promised that equal access to books would enable African Americans "to advance our causes by becoming informed through reading . . . [and allow us to] participate in the great ethical and great social debates of our time" as "an integral part of the leadership of the New Democratic South." All of this must be done "for democracy's sake"; for a good reader was a good citizen—even if parts of white America did not yet recognize African Americans as citizens of any kind. The "challenge" for black educators, librarians, and readers was "to regard their heritage of America with positive and affirmative action toward a realization of what America should be for its entire citizenry."[24]

Many Cold War African Americans answered these calls and sought books, education, and library access in greater numbers than ever before. African American book clubs flourished in major cities, and subscription book clubs such as the Negro Book Club, the Frederick Douglass Book Club, and the Progressive Book Club became popular. African American newspapers increasingly included book columns and book reviews, and the Book of the Month Club advertised in *Ebony.* Independent African American publishing houses continued to expand their numbers, and educators and publishers called for more books representing varied African American experiences for readers of all ages.[25] The American Library Association, which at times had failed to challenge segregation and race prejudice, began calling openly for increased resources and programs to address the needs of African American libraries, readers, communities, and youth: "we cannot say to Negro youth 'Open Your Future—Read,' and at the same time make no effort to help him read. Negro youth and all American youth may be aided by improving the nation's school libraries."[26] Efforts to desegregate libraries escalated in the 1950s and 1960s, with read-ins in Mississippi and elsewhere garnering national coverage in magazines such as *Library Journal* and *Newsweek.*[27]

At the same time, changes were evident in African American education. According to a 1952 study of Negro colleges and universities, student enrollment had increased from 2,624 in 1900 to 76,561 in 1950. The number of bachelors' degrees had also increased, from 156 in 1900 to 13,108 in 1950. Likewise, the number of masters' degrees had increased, from 2 in 1899 to 768 in 1950, as had the number of African American faculty: from 1,555 in 1900 to 6,600 in 1950.[28] According to another study, the number of African American students attending unaccredited institutions had dropped to 10 percent; now most undergraduates and graduates attended accredited institutions, many of them liberal arts colleges. In a single year, 1949–1950, the total number of African American college graduates had swelled by 20.4 percent, the number of African American graduate students had increased by 12 percent, and the number of African Americans receiving masters' degrees had jumped a staggering 48 percent.[29] However, the *relative* enrollment of black to white students revealed a persistent racial gap in rates of educational access and accomplishment. On the whole, nonwhite attendance at public elementary schools, high schools, and postsecondary schools was up, but it still was significantly lower than white attendance. In fact, the gap in high school attendance was closing so slowly that it would take "280 years for the level of education of non-whites to equal that of whites." In 1953, whites were still two times more likely than blacks to attend college.[30] Thus, while progress was visible, economic and political obstacles still prevented African Americans from reaching full educational and social equality.

Hence, as increasing numbers of African Americans accessed books, libraries, and higher education while still facing job, housing, social, and political discrimination, many questioned the relationship between freedom and literacy, calling such assumptions hollow or at least naïve. Being able to read did not guarantee that one would get a job, find housing in a racially restricted area, or avoid daily indignities.[31] As a result, "a distrust of the printed word, especially when it concerns or presumes to represent black experience, . . . [arose in] much black literature after World War II." In the 1950s, a younger generation of civil rights activists began to assert that the problem was not merely white supremacist custom or prejudicial interpretation of American statutes; rather, the very letter of the law was racist and exclusionary. During a commencement address at the College of William and Mary, Ellison spoke directly about this issue: "The moral conflict which marks the world into which you go was present even in our sacred documents of state, even in the clerical forms which made it possible for our bureaucracies to get on with their work. . . . They were woven into the texture of our society."[32]

A central assumption of Cold War reading theories was that literacy is the ultimate stage in humanity's "history of progress" and the primary signifier of civilization. This assumption created a sort of "mythical charter for the dominant social order and its ideals . . . which in effect sanction[ed] existing interests and explanations by an apparently incontrovertible authority transcending (but supporting) the current establishment." Yet as the philosopher J. Elspeth Stuckey contends in *The Violence of Literacy* (1991), literacy is always a "system of oppression" that works to "replicate, or at least not to disturb, social division and class privilege." After World War II, African American letters increasingly interrogated, revised, and reread the "sacred documents" and "clerical forms" so central to Cold War ideas about literacy.[33] At the same time, however, white politicians, educators, and linguists, both benevolent and malevolent, were marking African American reading and speech as "deficient" and therefore requiring top-down "correction" and control.[34] Such "Eurocentric bias and racism" elevated and normalized white ideologies of literacy, reproducing social inequity and "serving mainly the purposes of the elite."[35] By denigrating their culture, this attitude perpetuated great violence against African Americans, demanding they conform to an arbitrary white standard and setting them up to fail educationally, socially, economically, and politically.

Systemic violence prompted James Baldwin to declare that American society "is desperately menaced, not by Khrushchev, but from within." In a 1963 speech to educators, he charged America's educational system with seeking to preserve white supremacy and the racial status quo, behaviors that made it, he said, more dangerous than communism. His words echoed those of the NAACP's 1947 "An Appeal to the World," written primarily by W.E.B. Du Bois: "It is not Russia that threatens the United States so much as Mississippi; not Stalin and Molotov but Bilbo and Rankin; internal injustice done to one's brothers is far more dangerous than the aggression of strangers from abroad." The specter of the Cold War haunts African Americans' midcentury writings about reading and citizenship. They watched as the *Brown v. Board of Education* decision, the fight for school integration in Little Rock, Arkansas, and the college-student sit-ins around the country "exposed [to the world] the hypocrisy of the United States' treatment of blacks." In 1950, Caliver noted that "the relation of Negroes in this new world order has gained new prominence," and he declared that education would be key to the struggle. Others condemned the "cotton curtain" constructed of white supremacist ideas of race and knowledge, arguing that denying African Americans the right to read forced much of the nation "to remain out of step with . . . the world." Those challenging library segregation declared that "separate but equal" codes were illegal, "whether in Mississippi or Soviet Russia." Time and again, African Americans confronted and forced others to confront a key question: "How could American democracy be a beacon during the Cold War, and a model

FIGURE 5. Photograph of a civil rights protest in Farmville, Virginia, circa July 1963. Published in Bill McKelway, "Our Nation Has a Date with Destiny," *Richmond Times-Dispatch*, 24 August 2013. Reprinted by permission of the *Richmond Times-Dispatch*.

for those struggling against Soviet oppression, if the United States itself practiced brutal discrimination against minorities within its own borders?"[36]

At the same time, many African Americans were skeptical about court rulings, policy changes, and integration concessions, believing that these laws and rulings were window dressing for an international audience rather than signs of a legitimate change of heart. As Baldwin wrote,

> Most of the Negroes I know do not believe that this immense concession [*Brown v. Board of Education*] would ever have been made if it had not been for the competition of the Cold War, and the fact that Africa was clearly liberating herself and therefore had, for political reasons, to be wooed by the descendants of her former masters. Had it been a matter of love or justice, the 1954 decision would surely have occurred sooner; were it not for the

realities of power in this difficult era, it might very well not have occurred yet.[37]

People also questioned the validity and enforceability of these laws and rulings. So often in the past, written texts that had seemed to guarantee freedoms had been left to the interpretation and implementation of the whites in power.

Weariness and wariness marked many African Americans' reception of civil rights legislation and its public, international dimension. At the same time, a number of black writers, educators, activists, and politicians continued to warn that discriminatory uses, denials, and inhibitions of African American literacy and learning would destroy democracy at home and undermine national efforts abroad. In 1951, the educator A. D. Beittel wrote, "When for our own safety we need to win the cooperation of colored peoples all over the world, segregated education is a great obstacle making it difficult for us to convince the world that we know how to make democracy work." United Nations ambassador Ralph Bunche agreed: "The position of world leadership which our nation now enjoys is made vulnerable and morally undefensible by the harsh rattling of the race-relations skeletons in our closet. We cannot afford, the world cannot afford, to have this nation made ineffective by the taunt 'Your undemocratic deeds speak so loudly that your democratic professions cannot be heard.'"[38]

To some, however, these outspoken African Americans seemed to threaten the established order, and they often were dismissed as Communists. Civil rights organizations "had to walk a fine line, making it clear that their reform efforts were meant to fill out the contours of American democracy, and not to challenge or undermine it." As Dudziak has noted, the NAACP took great care to "cast its efforts at racial reform as part of the struggle against communism," and groups such as the Southern Christian Leadership Council and the Fellowship of Reconciliation repeatedly professed their faith in American democracy to forestall red baiting. Volunteers associated with Freedom Summer schools and libraries and those who were helping African American citizens prepare for literacy tests and register to vote also faced the terrors of red baiting and blatant racism: in the space of ten weeks in 1964, at least 425 incidents of white supremacist violence were recorded. Ironically, by that decade, even the older generation of African American community leaders were throwing around the term *Communist* in efforts to stall increasingly activist, "trouble-making" civil rights efforts.[39]

Many black writers and publishers had to contend with FBI surveillance and charges of un-American activity. Between 1919 and 1972, Hoover's bureau accumulated more than 13,000 pages of material on African American writers labeled as radicals or merely suspected to be potential challengers of the status quo. Further, the "FBI readied preventative arrests of more than half of the black authors shadowed in its archive," engaging in what William Maxwell calls "editorial federalism"—that is, the practice of perpetuating narratives that "represent the national security state's collective interests." Hoover's counterintelligence program, known as COINTELPRO, closely monitored the activities, correspondence, and publications of prominent civil rights figures, from Martin Luther King, Jr., to Malcolm X, using poison-pen letters, false flyers, and other reading materials to undermine movements for racial equality.[40]

Nevertheless, civil rights activists saw reading as a valuable weapon against racial prejudice, one that could be used in service of a truer democracy. In a 1965 memoir of her work as a Freedom Summer librarian, Miriam Braverman saw the "widespread interest and enthusiasm for the library as integral to the arsenal of weapons of the nonviolent movement" and noted that "each civil rights headquarters houses a library, which is used by students, parents, and teachers." The educator and librarian E. J. Josey contended that libraries and "good books" have "a very important role to play" in the civil rights movement: "[they] are powerful weapons to use in the battle to overcome the cultural lag that Negro youth have suffered because of segregation and discrimination." In an article in the American Library Association's *Bulletin*, Charles Morgan claimed that "the library is a major battlefield, its books most important weapons" for defeating institutional racism and homegrown "totalitarianism."[41] Here and elsewhere, activists saw reading as a way to disarm white supremacy and destroy institutional discrimination. While this stance resonated with core beliefs of Cold War reading discourses, it was now being used as a weapon against those very institutions that had claimed to be quintessentially American but were in truth failing to be democratic. To those in power, such rhetoric was treasonous; to the oppressed, it was a revolutionary reclamation of the ideas and ideals of America's founding.

As they languished in the jails of Mississippi, Freedom Summer volunteers read books to pass the time. A young man named Morton wrote to his parents from prison, saying, "I can't sleep, though I've finished *Borstal Boy* and reread *Invisible Man* and *The Stranger*." Notably, he grouped Ellison's book with Brendan Behan's political memoir and Albert Camus's existential urtext. Like them, *Invisible Man* questioned oppressive ideologies and racist systems and sought a means of creating a more equitable and just society. Although Ellison later wrote that "*I would always write as though the governor of Mississippi was looking over my shoulder,*" it was less his overt political writings and more the act of opposition that was his novel that garnered a civil rights readership and triggered activist sympathies.[42]

Reading Ellison Anew

Invisible Man can be read as a cautionary tale about the pitfalls of misreading. The invisible man is a poor reader who allows others to dictate what, why, and how he reads, relinquishing his agency and assisting in his own disenfranchisement. In many ways, he is the opposite of the ideal reader whom Ellison sketches in his essay "The Little Man at Chehaw Station." Whereas the little man challenges assumptions, prompts questions, suggests answers, defies categories, promotes collaboration, and assumes an agency of expression, the invisible man spends most of the novel toeing the line, following the program, and seeing the world as he has been taught to see it.[43] Because he ingests the sanctioned narratives his leaders have authored and perpetuates the psychological and social violence written therein, he represents the type of poor reader that midcentury African American educators, writers, and politicians were struggling to eliminate. Although the novel is set in prewar America, the invisible man's history, education, social position, and reading skills speak to African Americans' postwar concerns about discriminatory institutions, ideologies, and interpretations. Likewise, his journey mirrors that of the era's civil rights activists—a growing awareness of the social, political, economic, and interpretive possibilities available to him as a human being (580). Cold War America's emphasis on reading, citizenship, and nationhood is key to the invisible man's struggle and possible awakening and therefore key to *Invisible Man* itself.

Lesley Larkin, Alan Nadel, and Henry Louis Gates, Jr., have studied ways in which readers have approached Ellison's novel. However, few literary scholars have examined the role of reading within the novel itself.[44] Yet as in *The Catcher in the Rye*, *Invisible Man*'s opening paragraph and prologue immediately establish the narrator as a reader and the novel as a readerly text. The narrator quickly reveals his familiarity with Dante, the Bible, American authors such as Edgar Allan Poe, African American folk texts, low-brow texts such as the gossipy *New York Daily News*, and American hero myths about "Ford, Edison and Franklin" (6–10). The opening of *Invisible Man* leads the reader back into the past world of his picaresque narrative; in other words, at the beginning of the novel, we meet the broad readerly self that the narrator has become. So where did he start? If "responsibility" and "recognition" are the goals of a well-formed and -informed citizen-reader, how did the invisible man reach them (14)?

The invisible man's journey is a series of traumatic events triggered by a series of texts he fails to read—from the "official looking document" he receives after winning the Battle Royal (a brutal boxing match involving several blindfolded black schoolboys fighting for the entertainment of the town's white leaders), to the "important papers" his white high school superintendent foretells he will carry as a race leader, to the seven letters he receives after his college expulsion "addressed to men with impressive names," to the job reference from the supposedly enlightened race ally Mr. Emerson, to the hospital affidavit sanctioning his shock therapy, to the documents from the Brotherhood—the Harlem political organization for which he becomes a spokesperson (32, 31). As a high school student in a segregated school and town, he learns to read, see, speak, and do under the control of a power structure that wishes to keep him in "place" (16). In a speech before the town leaders, he quotes Booker T. Washington's "Atlanta Compromise," thus revealing himself to be the ideal product of a manipulated reading curriculum (30). "The wisdom of that great leader and educator" calls for a separation of peoples, imposing an interpretation of African American potential that reinforces the status quo (29).

Thanks to a scholarship from the town's white leaders, the young man continues his education at a Tuskegee-like institution, where he is taught not to "suspect there is more" to life or be "curious about what lies behind the face of things" (188). Rather, he is told to rely on those in power—for instance, Dr. Bledsoe, the school's president—who "know what's best for me" (189). As the scholar Roderick Ferguson points out, "[the] canonically driven . . . Western university has historically worked to socialize subjects into the state"; the pressure is even greater in institutions that have historically worked to subject persons of color to prevailing standards. Taught to defer to authority, the invisible man does not learn how to read for himself. He trusts in appearances, "always tr[ying] to do the right thing" according to the rules that others establish and enforce (191).[45]

When texts deviate from familiar methods, myths, and narratives, the invisible man gets "lost," so he retreats into the ideas and "phrases that I had learned all my life" (238, 275). He clings to knowable systems: speaking with dismay to a Harlem mob, he asserts, "We're a law-abiding people and a slow-to-anger people" (275). He continues to read the law as neutral and universal and does not question who or what has created, controls, or benefits from it. His call to the mob echoes both Washington's Atlanta speech and the white power structure's demand that African Americans be docile, tractable, and compliant.[46] His impulse to cling to these phrases and narratives underscores the totalizing nature of his reading education and makes him an easy target for those who wish to use and control him—for instance, the Brotherhood, which is seeking the next "Booker T." to "follow instructions" and represent the organization after a "period of intense study and indoctrination" (305, 308, 351). As a reader, the invisible man follows rules, schedules, discussions, and meetings. When he joins the Brotherhood, where "every occasion [becomes] a study situation," he simply becomes another party's man (357).

Significantly, the invisible man's reading education and indoctrination blind him not only to other modes of meaning making but also to the reality of his subservient position and his own part in his oppression. For instance, he does not think it is "honorable or safe to tamper with" the letters Dr. Bledsoe has given him, even after that leader reveals himself to be duplicitous and dangerous. The invisible man continues to invest value into doing what he is told. Thus, he takes the texts' outer appearance for reality: he calls his letters of recommendation a "hand of high trump cards," not realizing that he will always be trumped by the people who have dealt those cards (163). His conversation with Emerson's son reveals the extent to which the lessons of his leaders have blinded him to the realities of his position (185). Whereas Trustee Emerson's son claims there is "tyranny involved" in these letters, the invisible man struggles to see through the veil of his reading education (187).

The invisible man's blindness is further evidenced when he receives an anonymous letter "from a friend who has been watching" him closely, which warns him to "go easy so that you can keep on helping the colored people" (383). The invisible man misinterprets the letter; rather, he interprets it exactly as the controlling Brotherhood might wish him to read it. The letter's text adopts an us-them division based on race; but instead of examining those around him and questioning the note's provenance, the invisible man follows the track the Brotherhood has laid, convincing himself that "whoever sent the message [was] trying to confuse me; . . . trying to halt our progress by destroying my faith through touching upon my old southern distrust, our fear of white betrayal" (390–391). Because he has bought into the Brotherhood's falsities, he becomes his own worst enemy.

Indoctrination keeps the invisible man from reading other signs and symbols that could help free him from his narrow interpretive confines. Like segregation, it is "a device to keep the Negro in an inferior position" and to prevent African Americans from being able to comprehend and address the diverse challenges and demands of contemporary society.[47] The invisible man struggles to make sense of symbols such as the chain link his elder Harlem comrade Brother Tarp gives him or the racist dolls he finds his former Brotherhood comrade Tod Clifton selling on the street. Tarp tells him that there's a "heap of signifying wrapped up in" this broken, open link, yet it unsettles the invisible man because his mode of reading is precisely the opposite of signifying (388). He has been trained to follow a logic that claims to hold singular truth and be the key to all mythologies. He has been inoculated against signifying and its transgressive meaning-making practices by the oppressive forces arrayed against him and others.

Thus, when the invisible man runs into Clifton, his former Brotherhood comrade, selling racist paper dolls, his "mind grappl[es] for meaning" as "bits of paper [whirl] up" around him in the subway station (435, 438). The disorder prompts a new range of *what* and *why* questions that refute the Brotherhood's interpretative schema and frighten the narrator. In response, he retreats into the shelter of the Brotherhood, frustrated that he has failed "to educate" others or to situate symbols and events within the proper "apparatus" (445, 470).

"Only the correct ideas for the correct occasion" feels like a safe way to approach life, for the invisible man knows that asking questions is not safe in the world that others have created (470). Whenever he does pose questions or reflects on what and how he knows, oppressive institutions and their representatives force him back into line, meeting his deviations with threats of violence. For instance, when he "slips" in his Battle Royale speech and calls for "social equality" instead of "social responsibility," he is met with "sudden stillness," "sounds of displeasure," and "hostile phrases" from the town's white power structure. These powerful men are quick to correct him, and he is quick to acquiesce because he is "afraid" (31). When he threatens the power structure at Liberty Paints by asking questions, he is tricked into triggering an explosion, injured, and given shock therapy without justifiable cause or consent. He is forced into a reeducation program of the hospital's making, the "power" represented by the electric current shocking him back into his place and helping him "becoming adjusted, as it were," to the docility that others expect (247). He is never the source of power but always a conductor or receiver. As a result, he cannot wholly break free from the currents that shape his thought, sensing himself to be in "a kind of combat with myself," feeling "criminal" but "why ... I didn't know" (242).

During his first speech for the Brotherhood, the invisible man is warned to be "careful now" when he flirts with going "off script" and reading the crowd and situation as he sees them (345). Afterward, the "grim" leadership chastises him, calling his speech "backward and reactionary," "wild, hysterical, politically irresponsible and dangerous. . . . And worse than that, it was *incorrect*" (350, 349). He is prescribed a course of study that strips him of his individuality, teaches him "not to ask any questions," and emphasizes that he was "not hired to think" (356, 469). When he challenges Brother Jack's leadership and ideology—"Wouldn't it be better if they called you Marse Jack?"—the leader comes at him, "gripping the edge of the table, spluttering and lapsing into a foreign language, choking and coughing and shaking his head," and "pacing up and down, shouting" (473, 474).

Despite the perpetual threat of social, political, ideological, and physical violence, the invisible man does have moments in which he considers interpretative possibilities that fall outside of sanctioned narratives. Throughout the text he has moments of insight that draw his attention to the oppressive structures defining him and the possibility of alternate modes of reading and meaning making. As a young man, he dreams he is at a circus with his grandfather, who encourages him to open the "official envelope stamped with the state seal," inside of which he finds "another and another, endlessly," until he comes to one last "engraved document containing a short message in letters of gold" (33). The dream can be read as signifying the state's perpetual deferment of rights and citizenship for African Americans, and it highlights the controls of lawmakers, judicial appointees, and those in charge of the state's capital. Like the fake gold at the Battle Royal, the gold letters on this dream document reveal the lie inscribed in and on the nation state's founding documents: "To Whom It May Concern. . . . Keep This Nigger-Boy Running" (33).

The narrator's growing awareness is revealed in the eviction episode that follows his shock therapy. As he looks at an old couple's possessions on the curb, he feels "strange memories awakening that began an echoing in my head." It is significant that, once again, his awakening results from reading. Included in the various objects in the snow are literal texts: a card reading "God Bless Our Home," news clippings, and voided life insurance policies (271). He sees "an ornate greeting card with the message 'Grandma, I love you' in a childish scrawl," baseball scorecards, sheet music, and "a fragile paper, coming apart with age, written in black ink grown yellow. I read: FREE PAPERS. *Be it known to all men that my negro, Primus Provo, has been freed by me this sixth day of August, 1859. Signed: John Samuels. Macon*" (272). As the invisible man recognizes, these humble texts form an archive of African American life. They speak of family, work, community, art, folk culture, and freedom; they are a record of a people and emblems of a culture. Although he has not been schooled in such texts or readings, he experiences "a pang of vague recognition" and a "*discomfort so far beyond their intrinsic meaning as objects*" (273).

Removing the "veil" that his school leaders have placed over his eyes troubles the invisible man both physically and emotionally:

> I turned and stared again at the jumble, no longer looking at what was before my eyes, but inwardly-outwardly, around a corner into the dark, far-away-and-long-ago, not so much of my own memory as of remembered words, of linked verbal echoes, images, heard even when not listening at home. And it was as though I myself was being dispossessed of some painful yet precious thing which I could not bear to lose. (273)

Rather than looking forward into his great aspirations to lead and his grand narrative of progress, he finds himself looking backward into knowledge picked up in unconventional venues and from unofficial sources. To this point, he has always felt disconnected from aspects of black culture—his grandfather, the former slave cabins near the college, the disgraced sharecropper

Trueblood, the black veterans and asylum patients at the Golden Day bar, and the people he first meets in Harlem. Suddenly, however, he feels for and with the old couple, as if he, too, is being "dispossessed."

The invisible man is similarly unsettled when he attempts to understand ideas that resist interpellation by the Brotherhood's doctrine. In many ways, this recognition is like that for which the Black Arts Movement's Addison Gayle calls in "The Literature of Protest": "a confrontation between the white idealistic conception of reality and the pragmatic conception which negates the American Creed. In so doing, the white American is forced to turn inward upon himself, to question his most sacred ideals, and if he is at all sensitive to admit that they are, after all, more imaginary than real."[48] Although the invisible man is not white, he has, up to this point, accepted the white power structure's "idealistic conception of reality." But when he runs into Tod Clifton and his racist dolls, he is thrust into this "confrontation" and "forced to turn inward," "to question," and to admit that what he has embraced may be "imaginary." The whirlwind of interpretative possibilities that fall outside of the Brotherhood's sanctioned narratives and interpretative methods unmoors him. To understand, he at first tries his old method: "to step away and look at it from a distance of words read in books." Yet as he begins to ask *why* questions, he comes to recognize that "only those events that the recorder regards as important ... are put down, those lies his keepers keep their power by" (439).

The invisible man subsequently embarks on an unstructured and self-directed foray into new knowledge. His search is characterized by words such as "plunging," "roaring," and "sparks," signaling his descent into the underworld and foreshadowing his escape and enlightenment at the end of the novel (438, 439). Like many black educators, politicians, artists, and activists of the 1950s and 1960s, he identifies a central institutional apparatus that is keeping him down and others up, a realization that causes him to "tremble so violently" that he has "to lean against a refuse can"—perhaps the proper place for the Brotherhood's narrative (441). As he does at the end of the Battle Royale, after his expulsion from college, and during his shock treatment, the invisible man trembles violently because he is on the precipice of learning to read for himself.

Now that the narrator has awakened to the possibility of other modes of interpretation, he leaps into the interpretive void. He realizes that the Brotherhood "was all a swindle, an obscene swindle! They had set themselves up to describe the world," yet "what did they know of us" (507)? He recognizes that he has been tricked out of his name, his past, and his creative ability to author his own life and participate in his community. Like other oppressive white institutions, "they had set themselves up to describe the world" in order to perpetuate their own power. The invisible man chooses to reject such indoctrination. He attempts to see beyond the surface, "to look around corners," to read himself out of narratives and systems that would constrain him (508). He realizes that "Jack and Norton and Emerson . . . were very much the same, each attempting to force his picture of reality upon me and neither giving a hoot in hell for how things looked to me. I was simply a material, a natural resource to be used" (508). He discerns that "they kept us [blacks] dominated" by claiming "that success was a rising *upward.*" He even suspects that the narrative in which literacy equals freedom is itself a lie (510).[49] He has awakened to the possibility that he might have a perspective of his own, one unsanctioned by those in power.

Such thinking is revolutionary and, to the many institutions seeking to control the invisible man, "extreme treason" (192). Emerson indicates this possibility when he shows him Dr. Bledsoe's letter and exposes the reality hidden in the envelope. The secret workings of the power structure are made manifest, and the tyranny of knowledge is challenged. Although the invisible man is not yet able to understand fully this act, the cumulative weight of his insights eventually helps him to declare his independence and reject oppressive reading prescriptions and institutions.

The final chapter of the novel proper depicts a Harlem race riot that the Brotherhood's machinations have helped trigger in order to create a power vacuum for the organization to fill. Harlem is wracked with inter- and intraracial violence, and the invisible man realizes that as the Brotherhood's Booker T.—that is, as spokesperson, puppet, and man—he, too, is responsible for the riot. Yet as he faces his own destruction, the invisible man also recognizes "now who I was and where I was and . . . that I had no longer to run for or from the Jacks and the Emersons and the Bledsoes and Nortons" (559). He chooses to stop the running that started when he received and misread his first document and escapes the riot's violence by jumping into a manhole. Here he is literally and figuratively in the dark, and he chooses to burn his documents so that he can see his place with clarity. These once-cherished important papers, written by and for important men, become fodder for a feeble flame, therein marking their actual worth. "I started with my high-school diploma, applying one precious match with a feeling of remote irony," and then works through all of the papers he has accumulated—those texts that he has allowed to determine the course of his life (567). Burning these texts helps him expose the "illusions and lies" that he had read as the story of his life, and living underground allows him to "try to think things out in peace, or if not in peace, in quiet," without the noise of those discourses that are competing to direct and own him (569, 571).

This time the invisible man is really able to begin anew, choosing for himself what, how, and why he reads. A radical now, he burns the trappings of his oppression and works "belatedly to study the lesson of [his] own life" (572). In so doing, he performs the work for which the African American literary critic Stephen Henderson calls in *Understanding the New Black Poetry* (1972)—reading and studying blackness "in order to move . . . toward self-knowledge and collective freedom."[50] Unlike the invisible man we meet early in the novel proper, this version recognizes and begins to accept ambiguity. He comes to understand that interpretation is relative and relational, that "good and evil, honesty and dishonesty" are "shifting shapes" whose meaning depends "upon who happens to be looking through him at the time" (572). This is in direct contrast to the "security" of narratives and modes of reading that provide "facts," fixity, and a "world . . . nailed down" (573). While authorities and institutions try "to give pattern to the chaos which lives within the pattern of your certainties," the invisible man comes to see such singularity as false (580–581).

Like many postwar African American educators and politicians, the invisible man recognizes the violence in a "nailed down" world, particularly when others are doing the nailing. He admits that, to accept this world, he had to "choke myself until my eyes bulged and my tongue hung out and wagged like the door of an empty house in a high wind" (573). In *The Mis-Education of the Negro* (1933), Carter G. Woodson contended, "When you control a man's thinking you do not have to worry about his actions. . . . He will find his 'proper place' and stay in it." Woodson criticized schools for handicapping "a student by teaching him that his black face is a curse and that his struggle to change his condition is hopeless." This is "the worst sort of lynching. It kills one's aspirations and dooms him to vagabondage and crime." Because "Negroes have no control over their education," students end up being products of a flawed and racist system, "convinced of their inferiority."[51]

The psychologist Kenneth Clark also condemned the violence inherent in segregated education and the ways in which it contradicted basic civil, democratic, and human rights. His influential text *Prejudice and Your Child* (1955) demonstrated that "a segregated school gives children an indelible impression of the inferiority of a whole group of people—an impression that cannot be neutralized by any amount of classroom indoctrination in the ideals of democracy." Lerone Bennett, Jr., echoed this criticism in "The Negro in Textbooks: Reading, 'Riting and Racism," claiming that African Americans' exclusion and degradation at the hands of educational institutions "is a reflection of the pattern of exclusion in American life" and part of a system of oppression that relies on social and psychological violence: "in order to oppress people, you have to convince them of their social nothingness—you have to tie them up, either with ropes or words. And in the long run, words are far more effective than ropes and chains."[52] If people have been trained to pay obeisance to founders, leaders, and brotherhoods and to read the word and the world as these authorities dictate, they will always buy into narratives of their own inferiority and accept their second-class status. In contrast, if people challenge authority, question oppressive narratives, and propose alternatives, they commit themselves to revolutionizing reading and readership.

The invisible man teaches himself to critique either-or modes of reading that demand conformity, reject possibility, and neglect responsibility. He asserts that isolation and separation are not the answer, that to be "for" or "against" society is not "responsible" citizenship (573, 576). He questions America's "passion to make men conform to a pattern" and put "the world in a straight jacket" (576). In Morris Dickstein's view, the novel becomes "a black-accented version of the anticonformist discourse of the 1950s, the social critique of the lonely crowd and the organization man."[53] Yet the book is more than a variation on the theme of 1950s malaise; it addresses the very binary logic that divides America into conformist and anticonformist. The invisible man rejects all either-or systems in favor of the possibilities of both-and. While he recognizes that those in control may see his way of reading as "chaos," he calls it "imagination" and celebrates it for restoring creative authority to individual readers who are operating in particular cultural contexts (576, 572). These readers choose how they will use the "lesson of [their] own life" to make meaning from what they encounter. Such choice and creativity allows for "the possibility of action" and "responsible" participation in one's community and nation (579).

The invisible man models his new critical, creative, relational, and rebellious reading in the epilogue's much examined discussion of "the principle" (573, 574).[54] In a paragraph that is almost two pages long, he works to interpret his grandfather's deathbed advice, which he has come to understand has a "meaning deeper than I thought" (574). After more than 570 pages of miseducation, misreading, and mistaking others' methods and meanings for universal truths, he depends on his own imagination and creativity to decipher, from his grandfather's words, the principle, or idea, on which the nation was founded. Despite the definite article, however, the invisible man never defines the principle, nor does he force it into a particular pattern or narrative. Instead, he offers five possible interpretations and suggests that there could be many more. As his choice of "could it," "was it," and other conditional queries signal, he "can't decide" on a single interpretation (574). His paragraph becomes a series of "or" questions that interrogate his ideas and his methods of interpretation. At one point he even exclaims, "I can't figure it out; it escapes me" (575). Once, this would have terrified the invisible man, set him trembling, and sent him running for the next program, but now he turns inward to work.

The variations on the idea of the principle are significant because they point toward the invisible man's nascent understanding of his own citizen-readership. Must one accept foundational ideas and texts uncritically? Can one accept them without accepting the racist "men who did the violence" (574)? Must one "take the responsibility for all of it" or only "affirm the principle, the plan in whose name we had been brutalized and sacrificed" (574)? In these questions we hear echoes of the postwar African American educators, activists, writers, politicians, and intellectuals who were working through America's founding ideas and ideals and their own relative positions. Introducing a pluralism that Ellison develops further in his essays, the invisible man asks, "Weren't we *part of them* as well as apart from them" (575)? He proposes a "one yet many" philosophy in which various groups and individuals inform one another while remaining distinct. They are different, not deficient, just like their language, texts, and modes of reading. This principle does not demand conformity to a single pattern of reading or citizenship but sees variety, creativity, and possibility as safeguards against the "tyranny" of singularity and determinism (577).

By embracing a both-and philosophy—"So I denounce and I defend and I hate and I love"—the invisible man chooses his own course despite possible contradictions or conflicts: in "possibility" he finds a "socially responsible role to play" (579, 581). He discovers that "the equality offered by 'the principle' makes room for individuals to realize diverse possibilities." In so doing, he anticipates the radical student movements of the 1960s and the Black Arts Movement's black aesthetic—in particular, the calls for functional, collective, and committing modes of creation and interpretation to revolutionize black consciousness. Like these later revolutionaries, Ellison's novel and its protagonist strive to correct false ideas of blackness imposed by others and to create a new consciousness for black people that will allow them to see their own worth and "define the world in their own terms."[55] Citizen-readers who do not accept the party line must muddle through various options to find the role they are to play. The invisible man does not and cannot depict what this looks like, for to do so would be to supplant one set program with his own. Furthermore, even by the end of the novel, he has not yet come up from his hole. All we are left with is the possibility of his emergence.[56]

But perhaps this possibility is enough. In his explosive essay "Myth of a 'Negro Literature,'" LeRoi Jones (later known as Amiri Baraka) asserts that he sees potential in "a no man's land, a black country, almost completely invisible to white America, but so essentially part of it as to stain its whole being an ominous gray."⁵⁷ The potential of a space between borders, "a no man's land" that "white America" has neither claimed nor named, is radical because it cuts to the quick and recognizes the part that African Americans have played and continue to play in the nation's story. It allows for creation, movement, self-definition, and self-determination. It is ominous only to those whose power may be stolen by those who hitherto have been forced to the margins, because it violates the rules and does so from the shadows, because the possibility exists that violence may come out of the shadows and into the light. The invisible man admits "there's a possibility that even an invisible man has a socially responsible role to play" and that this role comes forth from "the mind" (581, 580). This individual's mind accepts its own and others' humanity while allowing for "conflict" and perhaps connection (580, 581). Here the possible becomes the actual; for in reading and studying his life, writing his narrative, and telling his story, the invisible man has come out of his hole on his own terms.

"Any and Every Book Possible"

Ralph Ellison published only one novel in his lifetime but was a prolific writer of essays, reviews, interviews, and articles, many of which address the function of art, readership, and citizenship in ways that build on the invisible man's final insights and continue to develop the author's vision of Cold War African American citizen-readership. In one of those essays, "Hidden Name and Complex Fate," Ellison uses his own literacy autobiography to narrate a history of twentieth-century African American reading and to suggest a more democratic understanding of reading.⁵⁸ His literacy history mirrors that of many southern African Americans. Recalling his childhood, he writes, "There was no library for Negroes in our city"; but on learning "that there was no law, only custom," forbidding one, the community quickly responded with "the renting of two large rooms in a Negro office building, . . . the hiring of a young Negro librarian, the installation of shelves and a hurried stocking of the walls with any and every book possible."⁵⁹

During his "formative period" as a reader, Ellison absorbed "the classics," "popular verse," "stories of Jesse James, of Negro outlaws and black United States marshals," "speech rhythms" of "Negro voices and their different idioms," "contests between fire-and-brimstone preachers," word play of "certain notorious bootleggers of corn whiskey," and the idiom of jazz musicians, bluesmen, blind street preachers, Negro hustlers, prostitutes, and "old ladies, those who had seen slavery and those were defiant of white folk and black folk alike." In his essay, he spends considerable time discussing "the places where a rich oral literature was truly functional" in his community—churches, barbershops, cotton-picking camps, and other public spaces "where folklore and gossip thrived."[60] Anticipating later black scholarship on literature and literacy, he recognizes that black texts, literacy, and folk traditions are different, not deficient, and are equally valuable parts of America's narrative tradition.

Here and elsewhere, Ellison resists the either-or impulse central to many Cold War reading initiatives and to postwar black nationalism, refusing to privilege one reading tradition over another and embracing a both-and literacy heritage. He celebrates what he "learned of the New Negro Movement of the twenties, of Langston Hughes, Countee Cullen, Claude McKay, James Weldon Johnson and the others. They had inspired pride and had given me a closer identification with poetry. . . . [I]t was good to know that there were Negro writers." Yet this pride did not preclude him from falling "under the spell" of T. S. Eliot's *The Waste Land,* Emily Brontë's *Wuthering Heights,* and Thomas Hardy's *Jude the Obscure,* nor did it prevent him from seeking out and "reading a whole range of subjects," "criticism," and the works of white American writers such as Sherwood Anderson, F. Scott Fitzgerald, Herman Melville, and Mark Twain. Ellison also counted Karl Marx, Sigmund Freud, Ezra Pound, Gertrude Stein, Ernest Hemingway, André Malraux, Fyodor Dostoevsky, and William Faulkner among his literary "ancestors." His literacy autobiography reveals his refusal to be pegged down as an X type of reader and his resistance to believing that only Y types of literature were fit for Z types of people. In this, it models a version of reading that refuses "to embrace uncritically values which are extended to us by others" but seeks a broader understanding of "social reality" that is "based upon our own hard-earned sense of reality."[61] He forwards an idea of individual citizen-readership that depends on neither the experts nor a predetermined set of values. Rather, it is informed by individual readers who create their own understanding and freedom and thus offers a radically democratic mode of canon formation and meaning making.

Some of Ellison's essays detail particular skills that challenge prescriptive reading schemata and enable readers to freely choose what and how to read. In "The World and the Jug," he discusses and models how he learned to read against "concepts which distorted the actual reality of my situation or my reactions to it," noting in particular Irving Howe's criticism of his work and Negro literature as a whole. Resisting interpretations that "whites impose . . . upon Negro experience," calling them "not only false but, in effect, a denial of Negro humanity," he relates how he "learned to outmaneuver" those trying to reduce him to imposed "ideas which defined me as no more than the *sum* of those laws and customs" of a racist institution and nation. His "outmaneuvering" is an act of self-determination and self-definition in the face of institutions that designate "another, politically weaker, less socially acceptable, people as the receptacle for one's own self-disgust, . . . for one's own fears of, and retreats from, reality."[62] In "The World and the Jug," Ellison reads Howe's words, parses them, situates them within their sociohistorical and cultural context (as opposed to accepting them as universals), and responds with his own interpretations. He rejects Howe's limited and limiting narrative and rewrites the story of black authorship to include a range of ideas, forms, inspirations, and experiences. He advocates a radical literary pluralism that refuses to accept one "right way" for blacks to write and read themselves into America's history and story. Such prescriptions manufacture and rely on us-them and better-worse binaries, another form of separation and segregation.

This radical literary pluralism "rejects all possibilities of escape [from prejudice] that do not involve a basic resuscitation of the *original* American ideals of social and political justice." Ellison claims that Americans need to get back to the root of "the principle" on which America was founded, charging that "social and political justice" have expired and are in need of reviving. This is not a nostalgic call to go back to the way things were but a call to inject life into those ideals to allow for greater "possibilities." Like other postwar African American thinkers, Ellison recognized that America's founding documents and fathers were constrained by the spirit and the letter of racial prejudice. It is significant that the essay uses the word "resuscitate" because this act "breathe[s] new life" and brings one "back to consciousness."[63] In calling for a resuscitation of "social and political justice," Ellison asks that we read "new life" into these principles and come to a new "consciousness" about them. He anticipates the central charge of both the Black Power and the New Left movements, which called for a change in or a corrective to consciousness to create a more just and democratic nation and world.[64]

The outmaneuvering in Ellison's novel and essays strives to resist oppressive structures, institutions, narratives, and ideologies; deny prescriptions their power; reject us-them binaries of any sort; and call for a radical pluralism that reinvests authority in individual citizen-readers, reanimates consciousness, and renews the possibility of an inclusive democracy and nation. During the Cold War, America was "the most powerful spokesman for the democratic way of life, as opposed to the principles of a totalitarian state," yet "the Russians publicize[d] our continued lynchings, our Jim Crow statues and customs, our anti-Semitic discriminations and our witch-hunts." *Invisible Man* calls for a revision of the script of Americanness and the long-standing prejudices on which racism has stood. It asks citizen-readers to become educated but not in the reductive manner of white-dominated reading curricula and discourses. Instead, it urges citizen-readers to learn how to access, read, and interpret "the actual reality" by outmaneuvering those institutions and individuals who would prevent such sight and insight.⁶⁵ It calls for reform of the kind of education that Ellison and his invisible man received—one that discouraged "the uses of the imagination, . . . attitudes of aggression and courage."⁶⁶

What does imaginative education look like? In a speech at a 1963 seminar titled "Education for Culturally Different Youth," Ellison asked educators to think of young African American readers as "products of a different cultural complex" rather than as "culturally deprived" and to realize that, to be educated, minority students "don't have to give up all of that which gives them their own sense of identity" because "the nation needs some of the very traits which they bring with them." He urged teachers to recognize that African Americans are "a people possessing great human potentialities and strengths" that should "be respected" and suggested that educators should focus less on correction and more on incorporation.⁶⁷ Importantly, he told teachers that schools must teach students how to think and read critically:

> Many American children have not been trained to reject enough of the negative values which our society presses upon them. Nor have they been trained sufficiently to preserve those values which sustained their forefathers and which constitute an important part of their heritage. Frequently they are not trained to identify those aspects of the environment to which it is to their best interest—and to the best interest of the nation—to say "No."⁶⁸

Like the invisible man, who has been taught to accept any idea, value, or reading pressed on him and to interpret the world obediently, "many American children" are taught to see and read the world as "society" says it is. Ellison challenges this notion and signals the violence that such "pressing" can have socially and psychologically. He stresses the importance of relearning how to read, "identify," and "preserve" those ideas, and values that are an "important part of [students'] heritage." True to his radical pluralism, he argues that educational deprivation hurts not only African Americans but also the nation as a whole and charges that changes in reading instruction will help African Americans see and act in "their best interest," which is also in "the best interest of the nation." In this way, he seeks to resuscitate reading to allow for a wider vision of Americanness and a new consciousness of and for its citizen-readers.

4

Reading against the Machine
Oedipa Maas and the Quest for Democracy in Thomas Pynchon's *The Crying of Lot 49*

Cold War fiction of the 1960s complicated accepted theories and practices of meaning making, redefining the postwar conception of a fit citizen-reader in hopes of further democratizing the act of reading. Oedipa Maas, the suburban housewife who is the protagonist of Thomas Pynchon's 1966 novel *The Crying of Lot 49*, typifies this transitional period.[1] When this suburban housewife is named executrix of her former lover's estate, her "good reading" skills fail her and her conception of reality becomes unhinged, forcing her to relearn how to read. As she works to make sense of the estate's apparent link to a renegade mail carrier organization called the Trystero, Oedipa uncovers what could be either an international conspiracy or an elaborate hoax created by her erstwhile lover, Pierce Inverarity. She becomes increasingly estranged from her suburban world and progressively more aware of an alternate one composed of those who are excluded from dominant narratives of America and Americanness. Although she never discovers for certain what the Trystero means or even if it exists, she does learn that there is more than one mode of reading and that the act of interpretation can have significant consequences.[2]

The heroine, the novel itself, and postmodernism were all part of a particular historical moment marked by a struggle to revise what one knew about self, others, and nation; to identify how one gained and communicated that knowledge; and to register the impact of these processes on nation formation.[3] As earlier chapters have demonstrated, reading in 1950s America was marked by a desire for stable meanings and understandings even as writers, educators, politicians, literary critics, and citizen-readers recognized that ambiguity, uncertainty, and complexity were their reality. The institutionalization of democratizing reading programs, mass-produced reading guides, and university curricula coincided with political rhetoric that privileged so-called facts and truths over ambiguity. By employing such rhetoric in speeches and published papers, President Eisenhower, his secretary of state John Foster Dulles, his advisor George Kennan, and other Cold War leaders spread an aura of American stability, enlightenment, and authority among citizens and allies, and helped create what Jacques Barzun has called a "national faith in facts and our distrust of mind."[4]

Like the neat, uniform rows of suburban houses masking great ideological, cultural, and individual differences, political rhetoric masked anxieties about a changing and mysterious world. Moreover, it was becoming clear that some of the most emphatic public supporters of these certainties—for instance, Senator Joseph McCarthy and FBI Director J. Edgar Hoover—were themselves skilled manipulators of information. By the period in which Pynchon's novel is set, students, activists, philosophers, and writers were beginning to contest facts and their use, whether benign, well intentioned, or malicious, seeking to reclaim interpretive authority from American institutions and relocate interpretive power in the readers of texts.

Oedipa's own readerly journey illustrates the complex relationship among reading, individuals, and community during this transitional time. She must come to terms with the contrast between the discourses of her formative years as a reader in the 1950s and those she encounters in the 1960s while seeking to make sense of Inverarity's will. Early in the novel, she displays her limited and limiting Cold War reading education as she endeavors to discern patterns in facts and to fit facts into patterns. As the novel progresses, however, we begin to recognize that Oedipa's (and America's) potential liberation from systematic alienation means that she must estrange herself from institutionalized processes of reading and reclaim interpretation for all individuals, including those who have traditionally been disempowered. Her development as a reader reflects a broader historical shift in reading discourse and practice away from mechanized modes of reading toward alternatives that are open to possibility.[5] The aim of this particular radical moment was to get to the root of what and how American democracy means and restore interpretive control to citizen-readers.

In Facts We Trust?

On the hit 1950s television show *Dragnet,* the character Sergeant Joe Friday constantly reiterated, "All we know are the facts," and "All we want are the facts," as he worked to protect law and order in Los Angeles. He was not alone: Barzun complained that America had an "addiction to fact" and argued that this "frantic clutch for a mental security card has something to do with the dread of all realities and the increasing difficulty of getting at them." Faced with a population newly initiated into atomic warfare, destabilized by changing racial, gender, and class codes, and conscripted into a Cold War "whose name could hardly be spoken" and whose "enemy . . . was faceless in a new way," institutions promoted the power of facts as a way to elicit a sense of calm. Political leaders repeatedly called for greater dissemination of democracy's truths as a way to combat communism's "shadow."[6] Yet in Cold War America, concrete knowledge, truth, and facts were anything but certain.

A faith in facts' ability to defend freedom and secure peace runs throughout President Eisenhower's early speeches. In his first inaugural address he asserted that "forces of good and evil are massed and armed and opposed as rarely before in history"; "this fact defines the meaning of this day." He stressed that "unity" could defeat "discord" only if Americans and the free world embraced his list of "fixed," "lived," and knowable "principles," which would make "this truth . . . clear before us." Likewise, his "Atoms for Peace" speech stated, "Clearly, if the peoples of the world are to conduct an intelligent search for peace, they must be armed with the significant facts of today's existence." As he sought to convince the United Nations that nuclear technology could be a tool for global harmony, he repeated the word *facts* five more times in the speech. In his 1953 State of the Union address, he again asserted that much of the solution to freedom from tyranny abroad and from discrimination at home "lies in the power of fact, fully publicized." These repeated invocations underscored his desire to create an atmosphere of stability, knowability, and peace; for as George Kennan said in his "Long Telegram," "there is nothing as dangerous or terrifying as the unknown."[7]

Kennan's telegram is itself an excellent illustration of the role that facts played in early Cold War American political rhetoric and policy. He framed it as an "objective analysis of the situation" in the Soviet Union, a contrast to communism's "honeyed promises." The telegram condemns what he saw as Communists' "disrespect . . . for objective truth. Indeed their disbelief in its existence leads them to view all stated facts as instruments for furtherance of one ulterior purpose or another." Kennan censured Russian Communists for treating the "vast fund of objective fact[s] about society" as a "grab bag" and for twisting facts to fit their "preconceived notions." The telegram emphasizes that the United States reveres truth and employs facts objectively, ethically, and dispassionately and warns that the Soviets' lack of faith in or corruption of "facts" makes their "apparatus" particularly dangerous, for its "amazing flexibility and versatility" allow it to "stimulate disunity" and destroy freedom. Meanwhile, the telegram explains, the Russian people are "too ignorant" and "mentally too dependent to question" what they are told, instead "making themselves believe what they find . . . comforting and convenient."

Kennan recommended a U.S. foreign policy approach that would counter Soviet factual flexibility and fabrication with actions predicated on "study," "thoroughness and care," and an "intelligent and constructive" understanding of the "facts." The telegram concludes that the United States can forestall communism and avoid war "if our public is enlightened and if our dealings with Russians are placed entirely on [a] realistic and matter-of-fact basis." Kennan's hopes for peace relied on "correct" interpretation: first, in authoring a fact-, truth-, and study-based foreign policy; second, in using facts to govern diplomatic dealings with the Soviets; and third, in informing and "enlighten[ing]" the American public so they can identify and read communism's "honeyed promises" in the clear light of democracy's truths.[8]

Dulles, whom Oedipa Maas recalls as one of her formative leaders, took a similar tack during his tenure as Eisenhower's secretary of state (104). A keen scholar, he methodically researched, organized, and narrativized facts and truths as he worked to promote U.S. interests abroad and avert another global conflict.[9] While he was writing and delivering many official policy papers on communism, he was simultaneously demonstrating his commitment to reaching and teaching average Cold War Americans about the dangers they were facing. In his two-part *Life* series, "Thoughts on Soviet Foreign Policy and What to Do about It," he worked to educate the American public about the "facts" of Soviet foreign policy: "the more closely Soviet policies are studied, and the more intimately they are known," the greater the need to alert and inform America's citizens about communism's ideology, methods, and endgame. Dulles wrote that "the makers of Soviet foreign policy take seriously the fact that the world *is* 'one world'" (that is, a world they wish to conquer). Thus, he argued, *Life*'s readers must take seriously the "facts" he will share about Soviet policy in order to preserve peace. Here and elsewhere he employed "an aggressive educational program aimed at convincing the public to support an activist, globalist foreign policy."[10]

Dulles used these articles to model studious factual interpretation and to demonstrate how "in the case of the Soviet Union there are many pieces" that "fit neatly together to form a coherent and logical whole." He sought to train the average American in interpreting the "phrases," "catchwords," and "slogans" of Soviet policy and in "understand[ing] the meaning which Soviet speakers and writers give to the words 'democracy,' 'fascist' and 'friendly.'" He apparently believed that readers with both "the facts" and the ability to read and correctly interpret Communist literature, ideas, and rhetoric would "better underst[an]d" the Soviets and thus "revive in [themselves] the spirit which led their forebears to pledge their lives, their fortunes and their sacred honor to secure their personal freedoms." He ultimately called on citizen-readers "to develop the facts which will make it apparent, even to those within the Kremlin, that present Soviet foreign policy will not succeed."[11]

Of course, facts and truth are subjective, contingent, and embedded in narrative; they are fictions authored to serve particular individual, social, or political needs in particular contexts. In the immediate postwar period, facts were a weapon in the battle to define America and Americanness against real and imagined threats to national stability and security. They were also a site of contest in which Americans from differing ideological positions asserted the primacy of their narratives. One need not believe in facts in order to deploy them in service of one's program or ideology. Nevertheless, as Kennan contended, that deployment itself revealed a great deal about individual and national character, and he advocated that Americans "cling to our own methods" (objective, truthful, systematic, transparent, and grounded in good scholarship) lest they start using facts less thoughtfully or ethically and thereby "become like those with whom we are coping."[12]

His warning was prescient, for some of facts' loudest postwar preachers (Hoover and McCarthy, among others) were the leaders who, as Pynchon writes, "mothered over Oedipa's so temperate youth" (104). Like Kennan's Russian Communists, they treated facts as items in a "grab bag," forcing them to fit their "preconceived notions" as they furthered their particular national security projects. Hoover's and McCarthy's language may have echoed that of their diplomatic contemporaries, but their methods and ends often differed. As Hoover wrote, his goal was "to assemble, organize, and present basic, everyday facts of communism which will be of maximum help to the people of our country in recognizing and fighting the enemy in our midst"—sounding a clarion call similar to those of Eisenhower, Kennan, and Dulles.[13] He also proposed that systems of reading, knowledge, and interpretation could help fortify and ground average Americans in their struggle against communism. Yet he diverged from the others when it came to his means and ends. Whereas they used facts in their attempts to understand Soviet policy, Hoover used facts as a way to examine those "in our midst"—American citizen-readers themselves. Rather than framing facts as tools for peace, he relied on them as he fought a series of battles on American soil. Eisenhower, Kennan, and Dulles focused on sharing their facts with the American public to teach them about current threats to the nation, but Hoover revealed his only when they suited his purposes. Granted, Hoover was not a diplomat but was in charge of maintaining domestic law and order. Nevertheless, what he ordered and how he ordered it often exceeded both his charge and the law he was appointed to defend.

Hoover regularly fed the House Committee on Un-American Activities with information gathered both legally and illegally. He created programs such as Communist Infiltration of the University of California Radiation Laboratory, Communist Infiltration of the Motion Picture Industry, and COINTELPRO to gather information and spread strategic misinformation. During his long tenure he enacted anti-Communist measures such as the Responsibilities Program (a "secret nationwide program to remove politically suspect teachers") and the Security Index ("a secret nationwide list of people whom FBI officials believed would be dangerous" during wartime). He composed poison pen letters to discredit alleged subversives and founded the Mass Media Program to facilitate the distribution of approved anti-Communist and pro-American news items.[14] Under Hoover, the FBI became a finely tuned fact-gathering and -fabricating machine that allowed him to craft a specific idea of America and Americanness.

McCarthy also relied on rhetoric of facts, truths, and order in his arguments about the postwar Communist threat. In a speech in Wheeling, West Virginia, he declared, "There is still a hope for peace if we finally decide that no longer can we safely blind our eyes and close our ears to those facts which are shaping up more and more clearly . . . and that is that we are now engaged in a show-down fight . . . not the usual war between nations for land areas or other material gains, but a war between two diametrically opposed ideologies." Like Eisenhower, Kennan, and Dulles, he claimed that global peace required Americans to open their eyes and ears to the facts of communism's evils and democracy's good. But he differed from the diplomats in his approach to outlining those facts, which he enumerated in order to ensure that "the whole sorry mess of twisted, warped thinkers are swept from the national scene so that we may have a new birth of honesty and decency in government."[15]

Like Hoover, McCarthy turned the interpretive gaze on Americans themselves—specifically, elected and appointed government officials. His book *Fight for America* (1952) proudly models the methods he used to "publicly expos[e] the truth about men who . . . were betraying this nation." McCarthy positioned himself as an objective and dispassionate expert, yet his ever-changing list of "known Communists" itself demonstrates the ways in which seemingly set and knowable facts were provisional, mutable, and uncertain. Beneath his bluster was a belief that facts were whatever one made them out to be and that whoever controlled their narrativization was in a position of power. He deployed facts like a blunt instrument, and he was successful until he appeared to start believing in his own fictions and politically self-destructed.[16]

As Ellen Schrecker and Seth Rosenfeld have detailed, pro-American groups such as the Chamber of Commerce and the American Legion offered key support to the FBI, the House Committee on Un-American Activities, Senator McCarthy's various investigative committees, and others who were gathering and distributing facts. According to Jack Beall of the American Legion, exposing communism "requires some degree of expertness, it requires knowledge, it requires experience, . . . it partakes very definitely of science."[17] By linking factual enlightenment to science, Beall positioned anti-communism and postwar American nationalism as empirical epistemologies, unlike Communist ideology, which was philosophical, ideological, mutable, and subject to interpretation. Moreover, anti-Communist science required experts, he said, thus reaffirming the authority of facts. Yet his persistent emphasis on science and authority suggests he recognized that skeptical readers might see these so-called facts as fictions.

Some of the popular how-to-read guides of the 1950s borrowed from this "expert" model, arguing that an ordered and systematic approach to reading would help unify America and strengthen citizen-readers.[18] The preface to *Good Times through Literature* (part of the *America Reads* series edited by Robert C. Pooley and William S. Gray of the University of Wisconsin and Chicago, respectively) promised that the book would help teachers "[carry] out a program of systematic review, maintenance, and refinement of those skills that contribute most to good interpretation," including reading activities and tests that function as a "diagnostic check" on students' abilities. While it also stressed the individuality of each reader and encouraged teachers to keep student differences in mind when designing lesson plans, the text incorporated the language of mechanical operations—"systems," "maintenance," "diagnostics"—and equated students with machine operators. "Good" literary experiences required the security and reliability of "good" texts, which promoted "good interpretation," "check[ed]" individual reader's "skills," and ran smoothly under the watchful eye of committed authorities.[19]

In an essay about reading drama, included in *The Wonderful World of Books,* John Gassner likened the reading process to examining a machine. Here the text itself rather than the student is part of the mechanical analogy. Gassner encouraged readers to look for evidence of order, systems, and structure in a text—"not only in what the machine grinds out but in its appearance and the manner in which it performs. No American, certainly, needs to be told what pleasure there is in knowing how a thing works . . . the over-all shape or mode of operation." Linking texts to the icon of American progress—the machine—he praised aesthetic and systemic "order," associating the "pleasure" found therein with Americanness. In so doing, he typified how "Americans have seized upon the machine as their birthright," associating it with economic, political, and metaphysical "progress." In the same volume, Thomas

Riggs, Jr.'s, essay "What Good Are Poems?" claims that order and correctness may save a reader's soul: "the shapeliness and the order tell us, secretly and without making speeches about it, that despite suffering, peace exists; that despite chaos, order exists; despite ugliness, beauty; despite evil, good."[20] Like Holden Caulfield's Museum of Natural History and the Brotherhood's idea of science, these texts echo postwar political rhetorics about the power of facts in the construction of peace, order, beauty, and good.

By the 1960s, many commercially successful reading programs had become well-oiled machines. In addition to old standbys such as the Book of the Month Club and the Great Books Program, newcomers such as the Readers' Subscription, the Mid-Century Book Society, and others promised to lead citizen-readers to the "pleasure and permanence" available from immersion in the best books. The desire to learn, be part of a community, and become anchored in a cultural tradition had long moved many people to join these groups; as early as 1953, the Great Books Program was operating discussion groups in more than "six hundred American communities." Yet by the 1960s, many observers were complaining that the readers themselves had become the programs' shaped and packaged commodities. Frank Jennings, *Saturday Review*'s editor-at-large, called the programs the "cult of the ready-mix and the instant pudding." In his popular book *This Is Reading,* he criticized organizations that "culled the 'total' intellectual heritage of the Western world . . . and presented some snippets in pamphlet form for those who would buy intellectual health and freedom at discount rates." In his view, these "snippets" and "mixes" turned reading into a predetermined process, churning out the same end product no matter who was doing the work. Other critics argued that the structure of commercial reading programs blatantly pressured readers to perform for and with "the group." These clubs, which had attracted readers with promises of "convenience; reading fulfillment; guidance by experts; [and] continuity," seemed to have become particularly heavy on the "continuity."[21]

Even *Mad* magazine, famous for targeting American popular culture, jumped in to critique the commodifying, normalizing, and numbing effect of these massive reading clubs. In 1959, *Mad*'s "Readin' and Writhin' Dept." satirically reported that, "in the good old days, people either bought their books in a store, or swiped them from their friends. Today, more and more people are building their libraries by joining monthly book clubs." Like other critics, *Mad* saw continuity as both the cause and the effect of an increasingly cookie-cutter approach to literature and culture. The magazine's "Spicy Abridged Book Club," "Millard Fillmore Book Club," "Useful Information Book Club," and "Ridiculously-Expensive Book Club" reflected the editors' contention that specialized clubs not only created homogenous readers but also compartmentalized them into "appropriate" social spheres and thus undermined democratic ideals of sociopolitical autonomy. Distrust of groups and group think is evident in the "Readin' and Writhin'" report, which characterized its members as mindless drones seeking neither comprehension nor understanding but only "the 'choicest'" or most "common" parts. *Mad* depicted these readers as a slobbering, animalistic mob—a group of "beady-eyed" bodies feeding off the herd's frenetic energy. National book clubs, once praised for putting good books into the hands of diverse readers, were now seen as perpetuating a "culture industry and the crass knowingness that it fostered."[22]

The domestication and institutionalization of New Critical theory also seemed to illustrate the cultural ordering and homogenizing impulse in Cold War America. Originally, New Critics did claim that the order missing from the modern world could be found in literature, but the diverse body of theorists refused to see literature as "a conscious retreat from reality" or a "system" of interpretation. Rather, they asserted that it offered readers complex textures, various orders, and multifaceted means of understanding the world. New Critics repeatedly denounced science's systematization and mechanization as the enemy of close reading, arguing that it was totalitarian, wrecked mystery, gave readers a false sense of superiority, alienated individuals, and destroyed communities with false and utopic promises of "progress."[23]

Nevertheless, after the academy accepted the tenets of New Criticism, the "*unreflective* and *monotonous* application of some of its precepts" neutered its revolutionary power. It was reduced from a set of complex theories to a reproducible "method" that turned out "mechanical imitation[s] of New Critical techniques." This diluted form was mass-produced and made into science of sorts, much to the dismay of its originators. Students became "a ready market" for the proliferation of anthologies, textbooks, " 'casebooks,' 'critical editions,' and 'reader's guides' . . . devoted to unlocking the difficulties of [modernist] works." These reductive and prescriptive interpretive guides made "the assimilation of modernism easier than ever," which, as critics like Trilling believed, "inevitably . . . meant domestication, the taming of modernism."[24]

Scholars were concerned about this shift, as Reuben Brower and Richard Poirier made clear in their introduction to *In Defense of Reading* (1962). They insisted that the book's contributors shared "a common experience, not a system; an action and an attitude, not a rigid method." They "wanted to avoid the most common fault of modern criticism, particularly evident in critical anthologies, of letting method determine in advance—like a sort of gridiron—what we see in the work and what we miss." Their goal was to counteract "some of the analytical criticism of this period, particularly when it has taken the form of teaching 'methods,' [which] has tended to become standardized and mechanical." The scholars condemned the ways in which domesticated criticism had dampened "the nearly spontaneous recognitions in any intelligent reader" and forced interpretations to be "abstracted and codified as if they formed a new system of knowledge."[25]

In Defense of Reading sought to reclaim the revolutionary potential of interpretation as originally conceived by New Criticism. Its editors emphasized that "we have tried simply to be as variously and flexibly intelligent as possible in the face of literary events, to be all things to all kinds of literary experience." Suggesting the degree to which close textual criticism had been mechanized and abstracted from its theoretical aims, they insisted, "We are against any limitation on the kinds of questions that may be put to a literary work." As they noted, New Criticism's mechanization had led many critics and theorists to confuse the institutionalized practice for its theory, mischaracterizing the interpretive philosophy as "minimiz[ing] . . . change, difference, and discontinuity in literary history and the concomitant stressing of stasis, repetition without difference, and continuity."[26] Whereas New Critical theory stressed multiplicity and democratic hermeneutics, its institutionalization often rendered these processes uniform, not only forwarding a singular and systematic way of approaching reading and interpretation but also distorting subsequent generations' understanding of the radical theory.

A Portrait of the Reader as a Young Woman

At the beginning of *The Crying of Lot 49*, Oedipa Maas seems like a typical middle-class female reader in postwar America. Clearly she has mastered the sciences of reading, homemaking, and consumerism. Pynchon tells us that she reads the latest book reviews in *Scientific American*, a popular science magazine of the time and typical of what Vance Packard has called a "service magazine": one that white-collar Americans read as they sought to get ahead in the world or at least keep up with their neighbors (10). Not all reading proponents approved of popular magazines' dominance in middle-class homes, arguing that they "[put] almost no strain upon the literacy of [their] purchaser." In her foundational text, *Living with Books*, Helen Haines contended, "Magazines . . . are no more than accessories or deterrents to reading; they do not signify that wide ranging and rich adventure in the world of books that is real reading. Magazines have their place, their own usefulness; but no magazine can take the place of standard books."[27] She and other reading advocates dismissed popular magazines as either elements of home decor or how-to guides for homemakers and handymen.[28] They were a source of information but not of education or critical elevation. In their reading study, William Gray and Bernice Rogers cited a research subject who told them "if she was going to raise a family, maybe she'd 'read up on how to do it'" and "that after she was married, she might read some recipes" in various magazines. While Pynchon tells us that Oedipa reads book reviews, he doesn't tell us if she then purchases and reads the recommended books. All we know is that, like many postwar Americans, she refers to expert reviewers to discover what she should read. As the University of Chicago researcher Lester Asheim concluded about female readers, she also seems "less imaginative about selecting books on [her] own."[29]

Postwar reading guides primarily addressed male readers, and Pynchon's early characterization of Oedipa plays on the era's assumption that women were a lesser class of readers. Between 1947 and 1955, male college students outnumbered female students by more than two to one, yet the male-centered rhetoric of reading books, guides, and curricula was not primarily influenced by this population disparity. More likely, it linked to educators' assumption that women weren't serious students, attended college only to find husbands, and had learning goals that differed from men's.[30] The literary scholar Mark Krupnick contends, for example, that the influential professor and critic Lionel Trilling "was never much concerned with the education of young women—who would, as he put it, be 'responsible for the welfare of the polity.'" Likewise, Jacques Barzun believed that "most young women are likely to lose touch with books, ideas, and current events on the far side of the altar." Clifton Fadiman went so far as to assert that suburban women like Oedipa were inferior readers: "these commuters' wives—there are tens of thousands of them—were not really in any active sense doing any reading at all. They were taking their daily novel in a numbed or somnambulistic state. They were using books not for purposes of entertainment, but as an anodyne, a time-killer, a life-killer. . . . Truth to tell, they have never read a book in their lives."[31] In her home in Kinneret-among-the-Pines, Oedipa at first seems to fit these postwar caricatures of "numbed," "insulated" women who "couldn't feel much of anything" and read merely to kill time during their endless, identical days (19, 11).

Gendered assumptions about literacy were informed and reinforced by what the activist Betty Friedan called "sex-directed education." In her influential book, *The Feminine Mystique* (1963), she traced the rise of gendered curricula, which tailored women's high school and college courses to their reproductive capability, replacing traditional liberal arts courses with home economics and family science. In her view, these changes were based on the false assumption that different biological functions led men and women to learn differently. Sex-directed educators claimed it was dangerous for future housewives to be educated "like men" because such an education would create intellectual disappointment, gender confusion, family disharmony, and possibly mental disease. According to many teachers and administrators, it was better to educate women to "adjustment within the world of home and children."[32]

In *The Wonderful World of Books,* Mary S. Switzer's essay, "Is a Woman's Work Never Done?," links reading to family science, encouraging homemakers to read so that they can perform their "multitude of jobs more easily, cheaper, faster, and more effectively." The homemaker should "[learn] from her reading how she can save five minutes of the time she takes to prepare the evening meal. That's 1,825 minutes a year." Armed with such salient facts and systems, homemakers could transform their homes into a more efficient and effective domestic machine. These sex-directed beliefs also undergird Bernard Berelson's essay, "Who Reads What Books and Why?," which appeared in the 1957 book *Mass Culture.* It caricatures an average woman, Mrs. Jones, who reads "books on child-rearing because she wants to do well by her children and to hold her own with other mothers."[33] Mrs. Jones doesn't read to develop her aesthetic sensibility, be transformed by great works, or understand her role in a functioning democracy but only in service of family science and status.

Oedipa likewise approaches homemaking as a science of sorts, following a particular order that links domestic science, reading, and citizenship. At the beginning of the novel, she is returning "from a Tupperware party," a gathering that uses peer pressure and social competition to increase the sales of kitchenware (9). The scene hints at the "conformity" that Friedan derided, which she argued was perpetuated by "colleges' failure to educate women for an identity beyond their sexual role."[34] Oedipa is characterized as the consummate suburban wife: she grocery-shops, tends her herb garden, makes lasagna, and mixes drinks—completing before "the arrival of her husband, Wendell ('Mucho') Maas from work" (10–11). Her home is a well-run machine, and her days are "more or less identical," mirroring the repetitive and monotonous days that Switzer described in "Is a Woman's Work Never Done?" (11). Oedipa is trapped in a suburban stupor, one of many women struggling with what Friedan called "the problem that has no name," what Barzun called a "drowsy . . . narcotic state," what Fadiman called "numbed . . . somnambulis[m]."[35]

Yet despite common assumptions about women's supposed lack of sophisticated reading skills, the language used to describe female readers suggests that they were, in fact, the ideal postwar fact seekers. Whereas mature readers engaged with complexity, asked questions, analyzed information, and embraced abstract ambiguities and paradoxes, fact seekers were objective, systematic, and truth-driven. Like one of the women in Gray and Rogers's study, they read books "to garner the facts and form an opinion." Indeed, all but two of the women featured in that study linked good reading with "'informative' material" (as opposed to "'too heavy reading' like the Great Books") and with practical functions such as "job success." The researchers concluded that the women examined were good at "reaching rational conclusions" and finding "information" but less good at "evaluating what was read," drawing "penetrating conclusions," and performing analytical thinking that required "consideration of two ideas in their relationship to each other."[36] Likewise, Barzun wrote that women are "practical enough to distrust [hokum]" but that "one constantly meets women of fine intelligence who use their brains exclusively about concrete things" and whose "imagination about the distant or the abstract is completely atrophied." While these critics looked down on female readers for allegedly having reading and thinking patterns that were "little short of brutish," many Cold War reading guides celebrated exactly these qualities.[37] A good fact seeker and reader would accept a fact at face value and look for the concrete, the rational, and the stable. Because she would not feel the need to analyze or analogize the information, she would feel secure in her knowledge. As it does for her female reading compatriots, "the word" works to buffer and "protect [Oedipa] from" danger, abstraction, complexity, and disorder (129). Like an airtight Tupperware container, her reading world appears to be sealed and secure.

In Oedipa's case, this portrait of a secure, systematic, and fact-seeking reader is linked to what she learned in college. Here, too, she reflects the experiences of Cold War students, for "the desire for stability" worked to create a "spirit of passivity and privatism [in colleges] that dominated the fifties." As Pynchon himself notes in his introduction to *Slow Learner* (1984), "I think, looking back, that there might have been a general nervousness in the whole college-age subculture. A tendency to self-censorship" that translated into a "sense of academic enclosure" instead of openness. Oedipa recalls that she "had undergone her own educating at a time of nerves, blandness and retreat among not only her fellow students but also most of the visible structure around and ahead of them, this having been a national reflex to certain pathologies in high places" (103). According to Henry Steele Commager, the "political intolerance" of the period created a mentality in which "loyalty was identified with conformity, and the American genius, which had been experimental and even rebellious, was required to conform to a pattern."[38]

In an era of tension, educators and students "became cautious"—overly so. Fears of being subpoenaed, dismissed, or blacklisted drove some Cold War educators to "dilute" curricula, avoid ideological complexity, and seemingly buy into a prescribed course of truths and facts. Both Robert W. Iversen's *Communists and the Schools* (1959) and Ellen Schrecker's *No Ivory Tower* (1986) detail the numerous ways in which educational bodies such as the PTA, school boards, and the American Association of University Professors responded to government pressures to cleanse schools of Communist influence. Many elected to preemptively clean their own houses and forestall government interference, instituting loyalty oaths, public hearings, book censorship, and class surveillance to protect their students and schools.[39] Hints of this nervousness surface in the postwar reading guide *Books, Young People, and Reading Guidance*, which advocates censoring reading material: "It is not that we wish to keep the facts of life from young people but that . . . their lack of experience makes it difficult for them to evaluate properly the characters and their problems and actions in many novels."[40] Censoring or removing texts, curricula, or instructors became a common practice; for, like Holden Caulfield in *The Catcher in the Rye*, school boards, administrators, teachers, and reading guides wanted to protect America's innocence.

Pynchon evokes a few of the novel's recurring images of narcosis to describe Oedipa's collegiate experience: "bland," "temperate," "somnolent." His descriptors echo widespread concerns about problems in the academy. As Iversen explains, in a 1951 "*New York Times* survey . . . of seventy-two major colleges . . . revealed 'a subtle, creeping paralysis of freedom of thought and speech . . . limiting both students and faculty in the area traditionally reserved for the free exploration of knowledge and truth.'"[41] Oedipa's instructors typify this paralysis, "limiting" not only her educational experience but "the visible structure[s] around and ahead" of her (103). Ironically, by censoring reading materials, guides had created the very situation they claimed to be preventing because students were unable to learn to evaluate difficult texts properly. Thus, when Oedipa, as an adult, finds herself in an interpretive situation for which she has not been prepared, her solution is to appeal to the authorities, "Secretaries James and Foster and Senator Joseph" (104).

The fruits of Oedipa's reading education are illustrated by her response to *The Courier's Tragedy*, Pynchon's parody of Jacobean drama, which she reads and sees performed during her investigation. Oedipa is "just a whiz at pursuing strange words in Jacobean texts"; for while her formal education was marked by blandness, temperance, and retreat, her Cold War birthright has also trained her to accumulate "facts" and "pursue" "strange[ness]" (104).[42] She is "able to collect a few fragments" of information "from obscure philatelic journals furnished [to] her by Genghis Cohen, an ambiguous footnote in Motley's *Rise of the Dutch Republic*, an 80-year-old pamphlet on the roots of modern anarchism, a book of sermons by Blobb's brother Augustine also among Bortz's Wharfingeriana, along with Blobb's original clues" (158). Pynchon's characterization of her methodology combines a reductive New Critical exploration of textual ambiguity with the archival and philological methods that New Criticism replaced. In his parody of literary exegesis, Oedipa struggles through "obscure" and "ambiguous" pamphlets, footnotes, sermons, and notes to unlock the play's many allusions and discover its internal logic. Her work mirrors the process of anti-Communist surveillance: as Schrecker reveals, the FBI "collected literally tons of press clippings, pamphlets, congressional reports, and other published items. Hoover's men also went to public meetings and demonstrations, mainly to take notes on the speeches and collect handouts. They even did research in libraries."[43]

In fact, *The Courier's Tragedy* subtly associates Cold War reading pursuits with witch hunts. Jacobean drama is distinguished by intrigue, machinations, violence, and political upheaval. Bloody and brutal, its excesses of language and plot are similar to the excesses feared, prophesied, and at times generated by Oedipa's Cold War leaders. The world that the play's director, Driblette, projects in *The Courier's Tragedy* is a shadow of the one in which Oedipa has been schooled—a world of spies, treachery, and political instability. The Duke in the play is a version of Senator McCarthy, paranoid and allegedly besieged by spies, unlawfully ruling with illegitimate power derived from manipulative uses of information. He commands a shadowy society "sworn / To punctual vendetta never sleep," with the goal of undermining a return to legitimate rule (72). The play includes "a travesty of a trial" not unlike McCarthy's Senate show trials, that ends in "a refreshingly simple mass stabbing" (73). As the trial and mass assassination demonstrate, words—what a person says, reads, knows, and tells—are the play's primary currency. One dies or is saved by the literality of the word—by the "naming of names" (71).

Oedipa's reveals her "Puritanical" devotion to and desire for facts in her dogged determination to uncover the truth about Pierce Inverarity's estate and its possible links to the Trystero (156).[44] Like the various bodies littering the stage in *The Courier's Tragedy*, the Trystero is a body bearing secrets that can only "be revealed in its terrible nakedness" after "indefinite black hours long" (54). In many ways, Oedipa's journey can be read as her endeavor to expose Pierce's truth through a careful distillation of facts. Yet over the course of the novel it is she, the good Cold War fact-seeking citizen-reader, who is stripped while Pierce's estate remains shrouded in mystery. The first instance of stripping occurs when she plays a game of Strip Botticelli (a version of Twenty Questions) with the co-executor to Pierce's estate, the attorney Metzger. Here, reading, warfare, science, and sex intersect. To discover the plot of the World War II film *Cashiered* (in which Metzger possibly starred as a child actor), Oedipa agrees to remove one article of clothing for every question posed. Each article she takes off equals a clue, the accumulation of which will lead her to the truth. Inquiry and exposure are linked in this "unusually exciting form of literary criticism," although, in this case, the exposure of Metzger's plot involves the potential exposure of his inquisitor.[45]

Soon Oedipa begins likening her quest for facts to witnessing "some unique performance" at a burlesque—"as if the breakaway gowns, net bras, jeweled garters and G-strings of historical figuration that would fall away were layered dense as Oedipa's own street-clothes in that game with Metzger" (54). Oedipa believes it is her job to witness the removal of the layers that complicate and clothe the body of history that is Pierce's estate because she's been taught that finding clarity and exposing truth is her duty. Yet in discharging this duty, she herself is exposed, which suggests that reductive Cold War reading practices can have a violent and violating effect on the reading body politic, making citizen-readers vulnerable to authorities and authoritative narratives.

The Crying of Lot 49 further illuminates the limits of Oedipa's formal education and interpretive training when the character's detective work takes her to the University of California at Berkeley. Oedipa's alma mater, "somnolent" Siwash College, is seen as an "alternate universe" and she as a "rare creature" when they are compared to the atmosphere at Berkeley, which she describes as one of those "universities you read about, those autonomous culture media where the most beloved of folklores may be brought into *doubt*, cataclysmic of dissents voiced, suicidal of commitments chosen—the sort that bring governments down" (103–104). The FBI and other government agencies had been monitoring Berkeley since World War II, on the alert for possible Communist party activity. Their actions came to a head during the investigation and 1954 security hearing of nuclear scientist Robert Oppenheimer. In the 1960s they continued to monitor student radicalism at the university, particularly during Ronald Reagan's tenure as California governor.[46]

J. Edgar Hoover campaigned to purify schools such as Berkeley, working to eliminate teachers who employed "an insidious and unsound educational quackery that would rule out all the principles of discipline and control which, if carried to its illogical conclusion, would produce a generation of iconoclastic morons and criminals." Yet he faced considerable resistance. As the historian and Berkeley alumnus Leon F. Litwack has written,

> Over the years the University of California at Berkeley has been denounced for godlessness, blasphemy, debauchery, freethinking, subversion, coddling Communists and radicals, and exposing students to "dangerous" ideas. Whenever I hear those charges, that is when I want to invoke the school mascot and shout, "Go Bears!" That is when I am proudest of my alma mater. That signifies to me that the University is fulfilling its historic mission.[47]

To Litwack and many of his peers, Berkeley's "historic mission" was free inquiry, speech, and thought without institutional, industrial, or government constraints. To its critics and to Oedipa, however, that mission was menacing. Her description of Berkeley as "the sort that bring governments down" echoes Hoover's condemnation of universities and professors that have "aided the Communist cause by tearing down respect for agencies of government, belittling traditional and moral custom and by creating doubts in the validity of the American way of life."[48] Both Oedipa and Hoover identify "doubt" as a great danger because uncertainty and distrust run counter to their belief in "discipline," knowability, and controllability. Unlike Oedipa's professors, who retreated from conflict, Berkeley's students and faculty seem to embrace it, and that unsettles her (104).

Significantly, Oedipa's visit to Berkeley takes place two years after the Free Speech Movement exploded on campus and led to the decentralization of university authority, increasing the power of students and inspiring various politically minded groups. In the introduction to *Revolution at Berkeley* (1965), Irving Howe recounts professors Sheldon S. Wolin and Jahn Schaar's claim that, "for some time now, the students, especially the undergraduates, have felt themselves to be an alien presence within the multiversity, an 'Other Academia' analogous to the 'Other America.'" They attribute this alienation to the increased emphasis on "research productivity" and the transformation of the university into a "research factory." In a speech, university president Clark Kerr, even called the university a "knowledge industry."[49]

Students staged protests in response to the university's increased ties to industry, the military, and the government, hoping to break the machine and gain recognition for both the "Other Academia" and the "Other America." They referred to President Kerr as a "mechanic servicing a vast educational machine" and asked him to return to the humanistic roots of the university. Various teach-ins, rallies, and occupations "brought masses of University people together and gave them opportunities to interact more extensively. . . . A community of learning rife with debate about politics, education, and life itself seemed to have emerged, generating genuine excitement and camaraderie."[50] "Masses" from the political left, right, and center sought "camaraderie" instead of containment, "excitement" instead of somnolence, disorder instead of order, self-determination instead of paternalistic direction, and humanism instead of mechanism, making Berkeley of the early 1960s the epicenter of epistemological movement and change.

When Oedipa wanders into this politically charged atmosphere, she is confused. Her interpretive difficulty demonstrates that her methods of inquiry do not work in the face of this body politic. She arrives on a summer afternoon, expecting sleepiness but finding instead "a plaza teeming with corduroy, denim, bare legs, blonde hair, hornrims, bicycle spokes in the sun, bookbags, swaying card tables, long paper petitions dangling to earth, posters for undecipherable FSM's, YAF's, VCD's, suds in the fountain, students in nose-to-nose dialogue" (103).[51] She comes up against multiple types of texts—petitions,

FIGURE 6. Students for a Democratic Society (SDS) table at Sather Gate [University of California, Berkeley], September 1964. Reprinted by permission of Ronald L. Enfield.

posters, acronyms, and rap sessions—all vying for attention. The ubiquitous social and political bodies typify movement, disorder, and a refusal to stay put. Unlike Oedipa, whose education made her "unfit . . . for marches and sit-ins," the Berkeley students refuse to accept the primacy of facts, truths, systems, and order as privileged by authorities and argue that reading and learning can be more democratic, pluralistic, and uncertain (104).[52]

Although Pynchon does not propose that Berkeley is the model or ideal of reading education, this and similar episodes waken Oedipa to alternate possibilities for reading and readership. She begins to question: "where were Secretaries James and Foster and Senator Joseph, those dear daft numina who'd mothered over Oedipa's so temperate youth?" Her initial shock at Berkeley is followed by a gradual and stuttering change in her epistemology as she realizes that McCarthy and his ilk are "in another world" (104). She has been taught that "each clue that comes is *supposed* to have its own clarity, its fine chances for permanence. But then she wonder[s] if the gemlike 'clues' were only some kind of compensation" (118). Is she being compensated for believing in the fictions of clarity and permanence? For embracing a limited and limiting mode of reading? Oedipa begins to question her faith in clues; she begins to see a difference between what she was taught about them and their actual function. In this moment of wonder, she discovers she must relearn how to interpret her place in her world.[53]

However, questioning established interpretive modes is a dangerous activity in Cold War America. In the introduction to *Slow Learner*, Pynchon writes that the character Lardass Levine's "conflict in ["The Small Rain" (1959)] is about where to put his loyalties, . . . a dilemma that most of us writing then had, in some way to deal with." Similarly, Oedipa must deal with the fallout that such choices produce.[54] The potential risks of her questioning are figured in Metzger's exclamation, "What next, picket the V.A.? March on Washington? God protect me . . . from these lib, overeducated broads with the soft heads and bleeding hearts. . . . She wants to right wrongs . . . Raise ghosts . . . Forgetting her first loyalty, legal and moral, is to the estate she represents" (75–76). Metzger's exasperation appropriates Cold War rhetoric in which "bleeding hearts," "soft heads," and "overeducated" are code for "disloyal" and "traitor."[55] Furthermore, his invective is gendered, reducing Oedipa to a "broad" who is "overeducated" because she is intruding into what he considers a masculine interpretive sphere. Although she has had a limited education, the minute she begins to step outside of prescribed boundaries she becomes associated with a Berkeley-esque intellectualism that can "bring governments down" and make one forget one's prescribed duty to the state (104). Oedipa herself later makes this association when she fears that her theories will mark her "as a redistributionist and pinko" (181).

Metzger counsels her to forget social causes and stick with the textual world enumerated in the estate. Nevertheless, she questions her project and the processes by which she has been operating. Her faith in ordered, direct, and knowable meanings is shaken by a "metaphor of God knew how many parts" (109). She no longer sees Pierce's estate as an accumulation of assets and facts through which she must sort but as a "metaphor"—a representation of something larger than herself—dependent on coincidences, encounters, interpenetrations, and intrusions of meaning on meaning, "as if there could be no barriers" (109, 123, 109, 127, 177). What may have seemed concrete and categorizable is made uncertain, and Oedipa comments that "either Trystero did exist, in its own right, or it was being presumed, perhaps fantasized" (109). She begins to suspect that facts, clues, and truth are fantasies fabricated in the service of a larger plot and starts to see the contingency in the seemingly concrete. The possibility, uncertainty, and doubt inherent to this realization causes her to feel "unfurrowed," as if she has "slipped sideways" (129). The images recall the invisible man and even metaphor itself, which depends on the slippage between two or more parts. Oedipa feels she has lost her bearings and is shaken by the possibility of moving outside the lines drawn by her Cold War guides. While she is freed by this slippage, she also feels lost, struggles with the metaphor and this world of many parts, and hopes that they are a "fantasy" that might be cured (132).

Nonetheless, after recognizing the "metaphor of many parts," Oedipa "decide[s] to drift" to see what and how she might learn (110).[56] While wandering through San Francisco, she becomes more than just a "voyeur and a listener" (123). She interacts with African Americans, Latinos, homosexuals, homeless individuals, and common laborers and begins to recognize that there is a world outside her white, middle-class suburb. She sees and makes apparently random connections everywhere, not only between Pierce's estate and the Trystero but also between herself and the parts of American society from which she had been separated. Without "barriers," Oedipa "connects" with people who are practicing "a calculated withdrawal, from the life of the Republic, from its machinery" (177, 124). Previously she has encountered many machines and images of mechanization, from San Narciso's circuitry, to Yoyodyne's plant, to Echo Court's sign (24, 26). Significantly, however, her encounters in San Francisco resist mechanistic modes of interpretation. Pynchon describes the city as a body, and Oedipa "ha[s] safe-passage tonight to its far blood's branchings, be they capillaries too small for more than peering into, or vessels mashed together in shameless municipal hickeys, out on the skin for all but tourists to see" (117). Instead of stripping this body to expose it, she becomes part of it, perceives how she is implicated in its functioning, and comprehends that there are multiple routes to understanding it.

Oedipa's repetition of the words "as if" in this episode signals a potential move away from a reductive, mechanical type of reading that takes facts (those "shameless municipal hickeys, out on the skin for all but tourists to see") at face value toward one that anticipates the existence of something more—the idea that if she "exfoliated the mere words," she could access multiple worlds of knowledge (163). Her use of the phrase "mere words" illustrates her move toward the point of view of the director of *The Courier's Tragedy:* "[words are] rote noises to hold line bashes with, to get past the bone barriers around an actor's memory" (79). Previously, words offered Oedipa a "buffer" from the world of meanings outside her immediate experience, but now they are mechanisms that help her get past barriers (129). She recognizes "she [will] have trouble sorting the night into real and dreamed" (117). Instead, she must make it up as she goes along, improvising and adapting her interpretive processes to particular moments and occasions and, in so doing, learning about new possibilities for connection.

She asks herself, "Where was the Oedipa who'd driven so bravely up here from San Narciso? That optimistic baby had come on so like the private eye in any long-ago radio drama . . . to solve any great mystery?" (124). Her question echoes her earlier one: "where were Secretaries James and Foster and Senator Joseph, those dear daft numina who'd mothered over Oedipa's so temperate youth?" (104). Both recognize the passing of time and herald an epistemological and ontological shift. Weaned from her Cold War nursemaids, Oedipa is no longer the "optimistic baby" reliant on the sociopolitical dramas from "long-ago." The private *I* that had been subdued and isolated from others is now part of a community comprised of the "Other America."[57] She no longer has blind faith in either authorities or authorized interpretive modes or texts. Yet she is an uncertain, fearful, and unmoored player in an unfinished and changing drama. The signs are "too much" (124). She feels "beat up on," "immobilize[ed]," "overcome," in a "blur" (124, 126, 125). Outside the safety of the system, she is exposed to the dangers of an unbuffered world.

Far from a wholehearted revelry about postmodern possibility, *Lot 49* warns there is danger in losing oneself in metaphor, multiplicity, and play, for they can lead to saturation, madness, isolation, and even totalization. Mucho Maas most obviously illustrates "how far it might be possible to get lost" in layers of meaning (95). At first he typifies reading metaphorically in all of its possibility, his name being the first indicator of his propensity toward multiplicity and excess. When we meet Mucho, he is recovering from his work as a used car salesman—a job that was an "exquisite torture to him" because of his hyperawareness of "what *that* profession had come to mean" (13, 12). He is distressed by the meanings imposed on used car salesmen and makes an excessively ridiculous effort to infuse the job with other meanings. What kept him in the job for so long was that he "believed in the cars"; however, that belief, too, was founded in "excess." He invested too much meaning in the cars, reading them metaphorically as "metal extensions of [the owners], of their families and what their whole lives must be like." The cars became "automotive projection[s] of somebody else's life," exchanged for other cars "as if it were the most natural thing" (13, 14).

Mucho's interpretive mode ends up isolating him from other people and preventing real human connection. At first he merely reads metaphor's multiplicity in everything; ultimately, he becomes an embodiment of (or conduit for) metaphor. After leaving the car lot, he becomes a radio disc jockey, performing work and playing songs that he "[does] not believe in" (23). He finds no inherent meaning to or value in anything—there is no center to hold him—and thus he constantly drifts. With the aid of LSD, he can "listen to anything and take it apart again. Spectrum analysis, in my head. I can break down chords, and timbres, and words too into all the basic frequencies and harmonics, with all their different loudnesses, and listen to them, each pure tone, but all at once" (142). Mucho claims that purity of meaning is not possible with any other means of interpretation; yet by hearing all possibility all at once, he is overwhelmed by its excess, and his individual self disappears. His boss claims that Mucho "hasn't been himself," "he's losing his identity," and he's "less himself and more generic. He enters a staff meeting and the room is suddenly full of people. . . . He's a walking assembly of a man" (140).

Even though Mucho's person is distinguished by the aggregation of parts, he becomes "more generic" because this excess overdetermines him. He proclaims, "the world is so abundant. No end to it, baby" (144). He attempts to embrace and immerse himself in pure abundance and eventually "dissipate[s]" (144). In this, he is like Tyrone Slothrop in Pynchon's novel *Gravity's Rainbow* (1973), whom few can see "as any sort of integral creature any more."[58] Mucho is everything and anything; he is totality in all of its excess. His saturation and dissipation anticipate the path of many radical postmodern epistemologies: the New Left's multiple and competing factions, the New Right's proliferation into various conservative interest groups, and the explosion of postmodern interpretive theories. At the same time, he demonstrates possibility's dangerous potential to totalize and overdetermine, and his characterization anticipates those critics of postmodernism who accuse its theories of "endless" deferral, substitution, possibility, and play and of being relativistic, nihilistic, hedonistic, and self-defeating.[59]

In her last meeting with her husband, Oedipa recognizes the danger of clinging to pure metaphor and getting lost in either drift or play, so she leaves

Mucho in order to find some form of grounding. Throughout her physical and epistemological travels, she has become increasingly self-conscious about her processes of interpretation and the individual and sociopolitical implications of totalizing reading discourses based either in the purity of facts or possibility. As she attempts to make sense out of the body of evidence in Pierce's estate, she learns that she needs more than her familiar facts, truths, systems, and methods and that possible meaning making depends on connections between multiple, uncontrollable, and seemingly contrary bodies. Yet she also learns that metaphoricity, possibility, and play have their limits and can be equally totalizing. Hence, she, Pynchon, and their readers seek a middle ground.

Pregnant with Possibility

At the novel's close, Oedipa seems to have come full circle; she is isolated and numb once again. However, this time her isolation results from her fears that the "revelations" proffered by her new understanding could "expand beyond a certain point" and possibly "grow larger than she" is (166). She illustrates this paranoia and its threat in a series of either-or constructions: either she has identified a huge conspiracy while executing Pierce's will, or she is the subject of an elaborate hoax; either all of these connections exist, or she is crazy; either there is "another mode of meaning behind the obvious, or none" (182). The novel ends with these either-ors unresolved—an ambiguous conclusion that leaves Oedipa, the novel, and its readers open to the possibility that either the world can sustain and rely on multiple modes of interpretation or it will be paralyzed under the weight of overdetermination.

The complex and at times menacing possibility that meanings might "grow larger than" Oedipa is represented by the image of pregnancy. As her epistemological quest progresses, Oedipa is figured as a bloom, a blossom, a dome, and a beach ball. These images of roundness and fullness correlate with her accumulation of information and her subsequent attempts to reproduce meaning. After meeting Driblette, she questions whether or not it is "part of her duty . . . to bestow life . . . to bring the estate into pulsing stelliferous Meaning, all in a soaring dome around her" (82). The immediate images in this passage are astral: Oedipa is responsible for projecting a constellation of meanings. At the same time, the passage's language links interpretation with pregnancy. To find "Meaning," give "life" to the estate, and provide it with a "pulse" requires Oedipa to be encompassed by a "dome."

Elsewhere, we read that Oedipa has been "saturated" or "interpenetrated with the dead man's estate" and that the estate is a "metaphor of God [knows] how many parts." (177, 109). Pierce counsels Oedipa to "keep it bouncing" during their affair, and she initially misreads this statement, concluding that Pierce "must have known, writing the will, facing the specter, how the bouncing would stop." In fact, the will does not mark the end of the bouncing but the possibility of a new generation—a "bouncing" baby of metaphor. The "enigma his efforts had created," the "headlong expansion of himself," is this child (178). Oedipa sets up a pregnancy test, only to realize that "your gynecologist has no test for what she [is] pregnant with"—the unsettling possibility provided by reading rooted in multiplicity and linguistic play (175).

The language with which Oedipa discusses this legacy suggests a complex relationship between the individual citizen-reader and the community. Although her reading education had taught her how to withdraw, locate, and isolate, therein troubling community formation, her travels have opened her to the possibility of connection and communion. She admits that in attempting to make "sense of what Inverarity had left behind, [she] never suspect[ed] that the legacy was America" (178). Her bouncing baby of metaphor is or will be America. Signaling her changing interpretive mode, she discusses America's potential with another unresolved either-or construction. For Oedipa's baby there is either something "beyond the appearance of the legacy of America, or there was just America and if there was just America then it seemed the only way she could continue, and manage to be at all relevant to it, was as an alien, unfurrowed, assumed full circle into some paranoia" (182). She questions the form of the legacy and what role she will play once she has delivered it. She reaches for the openness of possibility even as she appears to foreclose it with an either-or binary.

Is there a greater role for America, something beyond mere existence? Or, is its work merely appearance? If delivered, will it deliver? It is unclear to both Oedipa and Pynchon's readers whether America is a miracle or a symbol of the quotidian, the mundane, and the profane. One could argue that possibility rests in that lack of clarity: how will Oedipa deliver this metaphor? As Gerald Graff wrote in 1979, "this celebration of energy frequently seems to hover somewhere between revolutionary politics and sophisticated acquiescence to the agreeably meaningless surfaces of mass culture."[60] Is the possibility Oedipa finds revolutionary? Does it signal her surrender to relativism and a world without meaning? Or is it something else altogether? She is "unfurrowed," "alien," outside her old track, and occupying a zone "somewhere between" the "ones and zeroes," a space that is both promising and ominous (182).

Within a year of *The Crying of Lot 49*'s publication, two other important texts—Jacques Derrida's "Structure, Sign and Play in the Discourse of the Human Sciences" (1966) and Norman Mailer's *The Armies of the Night* (1968)—also invoked pregnancy to identify what they saw as emerging changes in textual interpretation. Derrida, like Pynchon, characterizes a tension between two modes of interpretation: one that tries to "decipher" and one that is "no longer turned toward the origin, [but] affirms play and tries to pass beyond man." He notes that what he sees (or hopes to see) is a move in interpretation toward an understanding that "there is always more." He uses words such as "*conception, formation, gestation*, and *labor*" to articulate the potentialities of this "new" epistemology, recognizing that he does so "with a glance towards the operations of childbearing." Like childbearing, his interpretive mode involves anticipation, ambiguity, deferral, and labor. His language of pregnancy not only draws attention to the epistemological "operations" he's exploring but also emphasizes the as-yet "unnamable which is proclaiming itself and which can do so . . . only under the species of the nonspecies, in the formless, mute, infant, and terrifying form of monstrosity." Whereas the object of previous critical practices was fixed and controlled, the "infant" heralding his new mode of inquiry is "unnamable" and "mute," and therein rests possibility. Derrida's essay is similar to Pynchon's novel in that it does not or cannot say what form that possibility will take; it is formless, mute, and unnamable in its infancy. Like Oedipa's baby, Derrida's infant is terrifying in its possibility; for because of its "newness," it can only adopt a "form of monstrosity."[61]

In the concluding section of *The Armies of the Night*, appropriately titled "The Metaphor Delivered," Mailer employs the metaphor of pregnancy to make an apocalyptic pronouncement about America's future. He imagines America as a woman "heavy with child"; and like Oedipa's baby and Derrida's infant, that offspring is ambiguous and indefinite. "She will probably give birth, and to what?—the most fearsome totalitarianism the world has ever known? or can she, poor giant, tormented lovely girl, deliver a babe of a new world brave and tender, artful and wild?" Mailer sets up an either-or equation, and both options flirt with totality and totalization. Will the child be the revolutionary savior of a fallen America, or will it be a destroying angel? Is the once beautiful America a virginal vessel of divinity, or a diseased whore offering up a bastardized ideal? Foreboding shades the gestation period: "we must end on the road to that mystery where courage, death, and the dream of love give promise of sleep."[62] Uncertainty offers freedom, but that freedom is terrifying because it may go either way, both of which may forestall further interpretation.

The students at Berkeley who appear in Pynchon's novel, the Paris activists who influenced Derrida's work, and the marchers in Washington, D.C., who formed the backdrop for Mailer's *Armies* believed that doubt, deferral, and disorder were more human and honest than were epistemologies based on facts, systems, structures, organizations, programs, and order. Thus, these overlapping texts identify a key moment in thinking about reading, interpretation, and nation. Like earlier generations of reading advocates, this generation of authors, educators, philosophers, and activists were forwarding theories of reading that worked to wrest interpretation away from the few for the many. Readers once again sought a model of reading and interpretation that made possible both readerly autonomy and community action.

5

Metafiction and Radical Democracy

Getting at the Heart of John Barth's *Lost in the Funhouse*

Reflecting on his tenure at the State University of New York in Buffalo during the late 1960s, John Barth writes that it was "altogether a stimulating place to work through those troubled years."[1] Even early in the Vietnam War, the school's student and faculty antiwar activists created storefront colleges and took part in poetry readings and teach-ins that drew large crowds. Students for a Democratic Society (SDS) was a key player in this radical movement. After the group released *The Port Huron Statement* in 1962, its membership swelled, and SUNY-Buffalo's chapter had approximately five hundred members by 1968. Frequent clashes with campus security, city police, and community members were common, prompting visits from legislators and the FBI, which "compiled 17,000 pages of files on just the SDS and the Buffalo Draft Resistance Union" between 1965 and 1973. By 1968, Barth's university resembled a war zone with altercations between anti- and pro-war students, between activists and law enforcement, and between campus and community.[2] Looking back on that time, he writes that radical social, political, and "artistic experiment was in the Buffalo air" and suggests that other airborne agents also affected his art: "I sniff traces of tear gas in its margins; I hear an echo of disruption between its lines."[3]

The phrase "echo of disruption" suggests that Barth's 1960s work engaged with his current radical context, yet he has resisted explicitly aligning it with a political or an ethical project. Instead, he claims to have been "more of a deeply sympathetic spectator than a participator" in the political upheavals at

SUNY-Buffalo.[4] In his 1965 essay "Muse, Spare Me," he begs to be exempted "from social-historical responsibility, and in the last analysis from every other kind as well, except artistic. Your teller of tales will likely be responsive to his time; he needn't be responsible to it." He writes, "I'm not impressed by the apocalyptic character of the present age." Later, however, he recants: "For the posturing in my first paragraph . . . I apologize. If ever I wasn't [impressed by the apocalyptic character of the present age], I have certainly become so." Barth often contradicts himself when writing and speaking about his work, his responsibility as an artist, and his political context. Nevertheless, most critics, scholars, and writers adopt his language of disassociation when discussing his metafiction, asserting that it is necessarily abstracted from its political and social contexts. Because it is fiction about fiction, they argue, it is free from the demands made by or on realist or metaphysical fiction. John Carlos Rowe has written that postmodern writers such as Barth, Pynchon, and John Hawkes were "attracted to academic issues as a defense against their reluctance to write more politically specific work."[5] He is not alone; most of Barth's critics read the various echoes of disruption in his work as indicators of postmodern play. They treat texts such as *Lost in the Funhouse* primarily in terms of aesthetics and ask, like *Funhouse*'s character Ambrose, "What relevance does the war have to the story?"[6]

Yet if we read *Lost in the Funhouse* in the context of 1960s student and philosophical radicalism, we see that this seemingly apolitical, ahistorical, and academic work about the process of fiction making illustrates key ideas from "those troubled years." Its calls for self-consciousness, readerly participation, and "new human work" are similar to those found in the era's radical print, postmodern philosophies, global student activism, and texts by Barth's more overtly political peers, Norman Mailer and E. L. Doctorow. Although the act of reading is always participatory, *Lost in the Funhouse* calls for both responsive and responsible readership—"Can't you read between the lines?"—a type of reading that is self-aware, active, and creative (110). The text makes readers conscious of their role, work, and choices in the process of reading and thus suggests that the text is a living, evolving creation similar to the "living document[s]" that SDS and other student groups generated during this time.[7] Privileging paradox, digression, deferral, ambiguity, and fill-in-the-blank narration, *Funhouse* provides seemingly limitless points of access into the text that work to distribute and relocate textual authority in readers themselves.

Early Barth scholarship acknowledges *Funhouse*'s seemingly new relationship to reading. Edgar H. Knapp claims that the "funhouse for *man thinking* is a womb of possibility from which he may be reborn." Beth Boehm argues that Barth gives his readers the tools for interpreting future performances; he "make[s] us more self-conscious readers of literature." Michael Carey asserts that "the reader's active role in interpreting the text makes the reader equivalent to A [God], an active participant in the creation of a text." Brian Edwards contends that both Barth and Italo Calvino "create possibilities within uncertainty by inviting the reader into the process."[8] What these scholars and others have failed to recognize is that Barth's aesthetic is inherently political. Metafiction in general and Barth's work in particular purport to challenge modernist, New Critical, and Cold War liberal ideologies about authority, truth, and freedom—ideas that many writers, critics, philosophers, and student radicals claimed preserved power for those already on top. Dividing politics from metafiction's aesthetics is at best artificial and at worst a reaffirmation of the structures against which metafiction works. Putting Barth's metafictional urtext into conversation with student radical print and poststructuralist theory demonstrates that *Lost in the Funhouse*'s vision of and for narrative fiction was part of a larger, dynamic, radical discourse seeking to challenge authority and redefine interpretive processes in order to enliven moribund narratives, citizen-readers, and communities.

Reading and Writing a Living Document

Universities were a primary locus of radicalism and revolution in the late 1960s. The student radicals who participated in the various social movements that came to be known as the New Left were the generation for whom the Cold War was allegedly being waged.[9] Part of the postwar baby boom, these children had benefited from the increased access to books that Cold War reading initiatives, institutions, and infrastructures had provided. They had never known a world without local bookstores, affordable paperbacks, branch or mobile libraries, language arts funding, or youth-targeted publications such as the Classics Illustrated series, Scholastic Books, and controversial superhero comic books. They grew up in a reading culture and had access to books at school, home, libraries, churches, and clubs. Many attended some of the most prestigious private and land-grant universities in the United States. They were the students Oedipa Maas met in "nose-to-nose dialogue" at Berkeley.[10] They were the future of America.

Yet many a Johnny and Janey viewed their Cold War legacy with anything but gratitude. In the preamble to *The Port Huron Statement*, SDS representatives declared: "We are people of this generation, bred in at least modest comfort, housed now in universities, looking uncomfortably to the world we inherit." Student radicals saw their elders' efforts to keep their "mind on an even keel through the troubled waters of our dynamic political and social life" as a form of "sterilized, automated contentment" antithetical to the ideals of "freedom" and "democracy" that their leaders purported to defend. Rather than feeling secure, they felt smothered. They believed their Cold War caretakers were not keeping them free but were "the manifest of evil to this generation . . . who had covered the land with those suburbs where they stifled as children." They had grown up as part of what the historian David M. Potter called "the people of plenty," yet student radicals from Pynchon's Berkeley to Barth's Buffalo viewed their America with unease and fear. To them, it was a place in which nuclear weapons proliferated, conspicuous consumption reigned, universities became corporatized, Jim Crow laws and racially motivated violence persisted, and involvement in foreign wars was normal.[11]

Students who participated in Mississippi voter registration efforts, Freedom Ride campaigns, lunch counter sit-ins, the Free Speech Movement, anti–Vietnam War activities, anti-nuke protests, and other radical activities used their reading skills to challenge the "system of controls" and ideas of "social desirab[ility]" undergirding many early Cold War reading initiatives. These citizen-readers used their interpretive abilities to reframe the definitions, methods, and uses of good reading in order to save America's soul from a nationalism they believed was "ambiguous and tradition-bound instead of informed and clear, its democratic system apathetic and manipulated rather than 'of, by, and for the people.'" Declaring that "we may be the last generation in the experiment with living," they proposed a new epistemology— "truly democratic alternatives to the present"—to combat what they saw as "the stagnation of those who have closed their minds to the future," who have been the victims of institutions seeking to "blunt the minds of their potential critics," and who have been numbed like *Lot 49*'s somnolent Oedipa Maas or like Susan Lewin, a character in Doctorow's novel *The Book of Daniel*, who "died of a failure of analysis." They asserted that new modes of reading were necessary "to meet the conditions of cybernated abundance and organizational ascendance. Old definitions, goals, and tactics must be reappraised." For student radicals, "the aesthetic at last was in the politics," and they believed that form, style, and interpretation could explode oppressive structures just as effectively as a bomb could.[12]

The surging radical student energy of the 1960s caught many off guard. Parents, university presidents, liberal intellectuals, storied academics, cultural critics, and modernist writers seemed surprised and confused by students' rejection of their ethos, aesthetic, and politics. Was it philosophical? Was it political? Or was it merely bad behavior? Edward Bloomberg, a professor at the University of California at Davis, dismissed New Left charges of police brutality during sit-ins and protests as "simply the cry of the spoiled child who is, for the first time, not accorded special privileges." Scott Buchanan, a former professor at Saint John's College and a fellow at the Center for the Study of Democratic Institutions, also infantilized student radicals, expressing "a certain kind of anger at your playing house with the idea of power—that's what it seems to me you are doing. I don't want to call you children, but you act like children. You are grown-up but you are throwing yourself into the role of children. And you are talking about power in ways that make me want to spank you." In *Coming Apart: An Informal History of America in the 1960s* (1971), William O'Neill characterized SDS as childish even as he claimed to be celebrating the organization: "Defying authority in a good cause was fun. So were camping out for a week in university buildings, building temporary utopias, and standing guard dramatically against the enemy without. It was a mixture of living theater, cowboys and Indians, the Russian Revolution, and nursery school. Afterward, everyone got a good spanking for being naughty."[13]

Some government officials sensed the politics in the aesthetic and, like the authority figure in *Funhouse*'s "Life-Story," accused these radical readers of being "tireless," "shameless," violent, and unpredictable (124). Richard H. Ichord, chair of the House Committee on Internal Security, saw "a parallel . . . between the attitude of SDS activists and the well-known attitudes of Fascists and Communists." In response to such concerns, special congressional committees, the FBI, and local police units worked together to try to neutralize SDS and other New Left organizations.[14] Strategies involved planting agents in SDS meetings and branches to foment fractiousness and mimicking New Left reading and print culture programs. For instance, COINTELPRO created fraudulent pamphlets, letters, and circulars in an attempt to turn off new recruits, create dissent within the ranks, and discredit the organizations.[15]

When these efforts did not work, government bodies dealt with radical reading materials in much the same way as the House Committee on Un-American Activities had handled Communist literature in the 1950s. In 1968 and 1969, the current version of that congressional committee, along with the House Committee on Internal Security, held special hearings on SDS's political activities and used COINTELPRO's files as their primary evidence of the group's un-Americanness.[16] In December 1969, radical print materials and distribution methods were important elements in congressional hearings connected to SDS's antiwar activities near Fort Dix, New Jersey. Not only did the committee focus on the "numerous articles and leaflets distributed . . . [and] the regular left wing distribution of leaflets, propaganda material" as evidence of SDS's treasonous activities but it also underscored that no "pro-American literature [was] distributed," therein marking these groups and their ideas as anti-American. A 1969 House report titled "SDS Plans for America's High Schools" identified numerous problematic activities related to reading: "passing out SDS literature and talking with students," "literature all over the place," and "underground newspapers . . . [that criticize] the 'establishment,' government, school administration, law enforcement, the draft, and the

Vietnam war." The report saw these activities as part of a "virulent force which threatens the traditional values and institutions of our democratic society." Ironically, its proposed solution was exactly what SDS and other New Left groups were combating: "school officials must be prepared to wield firm and effective authority in dealing with young activists who seek to create chaos in our educational system."[17]

Members and supporters of the House Committee on Internal Security failed to understand how "firm and effective authority" could be in conflict with the values of "our democratic society." To these officials, the New Left was attempting to incite a civil war and needed to be stopped. Yet the New Left's various organizations believed that American society was already impaired, if not irremediably broken, by authoritarian government policies and paternalistic institutions that were sacrificing freedom on the altar of national security. Both sides claimed to want to protect or heal the Union, yet their goals were nearly opposite. In *Armies of the Night*, Norman Mailer's description of the 1967 march on the Pentagon captures this conflict:

> Out from that direction [the steps of the Lincoln Memorial] came the clear bitter-sweet excitation of a military trumpet resounding in the near distance, one peal which seemed to go all the way back through a galaxy of bugles to the cries of the Civil War and the first trumpet note to blow the attack. The ghosts of old battles were wheeling like clouds over Washington today. The trumpet sounded again. It was calling the troops. . . . They came walking up in all sizes, a citizens' army not ranked yet by height, an army of both sexes in numbers almost equal, and of all ages, although most were young.[18]

Though he is moved by the historical comparison, Mailer is excited by the new army's lack of rank, its celebration of equality, and its openness to all peoples and ideas. To him, this openness signals a return to democracy's root— the idea that democracy is a government of, by, and for the people.

Like their counterparts on the battlefield, this citizens' army believed that reading could defeat the enemy, strengthen democracy, and allow freedom to flourish. SDS's widely distributed foundational texts, *The Port Huron Statement* and *America and the New Era* (1963), focused on language as power and empowerment and argued that democracy could exist only when citizens were free to read, think, know, and participate as they chose. Like those who came before them, these citizen-readers saw their world as uncertain and believed that reading was a means of navigating it. Yet there were differences. The previous generation had seen uncertainty as a lamentable modern reality that could be temporarily transcended by textual order. In contrast, this younger group believed that uncertainty was significantly less threatening than the authorities' defined tracks, prescribed methods, and ordered world were. They claimed that manufactured certainty offered "no viable alternative" because it forced individuals to relinquish their agency as citizen-readers. Like their radical ancestors, SDS rejected institutions whose "policies and style flow from [their] necessary commitment to the preservation of the going system" and that offer a "surface promise of equality" while forwarding a "national stalemate."[19]

In place of these "exhausted" policies and systems, SDS texts offered images of life, birth, and rebirth that theorized individual creativity and linked it to democracy. Student radicals compared their revision project to an "embryonic upsurge," believing "that to become a radical was like giving birth to yourself." Both *The Port Huron Statement* and *America and the New Era* stressed the need to "recaptur[e] . . . the populist inheritance of liberalism." Describing its project as "an effort rooted in the ancient, still unfulfilled conception of man," SDS searched "for truly democratic alternatives to the present, and a commitment to social experimentation within them," in which "no existing mode of thought, nor entrenched institution will remain unchallenged."[20]

SDS's radical discourse emphasized both a return to an older democratic ideal and a need to "open the scope of alternatives." In other words, even as it privileged the new, SDS did not propose the complete destruction of the old. The group's idea of radical revision involved "drawing on what remains of the adult labor, academic and political communities, not just revolting in despair against them and the world they have designed for us." In particular, SDS believed in making use of the university, "no matter how dull the teaching, how paternalistic the rules, how irrelevant the research that goes on. Social relevance, the accessibility to knowledge, and the internal openness—these together make the university a potential base and agency in a movement of social change."[21] Challenging the idea that universities are founded on "principles of discipline and control," student radicals proposed they could be "functionally tied to society in new ways, revealing new potentialities, new levers for change," that would privilege students and communities rather than regents and investors.[22]

According to SDS, "the key to understanding the oppressive class structures now developing in American society is found less in the maldistribution of the nation's property than in the maldistribution of its knowledge." By working to change who accessed knowledge, how, and why, activists believed they could reverse the stifled "personal cultivation of the mind" and a widespread inability "to deal with confusion, anxiety, and the enormity of events," which, they claimed, earlier Cold War interpretive methods had wrought. The inspiration for the Port Huron meetings was borrowed from the writings of the sociologist C. Wright Mills, who emphasized that democracy is only possible "when there exists a free and knowledgeable public, to which

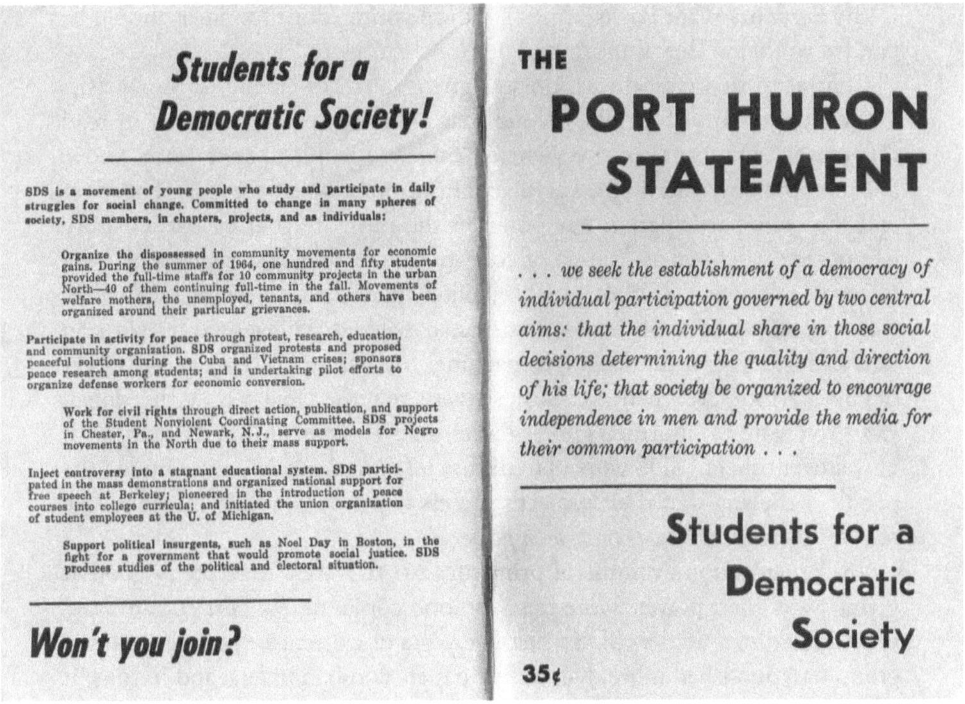

Students for a Democratic Society!

SDS is a movement of young people who study and participate in daily struggles for social change. Committed to change in many spheres of society, SDS members, in chapters, projects, and as individuals:

Organize the dispossessed in community movements for economic gains. During the summer of 1964, one hundred and fifty students provided the full-time staffs for 10 community projects in the urban North—40 of them continuing full-time in the fall. Movements of welfare mothers, the unemployed, tenants, and others have been organized around their particular grievances.

Participate in activity for peace through protest, research, education, and community organization. SDS organized protests and proposed peaceful solutions during the Cuba and Vietnam crises; sponsors peace research among students; and is undertaking pilot efforts to organize defense workers for economic conversion.

Work for civil rights through direct action, publication, and support of the Student Nonviolent Coordinating Committee. SDS projects in Chester, Pa., and Newark, N.J., serve as models for Negro movements in the North due to their mass support.

Inject controversy into a stagnant educational system. SDS participated in the mass demonstrations and organized national support for free speech at Berkeley; pioneered in the introduction of peace courses into college curricula; and initiated the union organization of student employees at the U. of Michigan.

Support political insurgents, such as Noel Day in Boston, in the fight for a government that would promote social justice. SDS produces studies of the political and electoral situation.

Won't you join?

THE

PORT HURON STATEMENT

. . . we seek the establishment of a democracy of individual participation governed by two central aims: that the individual share in those social decisions determining the quality and direction of his life; that society be organized to encourage independence in men and provide the media for their common participation . . .

Students for a Democratic Society

35¢

FIGURE 7. The cover of *The Port Huron Statement,* published by Students for a Democratic Society (SDS), 1964.

men of knowledge may address themselves, and to which men of power are truly responsible. Such a public and such men—either of power and knowledge—do not now prevail, and accordingly, knowledge does not now have democratic relevance in America."[23]

Mills's acolytes believed that "a good reader is a good citizen" but claimed that current reading methods and programs were limited and restrictive; only greater openness and exchange could "establish an environment for people to live in with dignity and creativeness." As early as 1961, the activist Tom Hayden was inviting "the peoples of the world" to join SDS's battle against "the endless repressions of free speech and thought, the stifling paternalism that infects the student's whole perception of what is real and possible and enforces a parent-child relationship until the youth is suddenly transplanted into 'the world.'" Student radical organizations throughout the decade sought access to information, knowledge, and authority, believing that they could help average Americans throw off "paternalistic" institutions and gain access to non-sanitized, non-sanctioned, non-official stories that would help them reclaim reading's democratizing function. As Steven Roberts noted in

"Why Students Want Power" (1967), radical youth "don't feel ideas should be handed to them. They want to find out for themselves."[24]

Central to this radical revision was giving birth to "living document[s]," a new conception of an old lineage that would help train citizens to read differently. SDS print was everywhere, "call[ing] people to read, learn, know, and do, thereby asserting a causal connection between the act of reading and the civic participation embodied in the ultimate goal of 'participatory democracy,'" defined as "the art of collectively creating an acceptable pattern of social relations." SDS materials typified "participatory democracy": they were produced by anybody (sometimes, it seemed, by everybody) with an idea and access to a mimeograph machine. In "Young Radicals and the Fear of Power" (1968), Kenneth Keniston suggests that the "goal behind this slogan [was] to create an informed group, rather than a single informed person with power over others." SDS worked to diffuse information and power among the people, believing that their project's success depended "largely . . . [on] *how successfully they gave away their own power.*"[25]

The organization's volume of print suggests that they were pretty good at giving away their power. More than 100,000 copies of *The Port Huron Statement* were distributed in SDS's first five years of existence. By mid-1964, the group had published more than ninety papers and pamphlets; and in 1965, it distributed more than 400,000 pieces of literature during antiwar teach-ins. Roughly a thousand SDS members handed out more than 500,000 copies of the group's four-page "National Vietnam Examination" to those taking the Selective Service exam in 1966.[26]

SDS believed that "we have access to more knowledge, more potential and actual and varied power than ever before, and in the endlessness of change lies always the possibility of making new and revolutionary departures."[27] However, citizen-readers must know how to process the knowledge they have accessed. Accordingly, the group proposed new methods of interpretation rooted in "a willingness to continually press forward with the query: Why? Radicalism finds no rest in conclusions; answers are seen as provisional, to be discarded in the face of new evidence or changed conditions. This is, in one sense, a difficult mental task and, in a more profound moral sense, it represents a serious personal decision to be introspective, to be exposed always to the stinging glare of change, to be willing always to reconstruct our social views."[28]

According to Hayden's vision, the radical reader cultivates an active intellect because it is the ethical thing to do. While resonating with earlier postwar emphases on reading and citizenship, this version differs because it works to be transparent and consciously emphasizes questioning, challenging assumptions, examining evidence, and reviewing and revising understandings.

Student radicals expressed confidence that everyone could be trained to "meet with increasing skill the complexities and responsibilities of their situation." They believed that people

> have unrealized potential for . . . creativity, . . . a quality of mind not compulsively driven by a sense of powerlessness, nor one which unthinkingly adopts status values, nor one which represses all threats to its habits, but one which has full, spontaneous access to present and past experiences, one which easily unites the fragmented parts of personal history, one which openly faces problems which are troubling and unresolved; one with an intuitive awareness of possibilities, an active sense of curiosity, an ability and willingness to learn.[29]

In this somewhat romantic view, the ideal reader recognizes ambiguity, uncertainty, and language's mutability, as earlier readers also did. But unlike them, she is neither bothered nor anxious, instead recognizing that a lack of resolution offers her the possibility of further learning.

Documents such as *The Port Huron Statement* theorized that educated reader-citizens would step out of isolation into a readerly community as they confronted new textual possibilities. Pushing back against the stifling effects of reading primers, book lists, great works, and interpretive methods, SDS radicals stated that "we have no sure formulas, no closed theories," preferring what James Miller calls "an open invitation to embark on a shared adventure of political discovery."[30] *Open* was an important word in SDS documents, which expended much energy denouncing the closed or limited nature of current systems and the need to "open the scope of alternatives."[31] These documents linked openness to sociability—a "shared adventure"; but rather than defining key terms and mapping out a step-by-step program, their framers encouraged readers to be creative in their use of knowledge.

Nonetheless, many SDS documents assumed an implicit hierarchy between student intellectuals and "the people," replicating to some degree the power structure they were fighting to dismantle.[32] There is a definite classed dimension to these materials, suggesting more structure and less openness than the documents' authors may have liked to acknowledge. SDS's writerly leaders often positioned themselves as experts who could "transform modern complexity into issues that can be understood and felt close-up by every human being" and create a coalition "between a new left of young people, and an awakening community of allies." Here and elsewhere in their documents there is an echo of paternalism. For example, in "We've Got to Reach Our Own People" (1967) and "Getting Ready for the Firing Line" (1968), student organizers refer to the working poor as "these people" and members of "these communities," signaling that the pamphlets' "you" is a more learned student audience tasked to educate these distinctly different "others." In "Chicago: Organizing the Unemployed" (1964), Richard Flacks blatantly declared that "an extensive supply of literature on economic and social issues, suitable for working class readers needs to be created immediately." Such rhetoric "raise[d] the specter of an elite cadre of intellectuals claiming to speak on behalf of a mute public" and complicated SDS's claims about participatory democracy.[33]

Although many radical organizations worked to contest the system's mores, the New Left "reflected more than it challenged the underlying sexual stereotypes of these early years." Women did wield some authority in these groups, but they also had to negotiate the "cultural undertow of expectations that they would perform traditional feminine tasks" such as "virtually all of the typing and clerical work." As I will discuss in chapter 6, Mary King, Casey Hayden, Mary Varela, and others wrote position papers and organized meetings to raise awareness about the ways in which female activists were denied a voice in decision- and policymaking, ridiculed, and harassed, yet they found that their liberated male comrades often were too threatened to discuss these concerns openly and honestly. Often these male allies responded immaturely, as evidenced in an issue of *New Left Notes*, which responded to women's concerns by publishing a "cartoon of a girl—with earrings, polkadot minidress, and matching visible panties—holding a sign: 'We Want Our Rights and We Want Them Now.'"[34] Yet despite these limitations, SDS and other radical student organizations did clear the path for many American citizen-readers to access, interpret, and create new knowledge in ways they hadn't previously. Even when SDS began to fragment in the late 1960s, its various factions continue to pursue the organization's original goal: moving individuals to define their own terms and participate in the workings of the nation as they chose.

"Lost" in the Funhouse of Language

The philosophies of reading, interpretation, and civic participation that student radicals offered in the 1960s were echoed in the theories of literary interpretation that came to be known as postmodernism. In October 1966, a conference titled "The Languages of Criticism and the Sciences of Man: The Structuralist Controversy," held at Johns Hopkins University, introduced European structuralist and poststructuralist theories to the American academy. Derrida's "Structure, Sign and Play" had its first audience at this conference, as did Eugenio Donato's "The Two Languages of Criticism." Frank Lentricchia recalls the impact of the conference: "Though on the Continent the attack on phenomenology and existentialism had long been explicitly underway, in the work of Lévi-Strauss and Barthes, and implied in the writings of neo-Saussurean linguists, in the mid-sixties the key figures of the structuralist movement were still virtually unknown in American literary critical circles." Yet, he notes, "American criticism was still fascinated, a good decade after the waning of the New Criticism, by perspectives which never succeeded in putting to rest basic formalist principles which structuralism, at least by intent, seemed sure to demolish."[35]

The Johns Hopkins conference challenged the preeminence of formalist and increasingly formulaic modes of interpretation that had become central to reading in the academy and helped give birth to a diverse body of postmodern philosophies and literary theories, which the scholar Terry Eagleton saw as "a product of that blend of euphoria and disillusionment, liberation and dissipation, carnival and catastrophe" that characterized the era. The context in which Barth worked on *Funhouse* was influenced by a number of the postmodern texts and ideas that came to prominence in the 1960s. For instance, many of the global student protests were marked by an "emphasis on the interplay between art and revolution." According to Richard Flacks, a member of SDS who later became a professor at the University of Chicago, the organization wanted "to redefine the vocation of the intellectual, . . . to find ways to connect intellectual work with the needs and realities of the disadvantaged and oppressed, . . . to expand the possibilities for effective social criticism."[36]

Both activists and literary theorists adopted the rhetoric of revolution as they articulated their visions for new modes of reading and creativity. In her essay "Post-'68: Theory Is in the Streets," Astra Taylor suggests that activism retreated into theoretical discourse because it was safer, and Eagleton concurs: "the student movement was flushed off the streets and driven underground into discourse. Nobody, at least, was likely to beat you over the head for doing so." Yet SDS members such as Hayden, Mario Savio, Mark Rudd, and Carl Oglesby recognized that discourse was playing two roles during the 1960s: members of the power structure manipulated it to repress student protests, and activists manipulated it to dismantle the system. As Rudd said about the 1968 SDS takeover of Columbia University, "a leaflet or dorm-canvassing is no less radical activity than seizing a building." In other words, discourse was not separate from action; both were living documents. In John Carlos Rowe's explanation, "the postmoderns' claims to understand how language functions by means of the strategic deformation of verbal conventions implied that any significant social change would depend on our knowledge of language and its determination of thought and values."[37]

Radicalism was a defining element of postmodern theories that purported to interrogate the ideological, political, social, and linguistic roots of the ways in which readers interpret and represent their world. This questioning resonated with Hayden's call to "continually press forward the query: Why?

Radicalism finds no rest in conclusions; answers are seen as provisional, to be discarded in the face of new evidence or changed considerations."[38] He and his comrades questioned and called others to question the systems that restrictively arranged them, just as postmodern theorists put "into question the system" that structured and ordered interpretation to get at the root of meaning making. Like the student radicals, the theorists revisited old materials but used them in new ways: "the passage beyond philosophy does not consist in turning the page of philosophy (which usually amounts to philosophizing badly), but in continuing to read philosophers *in a certain way*."[39] They recognized that "there are many ways to transcend formalism, but the worst is not to study forms."[40]

One might easily romanticize postmodernism's role in "liberat[ing] the reader from the tyranny of the text," yet that perspective ignores the "persistence of New Critical ideas in theories that tr[ied] to overcome them."[41] Both the New Criticism and postmodern theories shared the premise that the modern poetic world "resists mastery, is more mysterious than intelligible, . . . [and is] antipathetic to the modern everyday world of business, science, and positivism." Rather, they argued, this world is "pluralist, relativist, and irrational." Similarly, both drew readers' attention back to texts, demonstrating "a commitment to close attention to literary texture and what is embodied there" as they ground their reading of language's ambiguities, paradoxes, and opacities in predominantly standard western canonical works.[42] Both showed antipathy toward authorial intent, strategically focused the reader, recognized language's instability, worked to develop readerly skepticism, demanded readerly responsibility, and believed that interpretation is "the supreme task of critical inquiry."[43] As a radical philosophy, postmodern theory "owed its very conception of politics largely to the modernist doctrines the New Criticism had purveyed"; the differences between the two are, in fact, "differences between factions of the vanguard."[44]

Various critics see the postmodern turn as generational posturing, theoretical positioning, or epistemological revolution. However, the theorists themselves asserted that their aim was to challenge authority, redistribute interpretive power, and rethink readership in freeing ways. Just as radical student groups advocated training citizen-readers to interpret the "lies and half-lies" being sold to them and to participate politically by rereading old texts to make them new, foundational postmodern texts such as Derrida's "Structure, Sign and Play" as well as Roland Barthes's "From Work to Text" (1971) and *The Pleasure of the Text* (1973) insisted that readers must "interpret interpretation," theorizing it anew to clarify the relationship between discourse and power, challenge authority's law and order, and reclaim interpretive agency from systems and structures—all while showing one's "behind to the Political Father."[45]

These rebellious efforts are particularly well illustrated in "From Work to Text," which challenges ideas and methods that position literature as a concrete, structured, and authored object and instead sees it as an unbound series of networks created by readerly activity.[46] "Work" was Barthes's generalized term for the Great Books approach that had been the bedrock of many postwar reading programs. In previous interpretive systems, he argued, "the work [was] caught up in a process of filiation.... The author [was] reputed the father and the owner of his work: literary science therefore [taught] *respect* for the manuscript and the author's declared intentions." If one couldn't unlock the meaning an author intended, she proved herself to be a poor reader. Instead, Barthes proposed a theory of interpretation rooted in intertextuality, readerly interaction, and play produced by a "Text" that "reads without the inscription of the Father" and whose "metaphor ... is that of the *network*." The author-father would no longer be revered as the origin of the text but be seen as a "paper-I," one of many contributors to the text, including the readers themselves. The text "asks of the reader a practical collaboration."[47] In *The Implied Reader* (1974), Wolfgang Iser also emphasized the interactive and collaborative dimension of textuality: "the convergence of text and reader brings the literary work into existence, and this convergence can never be precisely pinpointed, but must always remain virtual.... [I]t is the virtuality of the work that gives rise to its dynamic nature."[48]

In some ways, these postmodern theorists (like the framers of *The Port Huron Statement,* who wrote of giving birth to their radical selves) were resurrecting Ransom's earlier theory of texture and reinvesting it with new meaning and life.[49] They saw reading as a participatory democracy because all readers have access to and play a creative role in the media, texts, and forums that shape their lives. Iser, Barthes, Derrida, Hélène Cixous, and others celebrated this potential, insisting that "reading is only a pleasure when it is active and creative," asserting that the reader has the "task of working things out for himself," and promising the "joyous affirmation of the play of the world and of the innocence of becoming."[50] The joy they felt is clear in the proliferation of critical theories that emerged in the 1960s, most of them claiming to tear down interpretive walls and dissolve conceptual borders. Like the diverse political activists of the New Left, the theorists argued that they offered a more ethical means for engaging with and participating in the construction of community.

Of course, these theories had their limits. Postmodern ideas circulated predominantly within the academic sphere rather than among mainstream readers.[51] Productive textual engagement required readers to have a certain facility with linguistics, languages, and continental philosophy. Structural and poststructural theorists were charged with elitism because they seemed to be speaking to a privileged few. Perhaps the greatest evidence of these limits is seen in the emergence of other postmodernisms in the late 1970s and 1980s: African-American studies, women's studies, Marxist studies, cultural studies, and queer theory all sought to address the particularities of race, gender, class, and sexuality ignored in structuralist, poststructuralist, and deconstructionist theories. This wave of theorists argued that discourse and texts are socially mediated and contingent and that erasing particularities reinforced current power dynamics and made the perspectives of straight white men the interpretive norm. In other words, the revolutionary power offered by postmodernism's earliest schools of thought was insulated and limited. Even so, it opened up new ways to read and interpret texts, and its gaps and limitations ironically worked to invite others to contribute to the conversation.

Radical Reading, Radical Work

John Barth published his novel *Lost in the Funhouse* in the explosive year 1968, and the book was subsequently nominated for a National Book Award. Thanks to the success of his earlier books—*The Floating Opera* (1956), *The End of the Road* (1958), *The Sot-Weed Factor* (1960), and *Giles Goat-Boy* (1966)—he had become a critical darling of sorts, collecting grants from the National Institute of Arts and Literature and the Rockefeller Foundation and receiving various awards and award nominations. His first two books reflected the postwar fascination with existentialism, but *Sot-Weed Factor* and *Giles Goat-Boy* moved toward literary postmodernism and metafictional experimentation.[52] *Funhouse*'s subtitle, *Fiction for Print, Tape, Live Voice*, announced a further break from conventional narrative form and fiction, and the original "Author's Note" declared that much of the text was intended to be read aloud to listeners. Describing the book as a "series" rather than a collection or selection of tales (ix), the "Author's Note" immediately signaled its resistance to conventional modes of meaning making, suggesting that engagement with *Funhouse* would require readers to do a different form of work (ix).

Early reviews were laudatory. *Time* celebrated the book's "enormous vitality and virtuosity" and the ways in which "these fictions interact to produce a series of constantly changing and enticingly illusive forms." In the *New York Times Book Review*, Guy Davenport concluded with pleasure that "we are on trial. We must not only read, but also think about what we are doing." The *New Republic* admired the way in which *Funhouse* "pick[ed] literature apart in a narrative, play[ed] with it, and finally [made] restoration just in time for it to accomplish its ancient purposes of amusement and revelation." *Newsweek* pointed out that Barth's work offers "truth between laughs and grotesque smiles of irony": "he has produced a finely drawn, and often funny and fascinating picture of, pardon the expression, the creative process."[53] Reviewers praised Barth's revision of "ancient" forms and purposes, his invitation of others into "the creative process," and his ability to create forms that "constantly chang[ed]" in productive ways.

In his oft-cited essay "The Literature of Exhaustion" (1967), Barth celebrated fiction that "confronts an intellectual dead end and employs it against itself to accomplish new human work." Here and elsewhere, he proposed a radical vision of narrative fiction that involved a recognition of "where we've been and where we are" as well as a commitment to "go to the roots of the novel and see whether [he] could bring back something new."[54] Though many critics have read the essay as a nihilistic cry of despair over the death of literature, it was, in fact, a call to rediscover "the artifices of language and literature" so that literary conventions might be "subverted, transcended, transformed, or even deployed against themselves to generate new and lively work" and thus "accomplish new human work."[55] The word "new" appears often in Barth's essays, usually in conjunction with action words describing a lively theory of narrative fiction that re-presents "old" matter.

In the final tale of *Lost in the Funhouse,* "Anonymiad," Barth uses a pun to illustrate this theory. The anonymous narrator/author figure reflects on his evolution as an artist, noting that, during his youth, "while other fellows played with their spears, I learned to play the lyre" (166). Taken literally, this claim suggests a künstlerroman—the portrait of an artist among a warlike people. Knowing he can never survive as a soldier, the narrator becomes a minstrel. By this point, however, readers have read most of *Lost in the Funhouse* and have encountered and participated in many puns, so most will identify the doubling within this apparently mundane claim: artistry is necessarily a fiction, and the artist is necessarily a liar. The central pun—to play the lyre/liar—situates Barth within the radical discourses of the 1960s, raising questions about the function of fiction, the role of the author, the connection between falsehood and selfhood, the nature of the text, and the relationship of readers to playing and lyre-ing.

Like *The Port Huron Statement,* which teaches readers how to negotiate the establishment's lies, *Lost in the Funhouse* trains readers how to approach and navigate texts that "play the lyre." By recognizing and foregrounding its fictitiousness, it engages with concerns similar to those voiced by postmodern theory and student radicalism: claims of truth and authority that privilege the strong and isolate the weak, faith in a reality that divests persons of creative authority, passive acceptance of others' constructions, and the sense that one is trapped in a closed system controlled by university, political, philosophical, linguistic, biological, and literary-historical fathers. Barth's metafiction plays the lyre thematically and structurally, confronting and troubling authorial primacy, generic conventions, and readerly expectations. As Carol Schloss and Khachig Tololyan have written, it "attempt[s] to move readers away from their traditional flaccid reading postures" and creates "a willingness to play with deceptions and the ability to learn, ultimately, what to do with them."[56]

There has been much critical discussion about the structure of *Lost in the Funhouse*. Uncertain whether to call it a novel, a series, or a short-story cycle, many critics have struggled to orient and reorient themselves, their anticipated readers, and Barth's text in relation to generic conventions.[57] The "Author's Note" takes note of the conventions and expectations that accompany "volumes of short fiction" and endeavors to clarify the text's form and suggest the best way to approach the text (ix). Significantly, this clarification requires "Seven Additional Author's Notes," which further play with readerly expectations about authors' notes and short fiction, setting the stage for more questions and the possibility of an unlimited number of self-conscious explanations (x–xi). The centrifugal motion of the "Author's Notes" suggests the structure of *Funhouse* as a whole; and in an interview Barth commented on this movement: "It's meant to be a series in that there is an exfoliation and a development, one with a double motion" like "a spiral."[58]

Mapping the series—forward, backward, and as a returning motion—has occupied many critics and also has implications for readers, for the "double motion" or "spiral" of the series may open our understanding of Barth's radical vision. First, its spin signals *Funhouse*'s radical recognition that one cannot break completely with what came before and therefore must work to reinvest old forms with new life. In the tale "Life-Story," a narrating voice suggests that "a chief task of civilized people at this hour of the world" is "not for an instant to throw out the baby while every instant discarding the bathwater." Contextually, this comment addresses the author figure's perpetual attempts to begin his tale afresh as well as his recognition that literary history's many "breaks" from period to period are, "it is to be remembered poles after all of the same cell" (116). Similarly, the author figure's attempts to produce a new text invoke various literary traditions: eighteenth-century novel, French *roman à clef*, and realist drama. Like theories of deconstruction, which "redeployed the discursive power of the New Criticism's representations of irony, author, the ideogram, propositional language, etc.," Barth's text revisits and revises established narrative forms as it tries "to accomplish new human work."[59]

In an interview Barth reflected on contemporary literature's complex relationship to the forms, theories, and texts that preceded them, acknowledging both the futility and wastefulness of assuming or asserting a complete break.

> If you acknowledge and embrace the artificial aspect of art, which you can't get rid of anyway, then it doesn't necessarily follow, for example, that you have to abandon certain kinds of literary devices simply because they're metaphors for notions that are no longer viable.... [E]xploit the outmoded conventions for all they're worth to get certain things done that you can't get done in any other way.[60]

In other words, as he suggests in *Funhouse*, all that came before is the "via negativa and its positive counterpart" (116). One can despair, entrench, or pretend to offer the wholly new, or one can return to the roots of various literary devices and conventions "to get certain things done that you can't get done in any other way."

The critic Charles Harris (and Steven Bell after him) calls Barth's approach "radical regression": by looking back, he increases the possibility of moving forward and creating more viable forms. Like Hayden, who charged that radicalism is "not just revolting in despair" but "drawing on what remains" to do productive work and effect social change, Barth creates new life out of "what remains."[61] For instance, in the tale "Echo," he uses a classical myth against itself to reexamine issues of authority, readership, self-consciousness, and language's resistance to fixity. Narcissus, not heeding Tiresius' warning about looking too deeply, falls in love with his own reflection. Meanwhile, Echo, a bodiless voice who can only repeat what she hears, is in love with Narcissus. Barth tells the tale in the third person, meaning that "none can tell teller from told" as "they come to the same" (99). The critic Michael Hinden suggests that Narcissus "is destroyed by self-observation" and "symbolizes passion turned to impotence, the exhaustion of the artist's voice and prophet's vision." The tale's final sentence, "our story's finished before it starts," hints at this exhaustion (100). One could read this as an instance of "play" or "openness," the perpetual deferral and indeterminacy of which flirts with overdetermination. Or one could read it as a reference to an exhausted genre that has been endowed with new life via its telling. Like the characters who constitute one voice, the author, the text, and the reader become one in the process of creating the tale. Their interaction is perennially new, creating infinite possibilities for new life. This echoes Barth's idea of myth more generally: "the myths themselves are produced by the collective narrative imagination (or whatever), partly to point down at our daily reality."[62]

Because it demands the reader's participation and textual responsibility, the structural, generic, and formal movement of Barth's text illuminates the reader's revised role in narrative fiction. The critic Brian Edwards suggests that the writer's retelling strategy succeeds in "recreating . . . precursors or their forms while inviting [his] reader into a game composed of echoes, allusions and variations on the known. Such procedures make special demands upon the reader and give a particular resonance to the view that texts are created by readers in the act of reading." Invoking the language of games in his argument, Edwards suggests that Barth's methods invest the reader with more authority, reveal texts to be living documents "created by readers in the act of reading," present the possibility that new forms will arise from this play, and contribute to the reader's joy and fun.[63] The work redefines the "coming of age" novel: "coming" becomes a continual process (paralleling SDS's), and maturity becomes a significant part of the revising and recycling process rather than an endpoint. The "funhouse for *man thinking* is a womb of possibility from which he may be reborn."[64]

In order for this to happen, however, the baby must develop and claim his own interpretive authority, and Barth's text emphasizes that such attempts at self-determination are central to its revision of readerly authority. Because self-consciousness about textual forms and reading processes allows for a degree of critical distance and reflection, *Funhouse* offers various lessons in which readers *of* the text engage with readers *in* the text. By participating in authorial successes and failures, citizen-readers may become more aware of their interpretive choices and the ways in which they are drawn from and contribute to their authority.

These lessons are particularly evident in the tales "Night-Sea Journey," "Autobiography," and the Ambrose stories ("Ambrose His Mark," "Water-Message," and "Lost in the Funhouse"). In "Night-Sea Journey," the seemingly naïve narrator/swimmer professes a belief in "a common Maker, Whose nature and motives we may not know, but Who engender[s] us in some mysterious wise and launched[s] us forth toward some end known but to Him" (3). The Maker invokes images of both the author as creator and the Judeo-Christian creation tradition. In both formulations, he has a plan, arranges matters, puts the plan into action, and watches it unfold. He holds authority and power while his seemingly powerless creations fumble along, hoping to surmise his unknown will. The naïve swimmer's image of the Maker is juxtaposed with a cynical swimmer's "heresy" that there could be millions of "Fathers" and that "Makers and swimmers *each generate the other*" (7, 8). In his vision, creation is collaborative, authority is displaced and distributed, and agency supplants predestination. Moreover, his supposition is marked by paradox and vagaries, further indicating the openness of his vision (10). Readers are invited to weigh these approaches to authority and make their own decisions about them.

The Ambrose tales also offer lessons about authority, interpretation, and self-consciousness. Ambrose's father, Hector, represents the limitations and failures of traditional ideas about authority. Purportedly a person of power—a school principal and a patriarch—he is in fact a nonentity. The narrative questions his potency from the start: early in "Ambrose His Mark," the reader learns that he was committed to the "Eastern Shore Asylum" before Ambrose was born because he suspected "that someone other than himself had fathered" the child (13, 18). His neighbor Willie also raises questions about Hector's potency when he shouts that Ambrose has "got no more father'n a drone bee," thus emasculating Hector and suggesting that many other bees have produced Ambrose, whose pet name is *Honig,* the German word for "honey" (27). "Water-Message" underscores Hector's impotency, even divesting him of his proper name and referring to him only as "he" (40). Eventually, in "Lost in the Funhouse," the narrator notes that the boy's "father is difficult to describe; no particular feature of his appearance or manner stood out" (72).

Because Ambrose's father is not "what he was supposed to be"—that is, he doesn't fit his son's expectations of fatherhood or of how an author should behave—Ambrose must read, interpret, and author himself (86). His readerly potential and vision are established early in "Ambrose's Mark," when we learn that a swarm of bees landed on his infant face. As Grandpa recalls, "the bees was more on this baby's eyes and ears than on his mouth," to which Uncle Konrad replies, "so he'll grow up to see things clear" (31). Thus, Ambrose's sight and insight are primary facets of his character, and his power as an author depends on his ability to read and engage with textual and contextual possibility. Throughout "Water-Message" and "Lost in the Funhouse," his "wide and clear" eyes take in much about the world and himself (16). In the funhouse mirror, he perceives that his self is comprised of multiple "I"s. He notes that "you think you're yourself, but there are other persons in you. . . . Ambrose watches them disagree; Ambrose watches him watch" (81). Although this passage describes his actual experience with the mirror, it also comments on the living and intertextual aspects of character, individual or written.

Over the course of a few short tales, readers meet various versions of Ambrose: an adolescent afraid to brush against Magda in the car, an adult making small talk with Magda by the pool, "a loving husband and father," the companion of another person lost in the funhouse who turns out to be "a Negro. A blind girl. President Roosevelt's son. Ambrose's former archenemy," a poet whose words are recorded by "an assistant operator of the funhouse, [who] happening to overhear him, crouched just behind the plyboard partition and wrote down his every word," the subject of "the unadventurous story of his life," an author, and the maker of funhouses (73, 80, 83, 92–94). The character's self-constructions tap into various literary traditions and expectations, trying them on for size and inviting readers to reevaluate their expectations about these conventions. In the process, Barth "makes the reader equivalent to A [God or another Maker], an active participant in the creation of a text," as opposed to being subject to a work.[65] As readers sort through and choose from among these various selves, they, like Ambrose, assume responsibility for their interpretive selves.

Again, the key to this responsibility is readerly self-consciousness. Just as SDS's Mark Rudd said that "reform, without a reform in consciousness, . . . will lead to co-optation" and Larry D. Spence argued that "men must be *conscious,* not hungry, to attempt the reconstruction of society," *Funhouse* works to make readers conscious of their reading expectations and practices so they can participate ethically in the text.[66] For instance, after introducing the major characters of his story with initials and blanks substituted for last names, Ambrose notes that "initials, blanks, or both were often substituted for proper names in nineteenth-century fiction to enhance the illusion of reality. It is as if the author felt it necessary to delete the names for reasons of tact or legal liability. Interestingly, as with other aspects of realism, it is an *illusion* that is being enhanced, by purely artificial means" (69–70). The narrator employs a convention, comments on the convention and its artificiality, and then comments on that comment: "Does it violate the principle of verisimilitude, that a thirteen-year-old boy could make such a sophisticated observation?" (70).

Similarly, the narrator in the tale "Autobiography" sardonically claims, "I've been speaking of myself without delight or alternative as self-consciousness pure and sour; I declare now that even that isn't true. I'm not aware of myself at all, as far as I know. I don't think . . . I know what I'm talking about" (35). Even as the passage communicates its awareness of self, it suggests that the text alone does not think; it only works when the reader's thinking calls it into being. The distance between "I don't think" and "I know what I'm talking about" invites the reader to fill in the blank, to read the statements as contradictory, or to find some continuity between the them. It asks the reader to participate in the text self-consciously, laying bare the processes involved in that work.

Like the dueling voices in the tale "Title," *Funhouse*'s reader is perpetually challenged "to fill in the blank," whether it be an actual typographical blank or a gap in a conventional narrative. "Title," for instance, both models and disrupts the model it presents. After offering an unconventional opening that problematizes teleological narratives, the text acknowledges what it has just done: "conventional startling opener. Sorry if I'm interrupting the Progress of Literature, she said, in a tone that adjective clause suggesting good-humored irony but in fact defensively and imperfectly masking a taunt" (102). In both performing and recognizing the performance, the text draws readers' attention to the text and calls on them to participate. (What *is* the "adjective clause" that suggests "good-humored irony" but is really a "taunt"?) There are many other moments in *Lost in the Funhouse* in which the reader must fill in a literal blank, supply text for which a punctuation mark has been substituted, or postulate what one could replace in an "et cetera" (122–123, 118). In these moments, the text "create[s] possibilities within uncertainty by inviting the reader into the process."[67]

While the scholar Carol Booth Olson sees these exchanges as depictions of "the process of a psychic breakdown," I see them as building readerly authority and membership in intertextual communities. The text's self-consciousness asks readers to reflect on their position and participation in meaning making, echoing a central tenet of radical thought that "we are free to the extent that we know what we are about."[68] Until an individual is aware of his provisional position vis-à-vis the powers that be and conscious of how that position affects others, he is part of the system. To challenge the system—whether it be the military-industrial complex or literary structures—citizen-readers must recognize, as well as they can, their positions within, biases about, and contributions to the text.

In performing active, collaborative, and self-conscious work, readers do the ethical work invoked in "Title": "The final possibility is to turn ultimacy, exhaustion, paralyzing self-consciousness and the adjective weight of accumulated history. . . . Go on. Go on. To turn ultimacy against itself to make something new and valid" (106). The book's demand is typified by a key exchange: "The final question is, Can nothing be made meaningful? Isn't that the final question? If not, the end is at hand. Literally, as it were. Can't stand any more of this" (102). The question "can nothing be made meaningful?" engages and replicates the primary hypotheses of Barth's essay "The Literature of Exhaustion." One of the narrative voices in "Title" states that "things have been kaput for some time" and that "everything's finished" (105, 104). Another narrative voice challenges this assertion: "Name eight." The first voice obliges with a list of seven: "Story, novel, literature, art, humanism, humanity, the self itself," thus leaving the claim unfinished and open to elaboration (104). The voices' interruptions, interactions, and injunctions defer closure and invite readers to inject their readings into the conversation. Here and throughout *Lost in the Funhouse,* meaning is collaborative and contingent, demonstrating that citizen-readers can resist the paralysis, overdetermination, and limits of postmodern play.

Nonetheless, some critics see Barth as a puppet master. They argue that he directs readers' participation via tone, word choice, and surrounding narrative and thus controls how they should fill in the blanks. Linda Westervelt, for instance, claims that the text "increases the reader's participation by making him attempt to determine who is speaking. At the same time, of course, [Barth] presents the reader with an unsolvable problem" that places the author firmly in control. Marjorie Worthington believes that Barth's metafictional text works "to cement the author into a position of authority over the text" and "to reauthorize . . . the author in twentieth century fiction." Beth A. Boehm's response is more nuanced: because "Barth writes for an audience steeped in the high modern aesthetic, . . . he must on the one hand make his readers self-conscious about their expectations of what literature should be and thus teach them the falseness of those expectations; and on the other hand, he must perform in ways that teach the reader to appreciate his virtuosity." She recognizes that Barth is doing the radical work of defamiliarizing and deprogramming but reduces this work to ego and a desire for mastery.[69]

Like his New Left and poststructuralist compatriots, Barth could be charged with self-aggrandizing elitism and accused of creating texts that attempt to provide the "key to all mythologies" for a new age. One could read Ambrose, a boy who wishes to be a funhouse maker, as a version of Barth himself. One could interpret Barth's text as a funhouse through which readers stumble only to discover that the author has covered all possible exits. To do so, however, requires turning a blind eye to the work the text invites and the work one actually does while reading it. Barth's text is "unsolvable" only if a reader is seeking one singular solution. If she is looking for *a* rather than *the* solution, then the problem no longer exists because this type of reading "finds no rest in conclusions; answers are seen as provisional, to be discarded in the face of new evidence or changed conditions."[70] With this approach, each time a reader opens *Funhouse,* she encounters a new text in which new problems, solutions, and meanings are created. "Makers and swimmers *each generate the other,*" blurring the boundaries between author, text, and reader as conventionally understood (8).[71] My path through the funhouse will not be your path, my discoveries will not be your discoveries, and my meaning will not be your meaning, even though both of us are active and self-reflective participants in the reading experience. As Barth's student radical counterparts noted, reading and thinking of this sort is "a difficult mental task and, in a more profound moral sense, it represents a serious personal decision to be introspective, to be exposed always to the stinging glare of change, to be willing always to reconstruct our social views."[72] There is a social responsibility in and to the search for meaning. To accept Barth's invitation into the funhouse is to accept the inevitability of change and one's obligation to persist in looking for meaning nonetheless.

Metafiction's Heart

In an interview, Barth spoke about the relationship among reading, history, possibility, and community:

> I don't know what my view of history is, but insofar as it involves some allowance for repetition and recurrence, reorchestration, and reprise (that *re-* prefix has become a house prefix at the Barth house), I would always want it to be more in the form of a thing circling out and out and becoming more inclusive each time—springing out . . . from a heart. If the technics of the fiction aren't part of an impassioned commitment to the enterprise and to the characters involved, then I've no interest in it.

Barth's emphasis on the "*re-* prefix" suggests the value he sees in rehearsing and revising former models, texts, and times. In his essay "From Work to Text," Barthes employs similar rhetoric: "the Text achieves, if not the transparence of social relations, that at least of language relations: the Text is that space where no language has a hold over any other, where languages circulate (keeping the circular sense of the term)."[73] Like Barthes, Barth assigns a social component to his work; his text is a circulation of discourses that move outward to include the reader in an ever-changing and evolving community. Unlike those who dismiss metafiction and other radical epistemologies as nihilistic, relativistic, or hedonistic, Barth articulates an ethical and social politic to his work, which he sees as rooted in "a heart."[74] The heart circulates meaning and authority; it makes life and work possible and is located within "technics" and form. The politic and the aesthetic are one in Barth's enterprise.

Barth's focus on hearts and passion reverberates with the discourses of living and loving central to the radical politics of the late 1960s. *The Port Huron Statement* elevates love as a key quality of its democratized vision: "we regard *men* as infinitely precious and possessed of unfulfilled capacities for reason, freedom, and love"; "these dominant tendencies cannot be overcome by better personnel management, nor by improved gadgets, but only when a love of man overcomes the idolatrous worship of things by man"; "we would replace power rooted in possession, privileged [*sic*] or circumstance by power and uniqueness rooted in love"; "*the United States' principal goal should be creating a world where hunger, poverty, disease, ignorance, violence, and exploitation are replaced as central features by abundance, reason, love, and international cooperation.*"[75] Love is central to the idea of participatory democracy. It makes *The Port Huron Statement* a living document. It is the "dream" to which Mailer refers at the close of *Armies of the Night*.[76] It constitutes the ethical and moral dimension of Barthes's *Music-Image-Text*. Love gave life to the radical revisionary and reclamation project in postwar America, moving its adherents to identify what was dead, what was still viable, and what had been neglected and was in need of resuscitation.

Rather than a stable point of origin, the concept of heart in *Funhouse* is an interaction, a relationship, and an exchange fueled by the reader's connection to and with the text. This circulating sociality regenerates with each reading. No two readings or readers will be the same, yet they are equally meaningful to those who create them. Barthes's work echoes the inclusivity of Barth's radical vision: "the Text is that *social* space which leaves no language safe, outside, nor any subject of the enunciation in the position as judge, master, analyst, confessor, decoder."[77] This social space is inclusive and resists replicating the power dynamics implicit in established interpretive modes. Such radical visions do not do away with Cold War reading rhetorics, programs, guides, or forms but attempt to open, build on, and extend their work and authority to even more citizen-readers. *Lost in the Funhouse* proposes that reading can be a radically regenerative process that perpetually revises and renews American literature, readers, and communities.

6

Confronting Difference, Confronting Difficulty

Culture Wars, Canon Wars, and Maxine Hong Kingston's *The Woman Warrior*

In a 1989 interview, Maxine Hong Kingston discussed the challenges of reading and writing ethically. She stressed that ethical literacy demands work because it requires a person to ask questions, challenge assumptions, and seek knowledge: "How do we acquire knowledge? One of the ways is go to the dictionary. One of the ways is go to the library. One way is to talk to the old people. Another way is to confront people who are difficult and keep your eyes open."[1] Throughout her work, language, texts, community, and confrontation are central to understanding oneself, the nation, and the world. Reading is an active process that makes individuals responsible for their methods and their meanings. Part of that responsibility is engaging with outside sources of meaning, including those that may challenge, contradict, or violate one's beliefs. To "confront people who are difficult and keep your eyes open" is to acknowledge difference and disagreement in order to see more clearly.

Kingston's advice seems particularly apt in light of the conflicts dominating America in the 1980s. Soon after his election, President Ronald Reagan renewed the nation's commitment to fighting communism. Using the "all-or-nothing rhetoric of a revived Cold War," he called the Soviet Union "the very heart of darkness"; and over the course of his presidency, he accelerated the nuclear arms race and involved the military in various proxy wars in Central and South America.[2] On the home front, hot-button social issues such as abortion, AIDS, capital punishment, affirmative action, social welfare policies, and art-versus-obscenity deepened existing political divisions and captivated the media.

Within these so-called culture wars was the subset known as the canon wars—a struggle to define great literature that pitted different versions of Americanism against each other. Some people advocated for a multicultural approach, asserting that opening the canon to reflect diverse American individuals and experiences would magnify the nation's liberal heritage. Others claimed that multiculturalism weakened the literary corpus and called for a return to the great-books tradition to restore the best America had to offer. Thus, it is fitting that Kingston's *The Woman Warrior: Memoirs of a Girlhood among Ghosts,* written amid these various battles, included the word *warrior* in its title.[3] Yet the author later regretted this choice: "Since writing [the book], I have become more of a pacifist. I keep wishing I could invent a peace language. Instead of a woman warrior with a sword, I could create one with a pen who would be just as dramatic." Nonetheless, by way of her pen, Kingston did wade into the various battles of the era—over what constituted an American narrative, who qualified as an American writer, and what texts American citizen-readers should read. As she said of Fa Mu Lan in the book, her "words in red and black files" were "like an army" (35).[4]

Many scholars have engaged with readers' responses to *The Woman Warrior*'s postmodern experiments.[5] Equally important, however, is a consideration of both the reader's function within the text and the book itself as product of and response to those issues that dominated the 1970s and into the 1980s.[6] While feminism and poststructuralism did shape the book's reception, divorcing that response from the text's own representations, models, and discussions of reading ignores the processes of interpretive exploration and collaboration central to the book and to Kingston's larger project. *The Woman Warrior* attempts to read and define Americanness against institutions, ideologies, and individuals that would exclude minority citizen-readers and texts from the nation's literary corpus. Just as the book works to claim its place inside this restrictive canon, so does the character Maxine work to learn how to read signs and interpret texts that might exclude her. She must translate back and forth between the dominant tradition and her marginalized mode of meaning making and vice versa, wrestling with the canon as it has been given her and finding a way to create a whole out of seemingly disparate parts. Like a woman warrior, who "learn[s] to make [her] mind large, as the universe is large, so that there is room for paradoxes," Kingston, Maxine, and the book as a whole call on readers to extend their interpretive expectations, practices, and understandings (29).[7] This is an inclusive and challenging mode of reading; but as Kingston has said elsewhere, "readers ought not to expect reading always to be as effortless as watching television." In the book, Maxine eventually learns to fuse these seemingly combative elements of literature, self, and community, modeling a reading ethic that is difficult, collaborative, pluralistic, yet necessary if individuals are to "become reader[s] of the world."[8] Ultimately, Kingston's book offers readers a new vision for democratizing reading, authoring national unity, and creating a greater potential for peace.

The Race to Define America

The social movements that dominated the late 1950s and the 1960s called for a radical rethinking of authority, knowledge, and power. Young organizers in the New Left relied on print culture and a democratized literacy to challenge the authorities who were writing the laws and controlling the narratives of America. Driven by their well-read student leaders, these groups rejected restrictive definitions of Americanness that attempted to position and exclude them from full participation in the processes governing their lives. By reclaiming definitional power and assuming their right to read, interpret, name, and author, they believed they could dismantle violent and oppressive social hierarchies and create a heart-based community that would allow creativity, individuality, and democracy to flourish for all.

All males, that is. Radical women discovered that they were second-class citizens in the movement—the workers rather than the thinkers, the maids rather then the organizers, the staff rather than the leaders. "Sisters were arbitrarily assigned to man the phones and the typewriters and the coffeepots. And when a few toughminded, no-messin'-around politico Sisters began pushing for the right to participate in policy-making, the right to help compose position papers for the emerging organization, the group leader would drop his voice into that mellow register . . . and say something about the need to be feminine and supportive and blah, blah, blah." In fact, "in 1964 black women in the [Student Nonviolent Coordinating Committee] office held a half-serious, half-joking sit-in to protest these conditions."[9]

Many female activists believed that only a break with male-dominated groups would allow a women-centered agenda to develop. The feminist Charlotte Bunch has recalled that "women's caucuses in leftist organizations fought first for our right to exist and then joined with the more radical elements from such establishment women's groups as NOW to create an autonomous women's movement, and hence established women's liberation and radical feminism." Unlike earlier generations of feminists, who agitated for the vote, access to college education, and other basic rights associated with female suffrage, the women's movement that emerged in the 1970s focused on "analysis of patriarchy as the root cause of female oppression." These activists believed, as Kate Millett argued in *Sexual Politics* (1970), that "sex is a status category with political implications," sexual domination is "perhaps the most pervasive ideology of our culture and provides its most fundamental concept of power," and in America "every avenue of power . . . is entirely in male hands." These second-wave feminists sought to radically revise the idea of gender and define for themselves what it meant to be a woman in America and an American woman. As Kingston remarked in an interview, she and others used narrative to wage a "feminist war" against those who would exclude them from the full rights and practices of citizenship.[10]

Like the earlier civil rights, student, and antiwar movements, the women's movement believed that liberation necessitated a change in how women understood themselves and their world; thus, they needed to be able to read. "Literacy," they argued, "is a way to give individuals more information about their oppression and to assist their ability to think about and choose alternative courses of action for their lives. . . . Literacy should be a feminist issue, and teaching women to read, write, and think a priority in our movement." Title IX, a law passed in 1972 requiring gender equity in every educational program and institution that receives federal funding, was a move forward for women who could afford to go to college, but not all of them had the means to do so. Hence, advocates called for alternate forms of schooling that would educate all women in "the basics of reading and writing," which "are critical tools for creating change and thinking for oneself." In Washington, D.C., a newly founded women's liberation group immediately purchased a mimeograph machine and began producing its own literature; other feminist groups founded magazines, journals, and publishing houses to ensure that women's writings would get into the hands of other women. The groundbreaking Feminist Press was founded in 1970, Calyx Press in 1976, the Women's Press in 1978, Cleis Press in 1980, Aunt Lute Books in 1982, and HerBooks Feminist Press in 1982. The inaugural Women in Print Conference was held in 1976 in Omaha, with 127 women attending and more than twenty women's bookstores from across the country represented.[11]

Nonetheless, although the movement claimed to be authoring a universal sisterhood, many women of color saw it as predominantly white and middle class and felt excluded from its vision, dialogue, and literature. As the poet Kay Lindsey recognized, women of color who struggled for racial and gendered liberty were "on the outside of both political entities, in spite of the fact that [they were] the object of both forms of oppression." Those who tried to voice their position inside the movement often encountered "psychological signs saying **white women only.**" The activist and author Mitsuye Yamada said that women of color felt "invisible to white Americans," who noticed them only if they reinforced stereotypes of their minority culture; and she recalled that such women were allowed to speak "only . . . about harmless and inconsequential subjects." Kingston also contended that women and writers of color had to battle against the narrative and definitional disenfranchisement wrought by "colonialism" at home and abroad, where those in power "take away your local stories, your local customs, your local identity." Like the white feminists, women of color asserted the right to "define [their] own terms" and determine the issues central to their person and communities. They believed, as African American lesbian librarian and poet Audre Lorde did, that "we must establish authority over our own definition."[12]

Once again, reading and print culture played a significant part in establishing that authority and disseminating ways of coming to consciousness about one's subjectivity and power. In her introduction to the anthology *Making Face, Making Soul* (1990), the Chicana feminist Gloria Anzaldúa writes that being a Third World Woman intellectual, radical, and feminist "means being in alien territory and suspicious of the laws and walls. It means being concerned about the ways knowledges are invented. It means continually challenging institutionalized discourses. It means being suspicious of the dominant culture's interpretation of 'our' experience, of the way they 'read' us." bell hooks contends that women of color had to be resisting readers because "living as we did—on the edge—we developed a particular way of seeing reality. We looked both from the outside in and . . . from the inside out. We focused our attention on the center as well as the margin. We understood both." Thus, organizations such as the groundbreaking Combahee River Collective of black feminists routinely developed "study group[s]. We had always shared our reading with each other, and some of us had written papers" to train readers to see and understand "the reality of our politics." Feminists of color "had to create a readership and teach it how to 'read' our work" by striving to "engage the reader's total person."[13]

The African American writer and womanist Alice Walker celebrated the revolutionary power of reading in her poem "Women," which opened the anthology *All the Women Are White, All the Blacks Are Men, But Some of Us Are Brave* (1982). She praised "my mama's generation," these "Headragged Generals" who "led / Armies . . . Across mined / Fields / Booby-trapped / Kitchens / To discover books / Desks / A place for us." In her preface to *Borderlands/ La Frontera* (1987), Anzaldúa claimed a similar power for literacy and the written word: "Books saved my sanity, knowledge opened the locked places in me and taught me first how to survive and then how to soar." In "Letter to Ma" (1981), Merle Woo celebrated reading and learning about Chinese- and Korean American history and culture: "the full awareness of being a woman [made] me want to sing." In an interview, Kingston declared that "maybe the greatest joy of my life is to read." Women of color repeatedly professed the power of the word to bring about not only liberated consciousness but also liberated people. In her foreword to *This Bridge Called My Back* (1981), Toni Cade Bambara said that reading was doing the work "to make revolution irresistible." In bell hooks's words, by "learning about other groups and writing about what we learn," people can "unlearn racism" and "challenge structures of domination."[14]

Nevertheless, like hooks, many feminists of color recognized that "literacy should be a goal for feminists even as we ensure that it doesn't become a requirement for participation in feminist education." They called for texts and tracts that were accessible to all women, not just those schooled in the latest philosophies or Ivy League terminologies. These feminists wanted writing that resisted jargon, abstraction, and "hard-to-access language that blocks communication [and] makes the general listener/reader feel bewildered and stupid," even if that meant teaching "academics to write in a way more people can read."[15] The activist Kit Yuen Quan warned that reading education often risked replicating a classist top-down structure: "A lot of times my language and the language of other working class, non-academic people become the target of scrutiny and criticism." She modeled and advocated for a type of reading that was cooperative and collective: "I read with [the people I tutored]. We did everything together. I didn't want them to feel like they were supposed to automatically know what to do, because I remembered how badly that used to make me feel." This was a challenging task, and some women—for instance, Kingston, who taught English in Hawaii—struggled with the "many problems of feeling like a missionary." They gradually learned that "I musn't [sic] just go into the classroom and tell them that English is the cash language and so, let's just learn it"; rather, they had to "show . . . respect" for their diverse languages and experiences.[16]

The need for "a pedagogy of liberation" was amplified in the late 1970s and early 1980s as a surging conservative coalition gained political and narrative control in the United States. "Hostility to communism" fused disparate arms of the postwar conservative movement, bringing together unlikely groups of allies: Catholics, southern evangelicals, unabashed racists, pro-business leaders, and disillusioned liberal intellectuals. The coalition was largely reactive, its "politics of backlash" fueled by the real and imagined gains made by women and minorities during the radical 1960s and early 1970s. At the end of that decade, amid massive inflation, energy uncertainty, a failed war against communism, and the dismantling of gender and racial codes, many white Americans longed for a sense of stability, order, and certainty.[17] Conservatism seemed to offer them that security.

By the late 1970s, the Right had coalesced into two distinct wings:

neoconservatism and the New Right. Neoconservatism traced its roots to the liberal anti-communism of the 1950s and 1960s. Many neocons were former liberal intellectuals who felt the Left had abandoned its principles and America to radicalism, and they had "spent the 1970s fighting against what liberalism had become." While they believed in liberalism's governing principle of equality, they did not believe in its legislation; and they took issue with the government's civil rights and social welfare legislation of the 1960s and 1970s.[18] Like the Left, the neocons used print to wage their battles, proclaiming, "We are engaged in a cultural war, a war about values. It is not a new war; it has been going on for centuries as part of a continuing struggle at national self-definition." Most were associated with elite universities such as Harvard, Stanford, and MIT or were members of prestigious think tanks such the RAND Corporation, the Aspen Institute, the Heritage Foundation, and the American Enterprise Institute. As journalists, professors, politicians, advisors, speechwriters, and lobbyists, the neocons were able to create intelligent, well-crafted messages, and their arguments were consistently on point. Their ranks included Irving Kristol, Daniel Bell, Nathan Glazer, James Q. Wilson, Edward Banfield, Robert Nisbet, and Daniel Moynihan, all of whom "had direct access to officeholders and the political elite generally."[19]

Although the neocons often complained of a liberal media bias, "their own position in the media . . . [has] never been weak." Their influence remains clear in highbrow publications such as *Commentary*, the *Public Interest*, the *New York Times Magazine*, the *Atlantic Monthly*, *Science*, *Encounter*, the *American Scholar*, and *Foreign Policy* as well as in popular periodicals such as *Fortune*, *Business Week*, *Reader's Digest*, and *U.S. News & World Report*. Like the radicals on the Left, these men used the printed word to craft a utopic national narrative, but theirs was rooted in a nostalgic longing for a stable, unified, Christian America that never really existed. Nonetheless, as William Simon, a cabinet member in both the Nixon and Ford administrations, did in *A Time for Truth* (1978), the neocons pressed the claim that people who challenged their narrative were "advocating that America cease being America."[20]

As the neocons came to prominence, the New Right was also ascending as a political force. Responding to what they saw as the moral degradation of American ideas and ideals in the 1960s and 1970s, national, local, and single-issue groups, including the National Rifle Association, the Eagle Forum, anti-abortion groups, the Moral Majority, and the National Conservative Political Action Committee, coalesced into a powerful force. Many on the New Right believed that America's decline was the result of misinformation, miseducation, and misreading. As the Moral Majority's Jerry Falwell declared, "for all too many years, Americans have been educated to dependence rather than to liberty. A whole generation of Americans has grown up brainwashed by television and textbooks to believe that it is the responsibility of government to take resources from some and bestow them upon others. This idea certainly was alien to the Founding Fathers of our country."[21]

Linking America's fall to bad texts, bad readers, and bad teachers, Falwell and other New Right leaders began producing and distributing their own literature in hopes of reeducating Americans. Using the direct-mail methods pioneered by Richard Viguerie, they distributed mountains of letters, pamphlets, and fundraising materials to tens of thousands of individuals. They perfected the mechanics of mass letter-writing campaigns, targeting politicians on issues from abortion to school busing to pro-Panama intervention. The New Right's print onslaught mobilized many conservative white Christians to take action against the ideas, policies, and groups that they believed were corrupting America.[22]

Bringing the Canon Back into the Cold

As the titles of James Davison Hunter's *Culture Wars: The Struggle to Define America* and Jonathan Zimmerman's *Whose America? Culture Wars in the Public Schools* suggest, citizens' disparate ideas about culture were major elements in the battle to define what constituted America and Americanness in the late 1970s and the 1980s. When they fought over which texts to include in a course or which courses to require in a curriculum, opponents were "debat[ing] over competing social agendas and concepts of morality, . . . over both the present and the future condition of American society." Their battle was "basically . . . [over] who has power and how it is exercised." For some combatants, these canon wars were a struggle to preserve America's heritage and to recover lost values. For others, they were a fight for a more inclusive vision of American literature and citizen-readership and against "a deeply nostalgic effort to revive the consensus and curriculum of the 1950s."[23]

Although women and people of color had always been writing in America, the political landscape had, for the most part, kept them from attracting publishers and readers to their work. Now, however, scores of texts representing previously unrepresented American identities were being published. In addition to memoirs and novels such as Kingston's *The Woman Warrior*, Toni Morrison's *The Bluest Eye* (1970), Alice Walker's *The Color Purple* (1982), and Sandra Cisneros's *The House on Mango Street* (1984), a flood of anthologies appeared: *Black-Eyed Susans* (1975), *Time to Greez!* (1975), *Ordinary Women* (1978), *American Born and Foreign* (1979), *The Remembered Earth* (1979), *The Third Woman* (1980), *This Bridge Called My Back* (1983), *Home Girls* (1983), *Making Face/Making Soul* (1990), and many others. By giving voice to an American experience that had yet to be formally recognized politically, socially, or aesthetically, they were calling for a change in how readers defined American literature.

Proponents of diverse American literatures believed that access to texts reflecting all of "our national cultures" was key "to shaping an equitable future" for all American students. Like Kingston, they said, "Look, there's more classics, more," and they challenged the literary establishment to make Americans better "readers of the world." They advocated changes in university majors, programs, curriculum, syllabi, and scholarship that would reflect a diverse body of letters. They believed that "a democratic polity and a curriculum that values, indeed focuses upon, difference opens a genuinely broader college education to far more citizens than any monologue, however well-intentioned." Books such as Paul Lauter's *Reconstructing American Literature* (1983) listed scores of diversity-driven curricula from the late 1970s and early 1980s, demonstrating the growing presence of texts by women and people of color and emphasizing the need for more. The creation of black, ethnic, and women's studies programs and the implementation of diversity and ethnic studies requirements demonstrated an increased university commitment to a more inclusive national narrative. Multiculturalists embraced the social dimension of literature and literacy, asserting that art is a social act, that diverse literatures and language can unite oppressed peoples, and that teaching them can undermine the "tyranny" of ethnocentrism in "Western aesthetics," thereby democratizing literary studies and welcoming more citizen-readers into the fold.[24]

Meanwhile, more conservative professors, politicians, and public intellectuals sought to protect traditional standards of literary excellence rooted in the western canon. To them, the proliferation of reading philosophies and identities had fractured the foundation of the American idea, reducing "one nation" to a seemingly endless series of interest groups and identities. They believed that a return to great works and good books would unite disparate people under the banner of universal themes, timeless values, and the classics, thus bringing stability and continuity to an unsettled nation and its people. Warning that "improving education in America" is "crucial to our national survival" and that "the cheapest defense of a nation is a good education," they decried what they saw as the sacrifice of quality literature to equality of "tokenism," arguing that the "damage done to the quality of higher education during the 1960's . . . persist[s] as a legacy of that period."[25] These critics blamed America's illiteracy problem on "the egalitarian and experimental trends of the protest period," "political activism," and the low standards and "lowered expectations" honed in an "era of permissiveness," when faculty kowtowed to students and "excellence was washed away."[26]

Of course, there never was a golden age of American culture—no time when all Americans were literate, embraced high culture, and performed their citizenship duties in the manner these advocates recommended. Reading guides in the 1950s were just as anxious about America's readerly mettle as were those compiled in the 1980s. Yet Reagan-era conservatives continued to invoke 1950s-style reading education as a lost ideal to which America could and should return.

In 1976, Richard Ohmann's "The Decline in Literacy Is a Fiction, If Not a Hoax" debunked the arguments, statistics, and conclusions forwarded by many of these critics. Yet it, too, advocated a return to great works, blaming innovations in reading education and modifications in the canon for damaging the prospects of not only minority, working-class, and rural students but also white students from the middle and upper classes. This purported failure of America's elite elicited great concern among commentators. Donna Woolfolk Cross worried that "now our middle-class kids are two to three grades behind in their reading skills." John Goodland foresaw the middle class's "decline." E. D. Hirsch, Jr., wrote ominously about a decline in the "top group," and Merrill Sheils lamented that the literacy skills of "even the best-educated young people [seem] to have fallen so far so fast." Like the 1950s reading experts, who linked failing literacy to cultural, social, and political decline, many people in the 1980s blamed reading education for America's perceived moral and political failures, both now and in the future. One of the most vocal was Allan Bloom, whose book *The Closing of the American Mind* (1987) blames changes in reading choice and education for the "decline of the family," the rise of "Nihilism, American Style," a "lack of respect for tradition," and an assault on the "moral order" on which America was founded.[27] He and others warned that the nation's economic power, political dominance, cultural reputation, and national security were at risk unless something was done to reverse the decline begun in the 1960s.

These reading proponents called for a return to classic texts, curricula, and reading methods; and in publications such as William J. Bennett's *To Reclaim a Legacy* (1984), they expressed their faith in traditional education's ability to promote order, stability, authority, and excellence. The National Education Association's report *Excellence in Our Schools* (1982) voiced the "need for greater structure and coherence" in both materials and education. Government-sponsored reports (such as *A Nation at Risk, Action for Excellence,* and *Excellence in Our Schools*) and curricular models (such as Lynne Cheney's *50 Hours: A Core Curriculum for College Students* and Mortimer Adler's *The Paideia Proposal*) dominated scholarly and popular discourse. Like their 1950s counterparts, these guides promised that their theories and methods would bring "needed order and coherence" to the world, engage "students with their democratic heritage," and strengthen America. They promised that reading "[classic] books that remain fresh, full of power to quicken thought and feeling, no matter how many times we open their pages," would return America to a position of global strength.[28]

Like-minded educators and intellectuals worked to fortify and unify America's citizen-readers with "the best their language has to offer." Detailing (as their subtitles claimed) *What Every American Needs to Know* and *What Our Children Need to Know*, E. D. Hirsch, Jr., compiled lists of foundational western texts, ideas, and philosophies that he believed would help Americans become culturally literate. His orderly approach to learning offered a corrective to what he saw as hobbyhorse curricula and promised to fill the gaps in everyday Americans' cultural knowledge. In *The Closing of the American Mind*, Bloom advocated a return to "the good old Great Books approach" and the "old Great Books conviction," in part to combat what he saw as the fracturing of Americanness into "unbridgeably separate 'cultures.'" He, like others, believed that emphasizing racial, gender, and class differences would only fragment America further. These critics railed against projects such as Lauter's *Heath Anthology of American Literature*, which reframed the American tradition in terms of its multicultural heritage. One editorial called the book a "disaster" that cut works of "literary excellence" in favor of literature "produced by an approved victim group."[29]

Critics of multicultural curricula often succumbed to hyperbolic, hysterical, and offensive language in their characterization of "the culture leeches" who were bleeding American literature and literary interpretation dry. Yet their staunchest foes also employed highly charged and emotional language, excoriating those "dull, arrogant, visionless men of affairs, who have no language but that of war and no object but that of control." Multiculturalists saw traditionalists as racist, sexist, and elitist relics who desired a "nostalgic return to what I think of as the 'antebellum aesthetic position,' when men were men, and men were white, when scholar-critics were white men, and when women and persons of color were voiceless, faceless servants and laborers, pouring tea and filling brandy snifters in the boardrooms of old boys' clubs." Today, most scholars commonly accept that any definition of civilization or culture is a political act; as Arnold Krupat has asserted, it is "inevitably a function of one's prior values and always implies a social vision; the canon proposed by William Bennett or suggested by Allan Bloom and Christopher Clausen is as fully determined by extrinsic factors as any canon [Edward] Said or [Terry] Eagleton or I might construct." Ultimately, the canon wars at the Cold War's end continued an old battle over the power to define nation and citizenship, and both sides believed "they [were] struggling for the very soul of America."[30]

Chapter Six

Barbarians in the Temple

Just as important as the scholars, theorists, and armchair critics who fought this battle were those "multicultural" writers at the heart of the contest. They were not merely terrain fought over but also committed combatants in the struggle to expand the canon and definitions of Americanness. Maxine Hong Kingston published *The Woman Warrior* to immediate acclaim. It received the National Book Critics Circle Award in 1976 and was listed as one of *Time*'s top books of the 1970s. Multiculturalists quickly incorporated it into college curricula, Kingston's work was "the most anthologized of any living American writer," and a 2011 Modern Language Association poll reveals that it is still the most frequently taught work of contemporary American literature in university classrooms.[31] Scholars continue to debate *The Woman Warrior*'s place in the canon and its role as a classic. Sau-ling Cynthia Wong contends that it "is arguably the only Asian American literary text securely canonized in American literature," and Marilyn Chin celebrates its longevity: "It survived the test of time, the test of great literature. It's already in the American canon." Shirley Geok-Lin Lim celebrates "the work's sheer literary luminosity, even as it transgresses and adds its weight of transformation to traditions and canons, makes it a classic."[32]

Yet the book has also had its critics—most vocally Fran Chin, who has accused Kingston of being "a fake" and of conspiring with the white publishing industry to emasculate male Asian American writers.[33] Others have charged her with orientalizing Chinese Americans, a claim Kingston strenuously rebuts in her essay "Cultural Mis-readings by American Reviewers," which demonstrates that the book's reviewers, not her, have exoticized the text.[34] Whether loved or hated, *The Woman Warrior* has made a significant impression on American letters. According to the Modern Language Association's *International Bibliography*, it is cited in more than six hundred articles, chapters, and books, most of which address issues of voice, silence, intergenerational conflicts, nationalism, body, autobiography, translation, feminism, postmodernist play, and challenges to form, genre, and canon. In *Approaches to Teaching "The Woman Warrior,"* Lim lauds it as an essential element of "the kind of multicultural literacy that E. D. Hirsch, Jr., had somehow omitted from his version of cultural literacy." Around the world, the book has become an ambassador of American literature, encouraging transnational connections and the study of Asian American literatures.[35]

The Woman Warrior's geographic, generic, formal, and national expansions attempt to delineate the varied ways in which people see, interpret, and represent life, particularly those who negotiate multiple or marginalized identities. In the book, Maxine says that "those of us in the first American generations have had to figure out how the invisible world the emigrants built around our childhoods fits into solid America" (5). One may read her comment as pointing toward the Chinese world of ghosts evoked in the subtitle and in contrast to an American world of materiality and materialism. Aspects of the text support such a reading—for instance, the character Brave Orchid's ghosts as well as her "talk-story" about China (19) that frame Maxine's understanding of her world and her maturing self. At the same time, America seems "solid" to Maxine and other "first American generations" because its rules, codes, and narratives seem to be fixed. America's heroes, myths, values, and founding principles are presented as concrete realities to which others from "the invisible world" must assimilate.

Ralph Ellison's invisible man declares that those in power "refuse to see me. . . . It as though I have been surrounded by mirrors of hard, distorting glass," an image that recalls Barth's funhouse mirrors. The metaphor is also applicable to the way in which immigrants' history and their contributions as citizen-readers have been distorted: "no matter what we say or do, the stereotype still hangs on"; people continue "looking right through and around us. . . . Asian American woman still remain in the background and we are heard but not really listened to." Yet *The Woman Warrior* complicates this assumption, revealing the elasticity of traditional worlds and words. The scholar Karoline Krauss contends that a central conflict in the book involves differences in interpretation.[36] Maxine herself claims to be neither substituting one world for another nor privileging one mode of understanding over another. Rather, she proposes that multiple peoples, traditions, literatures, and interpretations can exist together, and the book is devoted to discerning how these various worlds and words fit into and among each other.

Although Maxine is an academic success in the conventional sense—"They say I'm smart"; "I studied hard, [I] got straight A's"—she must learn how to read and interpret seemingly disparate traditions as part of the larger whole (201, 195). To do so, she must answer this question: "how do you separate what is peculiar to childhood, to poverty, insanities, one family, your mother who marked your growing with stories, from what is Chinese? What is Chinese tradition and what is the movies?" (5–6). That is, she has to learn to interpret the texts she's given and make sense of both their origins and their value. She also must figure out what it means to be "American-normal," sorting through sexist constructs of "American-feminine," racist practices, and aggressive labels such as "chink" and "gook" that contradict the American creed (87, 11, 48–49, 53). At the same time, she must cling to particular ideas of worth—"I wrap my American successes around me like a private shawl"—as she attempts to discern her place in the world (52).[37] As the cultural scholar Reed Way Dasenbrock has argued, this is "something we have to work at": readers mature as they encounter a "different way of using [a] word and hence . . . a different way of seeing the world."[38]

Yet the lines demarking Chinese, from American, from Chinese American culture are difficult to follow; and while Maxine struggles, she also revels in the possibility of expanding the lines and redrawing the boundaries. This is evident in the book's first section, "No Name Woman," in which she shares her mother's story of a fallen aunt and demonstrates how textual interpretation can be liberating. In response to her mother's claim that she "has told me once and for all the useful parts," Maxine finds herself interrogating both the revealed and unrevealed parts of the story as well as what "useful" literature entails. When Maxine gets her period, her mother finds value in telling the aunt's tale as a cautionary-cum-horror-story. But Maxine believes that "unless I see [my aunt's] life branching into mine, she gives me no ancestral help" (6, 8). For her, identification, connection, and communion are the valuable uses of reading and necessities for herself. She finds no comfort in the concept of literature's universality, nor would she agree with solely "using literary forms created by and for white, upper-class men." Rather, she sees the value in giving individuals opportunities to "pursu[e] a literary tradition of their own" and "read the works of our writers in our various ways"—even writing her own works to help herself understand her experience and self as a subject.[39] Although some scholars dismiss reading for identification as a lesser mode of interpretation, Maxine's words and methods suggest that reading for the "help" of identification may require a person to perform comparative, contrastive, analytical, and synthetic readings—to come at a story from multiple angles as she attempts to define and derive value from "the useful parts."

Here and elsewhere, Maxine's interpretations function like the weaving that the famed warrior woman Fa Mu Lan did after her fighting days, according to the stories that Maxine's mother told her: they tie together different narrative threads to craft a vibrant and multifaceted whole.[40] Maxine interprets the gaps in her aunt's story, repeating the word "perhaps" as she tries out alternate narratives that she may be able to apply to her Stockton, California, reality: rape as masculine, cultural violence, love and sex as choices and resistance, individuality rather than conformity, communion rather than isolation, the will to cross "boundaries not delineated in space" (6, 9, 8). Yet even though, as critic Silvia Schultermandl points out, Maxine reshapes "the aunt's story through a narrative act," she primarily derives power through readerly and interpretive acts.[41] Before she can revise and reshape her aunt's narrative, she must read and process the family myth—analyzing the text, engaging with its problems, and identifying its gaps. She does indeed use stories to help read her "immediate reality," but Maxine first understands through the process of interpretation, not merely by "reporting," as Joanne Frye has claimed.

As the critic Aleksandra Izgarjan writes, the various "barriers" in the aunt's tale compel Maxine "to actively search for the intelligibility and in so doing become part of the meaning of the text."[42] The aunt "haunts" her; she "waits silently by the water to pull down a substitute" (16). Thus, in interpreting her aunt's story, Maxine makes it her own and adopts both its possibility and its violence. What haunts her is the understanding that comes from her mode of interpretation: violence against women is not just her family's dirty little secret but also a gendered reality to which she is vulnerable.

Kingston immediately follows this tale of female vulnerability with a legend of female strength, and such textual weaving and interpretive shifting requires readerly work. In "No Name Woman," Maxine's period is a reason for speaking the unspeakable; but in "White Tigers," menstruation just *is:* it "did not stop my training; I was as strong as on any other day" (30). Maxine's reinterpretation of the Fa Mu Lan myth links the physical training of the young warrior woman with the training she herself receives in interpreting words and worlds, and by making this connection Kingston renders both revolutionary. The warrior's early lessons include learning "how to be quiet," how "to move my fingers, hands, feet, head, and entire body in circles . . . making the ideograph 'eight,' making the ideograph 'human,'" making the ideographs "bat" and "blessing" (23). Long before her family carves words of revenge on her back, the woman warrior's mastery of text begins to transform and empower her. It enables her mastery of the world, allowing her to run with the animals, manipulate time, and "invent new sights" (25, 27, 26). Words such as "understand," "recognize," and "watch" litter this section of the book as the young woman warrior is taught to see beyond convention, human construction, and surface meanings. Like John Barth's "heart," the one that the woman warrior discovers is multiple and changing, encompassing "Chinese lion dancers, African lion dancers, . . . Javanese bells, . . . Indian bells, Hindu Indian, American Indian" (27). As when Oedipa comes to understand metaphor and the invisible man comes to understand layers, the woman warrior sees that wisdom "contain[s] multitudes" and cannot be limited to one source or tradition.[43]

The abundance here is typified in the ritual cutting scene, which has drawn much critical attention. It represents the ways in which reading, creation, and bodies (whether individual, canonical, or national) are linked through sorrow, violence, reverence, and love. After the woman warrior returns to her parents' home, they cut a list of "grievances," "oaths and names" into her back and then "s[i]ng what they had written" on this "back covered entirely with words" (35, 34, 35). Most often read as part of Kingston's feminist critique, the scene can also be read as emblematic of her book as a whole, which works at "inscribing readers from other cultures inside their own textual dynamics."

The woman warrior's back links family, village, and nation, reproducing a collective body on a single body yet never claiming to be singular.[44]

The woman warrior does not see this multiplicity as diluting or fragmenting her potency. Rather, she sees the accumulated words as "an army." As she goes out to battle injustice, she draws soldiers from disparate communities and inspires, singing songs that are "loud enough for the whole encampment to hear" (35, 37). Wherever they go, she and her diverse army bring an "order" of inclusion and tolerance (37). Unlike the evil baron and the emperor, who, "like a god," oppressively dictate social, economic, and cultural codes, Fa Mu Lan invites difference and mutual respect, modeling a community and a canon that are inclusive and pluralistic (43).

The woman warrior's tale is juxtaposed to Maxine's claim that "my American life has been such a disappointment" (45). Fa Mu Lan is an ideal that Maxine must fight for and reconcile with her lived reality of sexism, racism, and economic oppression. Like the woman warrior, Maxine masters her letters—"I got straight A's"—but she struggles to integrate competing cultural demands and to recognize that the forces of racism, sexism, and classism are larger than any one woman can combat (195). Both her Chinese culture and "American-normal" require a woman to sacrifice herself, and many critics have read the book as a feminist critique of these codes (87).[45] In both cultures, Maxine endures demands for submissiveness, demureness, invisibility, and silence (172). For instance, Kingston describes her two American bosses, "business-suited in their modern . . . executive guise, each . . . two feet taller than I am and impossible to meet eye to eye" (48). Because she is a woman and less powerful, she is pushed around and fired. Because she attempts to see "eye to eye" with executive authority, she's terminated. Moreover, "it's not just the stupid racists that I have to do something about, but the tyrants who for whatever reason can deny my family food and work" (49). The narratives of racism, sexism, and classism frame Maxine's lived experience in America, and she must learn how to be a resisting reader in order to find the freedom she seeks.

Throughout *The Woman Warrior*, a pattern of contrastive analysis models a type of synthetic reading. Each section first presents Maxine's received texts—familial, mythical, historical, poetic. Then Maxine offers her own life as text, contrasting what she perceives as the takeaway message from those received texts with her own lived experience. "No Name Woman" contrasts the aunt's story with Maxine's attempts to understand and connect it to her own experience. "White Tigers" contrasts the fable of Fa Mu Lan with Maxine's sense of her life as a "disappointment." "Shaman" contrasts the story of Brave Orchid's medical education and healing prowess with Maxine's understanding of her mother in America and her own intellectual successes and perceived cultural failures. In each section, Maxine finds her own story and self wanting because they do not conform to the thematic and ideological dictates of the authoritative origin tale. She sees herself as a failure for participating in her family's silence or revealing its secrets, for not defeating the "stupid racists" and "tyrants," for being neither the daughter Brave Orchid left behind nor the success she believes Brave Orchid desires her to be in America (16, 49, 100–103). Words function as weapons: Maxine's textual interpretations cut her down emotionally and diminish her psychologically. Thus, at times she exaggerates her outsiderness—her silence, her nose picking, her neglected hygiene, her school failure.[46]

The book is a study in contrasts, one that pushes Maxine to think analytically and synthetically as she attempts to reconcile these various origin stories and make them her own, all the while believing that her own stories cannot measure up. Her struggle exemplifies the psychological, cultural, raced, gendered, and aesthetic violence that is canon formation—for instance, the claim that work by Asian American women writers does not meet the canon's standards of quality or excellence. At the same time, however, Maxine finds inspiration and possibility in these texts that demand her creative participation. As I have discussed previously, she attempts to fill in the gaps in her aunt's story to make it useful as a narrative of individuality, will, desire, and choice and therefore relevant to the new cultural context in which it circulates. Likewise, the stories of Fa Mu Lan and Brave Orchid model the type of heroine she could become and a version of womanhood that is more than being a "wife and a slave" (20). Maxine realizes that "the swordswoman and I are not so dissimilar. . . . What we have in common are the words at our backs" (53). By reporting these tales, she reads them into the record, making them material witnesses for herself and for readers beyond herself. Cumulatively, they allow her to possess "so many words—'chink' words and 'gook' words that they do not fit on my skin"—that they exceed any one tale or body of literature, either national or canonical (53). By weaving together these words, she becomes a healer; like Brave Orchid, she works to make the body, or corpus, whole.[47]

To be sure, Maxine does not cure herself, her family, or her nation, nor does she purge her archive of the pain and sickness that have shaped it. As in Toni Morrison's *Beloved* and Alice Walker's *The Color Purple,* scars and other evidence of violence remain. Yet she heals, regaining strength and function and embracing a more positive version of life. Though healing does not promise full restoration, it does involve the search for wholeness, a painful process because it is necessarily confrontational and active. One can see Maxine's reading as an illustration of the healing work that Paul Lauter, Arnold Krupat, Henry Louis Gates, Jr., Elaine Showalter, Nina Baym, and others were attempting in the 1980s as they actively worked to "heal" American literature, trying to restore texts that had been excised, neglected, or disfigured. By undertaking this difficult and painful task, they hoped to heal "a society under stress" from violence and intolerance, even as they faced those who continued to view feminism and multiculturalism as the sickness, not the salve.[48]

The relationship between Maxine and Brave Orchid offers another version of this struggle toward interpretive healing. In the book's final section, "A Song for a Barbarian Reed Pipe," Maxine's "throat burst[s] open" and she finally talks "directly at my mother and at my father" (201). The moment is conceived as a hemorrhage of words. In a torrent that addresses the relationships among nation, reading, and gender, the high schooler Maxine rejects what she sees as "Chinese" expectations of femininity—being an object who is "given" away "to freaks"—and embraces what she interprets as "American":

> Do you know what the Teacher ghosts say about me? They tell me I'm smart, and I can win scholarships. I can get into colleges. I've already applied. I'm smart. I can do all kinds of things. I know how to get A's, and they say I could be a scientist or a mathematician if I want. I can take care of myself. . . . I'm so smart, if they write ten pages, I can write fifteen. I can do ghost things even better than ghosts can. Not everybody thinks I'm nothing. (201)

Here, Maxine associates value with conventional ideas about literacy. She has learned to "take stories" and "turn them into essays," to embrace how "things follow in lines at school" as opposed to the circuitous paths of her parents' obfuscations: "I can't tell what's real and what you make up" (201, 202). For her, being someone means being able to "do ghost things even better than the ghosts can"—that is, to out-American the Americans and thus become a good citizen-reader and an American success.

Brave Orchid's response and Kingston's text complicate Maxine's simplistic binaries—Chinese/American, feminine/masculine, oral/written, myth/truth, scrambled/logical, and so on—illustrating that borders are porous and changeable. Brave Orchid counters Maxine's charge of obfuscation and illogic, arguing that Maxine "can't listen right. . . . You can't even tell a joke from real life. You're not so smart. Can't even tell real from false" (202). She contends that her daughter's inability to distinguish between different types of narratives indicates her immaturity and critiques the narrow mode of reading that Maxine privileges as American. Her daughter may be able to meet the prescribed standards of her school and her teachers, but she has yet to mature as a citizen-reader because she sees everything in terms of lines, limits, and order. Her desire for logic has cut her off from other possible ways of ordering and interpreting the world.

To Brave Orchid, being smart means being able to code-switch between the material and the immaterial, the concrete and the metaphorical. This is a lesson that Maxine has failed to learn. Because she has seen her mother only as a crazy Chinese lady obsessed with ghosts, she has failed to see her as a feminist readerly ideal. Brave Orchid counters, "I know about college. What makes you think you're the first one to think about college? I was a doctor. I went to medical school" (202). Although Maxine has associated educational and professional success with Americanness, her mother points out that American women aren't always encouraged to be successful, parroting a popular ad: "Learn to type if you want to be an American girl" (203). Brave Orchid contends that Maxine's feminine liberation lies within her Chinese legacy and that she has been blinded by her conventional education, becoming "very confused and lonely" and isolated (204). By working to exorcize the ghosts of her childhood and to embrace the material, the ordered, and the concrete, she has reduced her world: "now colors are gentler and fewer; smells are antiseptic." By attempting to place limits, to find "the simple explanation," to control and order language, to sort out "who's lying," she has sterilized reading, language, and narrative (205). While it may seem pure, it is really fruitless.

Like a good student, Maxine turns to books to try to understand her heritage and to translate that past into a usable present. She begins by trying to find translations for the name her mother calls her: Ho Chi Kuei. What she learns is that language, far from being fixed and logical, is also contradictory and confusing: "So far I have the following translations for *ho* and/or *chi*: 'centipede,' 'grub,' 'bastard carp,' 'chirping insect,' 'ju-jube tree,' 'pied wagtail,' 'grain sieve,' 'casket sacrifice,' 'water lily,' 'good frying,' 'non-eater,' 'dustpan-and-broom' (but that's a synonym for 'wife')." Like Oedipa, she gets lost among the definitions, unable to locate a single meaning and finding that possibilities multiply as she searches. Yet whereas Oedipa feels overwhelmed by such possibilities, Maxine begins repeating words such as "perhaps" and "could" (204). Though she seems to crave the safety of the simple and the sorted—"Oh, is that all?"—she also recognizes the openness in confronting the difficult and in keeping her eyes open (205).

As she prepares to share the tale of Ts'ai Yen, which appears in the final section of the book, Maxine says, "Here is a story my mother told me, not when I was young, but recently, when I told her I also talk story. The beginning is hers, the ending, mine" (206). This collaborative dimension signals Maxine's shift to seeing texts, reading, and interpretation as flexible and communal rather than fixed and individual.[49] She begins, "I like to think," signaling that she's now at home with questioning, uncertainty, and surmising (207). In "No Name Woman," such uncertainty felt like a dangerous and violent act. Now it has become a creative act that situates Maxine within an archive and helps her "keep the old Chinese myths alive . . . by telling them in a new American way."[50] Maxine and Kingston model a form of multicultural canon that illustrates the fruitfulness of violating boundaries by bringing together seemingly disparate texts. Although the critic Malini Schueller has argued that Kingston and "marginal groups" in general "have little investment in concepts of unity," this final section of *The Woman Warrior* typifies the painful work of creating a form of wholeness.[51]

Ts'ai Yen—a figure of political, economic, and poetic power—was kidnapped by raiders and lived with them for twenty years before she was ransomed, returned to her family, and married to Tung Ssu of the Hans. While in captivity, she heard flute music that "disturbed [her]," "made her ache," and made it impossible for her to "concentrate on her own thoughts." She attempted to escape the songs, but the music "filled the desert no matter how many dunes away she walked" (208). So eventually, she embraced it and made it her own, singing "a song so high and clear, it matched the flutes." "Ts'ai Yen sang about China and her family there. Her words seemed to be Chinese, but the barbarians understood their sadness and anger. Sometimes they thought they could catch barbarian phrases about forever wandering. Her children did not laugh, but eventually sang along when she left her tent to sit by the winter campfires, ringed by barbarians" (209). Like Fa Mu Lan, she expanded her mind to allow for paradox and thus was able to find use for and value in something that had initially seemed alien.

Ts'ai Yen's ability to juxtapose the two arts (we learn that "the barbarians understood" the sentiment of the Chinese and "could catch barbarian phrases" in the song) suggests that she had attempted to understand their language. Both traditions were positively changed when "she left her tent to sit by the winter campfires, ringed by barbarians." Likewise, when she returned to her family, "she brought her songs back from the savage lands" and incorporated them into the Chinese canon. The final words of the book, "It translated well," point toward the power and possibility of integration (209). A confrontation between difference and sameness allows for connection. Unity need not mean uniformity; rather, through a unity of difference, nations, civilizations, and cultures may find wholeness, strength, and peace.

Thus, a text that begins with isolation—"You must not tell anyone"—ends with an image of integration and communion (3). The fruitfulness of Ts'ai Yen's time with the barbarians—represented both by her two children and her epic poem "Eighteen Stanzas for a Barbarian Reed Pipe"—signal the use value of an open and integrated canon. While this beauty comes at a cost—violence, abduction, and dislocation—it intimates that healing and wholeness are possible and offers a compelling model of pluralism for America, its literary canon, and its citizen-readers.

A Broad Margin

Kingston's recent book-length poem, *I Love a Broad Margin to My Life* (2011), continues her work of connecting stories, genres, people, and nations via words. Yet another ostensible memoir, it weaves together family history, political history, travel narrative, fiction, myth, and many other texts. Drawing its title from the work of Henry David Thoreau, it also claims kinship with Jane Austen, Robert Louis Stevenson, John Mulligan, Anton Chekhov, Grace Paley, Miguel de Cervantes, Colette, Walt Whitman, Liu Shahe, the *I Ching*, Alice Walker, Zen Buddhism, Wen-chi, Du Fu, Li Bai, William Shakespeare, Franz Kafka, and Gilgamesh.[52] The text alludes to familiar tales: Ralph Waldo Emerson's "Self-Reliance," Whitman's "Crossing Brooklyn Ferry," T. S. Eliot's writings on "the objective correlative," the myth of Fa Mu Lan (here Fa Mook Lan), and the story of Ts'ai Yen's captivity (here Wen-chi). It refers to the family stories that Kingston has included elsewhere, such as the story of her aunt in *The Woman Warrior* and the story of her parents' immigration in *China Men*.[53] The book includes a glossary—a first in Kingston's work—defining Chinese, English, Hawaiian, Spanish, Vietnamese, and other words that appear in the poem and emphasizing the author's connective cosmopolitanism and her desire for inclusiveness. Stories set in diverse locales intersect on issues such as immigration, workers' rights, disaster relief, ending war, and post-traumatic stress disorder, indicating that these are world rather than national issues. What Kingston said of *The Woman Warrior* holds true for *I Love a Broad Margin:* "I feel I've written a political and artistic work. It's important for me to show that both are possible. . . . It's important for me to show that racial or feminist writing doesn't have to sound like polemics. It can dramatize events and make them brighter."[54]

There is an urgency in Kingston's call for better reading that bespeaks her continued commitment to peace and preventing discrimination and oppression. She speaks of the artist's obligation "to have a vision of a future. We need an idea before we can create who we are and what our society is. It seems to me there's a horrible emergency right now. We seem to be on the brink of destroying everything." Artists have to figure out "how to make beauty" from ugliness and provide light and hope; they must not accept militarism and tragedy. She charges readers to strive for community, for only through connection can they create global peace. She describes her audience as "very wide, . . . in a sense, the universe." She strives for a global community that remains aware of the connections among seemingly disparate peoples. She works to answer the question her mother poses to her in a recurring dream: "Have you educated America yet? . . . What have you done to educate the world lately?"[55] Her goal is to help others to live "a meaningful life" "where you are becoming a humane being, . . . able to form a community, a harmonious, non-warlike community. Which means that you have to be a human being who can take action. You are able to form bonds with other human beings and figure out a way to love each other." By creating literature about "a citizen whose work improves life," by working "in a community project, my portion of which was to get dropouts to drop in and learn how to read," by teaching "readers . . . not to worship tragedy as the highest art anymore" but to embrace hope, she attempts to fashion an ethical, humane, and global citizen-reader.[56]

Yet being a humane citizen-reader of the word and the world takes work. It means "teaching readers to enjoy the slowness" of reading texts. It means allowing for identification so that, "when the reader reads the first person narration, the 'I' becomes the 'I' of the reader, so the reader becomes me." This type of connection is based on what the poet June Jordan called "what we can do for each other." As Maxine recognizes in *The Woman Warrior,* "unless I see [my aunt's] life branching into mine, she gives me no ancestral help" (8). As the scholar Lynet Uttal has written, "*creating* a sense of unity that comes from all of us working together, building on our diverse experiences" necessarily involves messiness, difficulty, and possible conflict—all of which are modeled in the healing process in *The Woman Warrior.* Kingston believes that readers need to "allow themselves to change as they are reading the books. I hope that they will become different people by the time they finish"—that they will see a self beyond their own needs, concerns, and grievances and become someone who is socially responsible. She contends that "reading and writing should expand and transform the self" because "words can get through all kinds of barriers; they can get through skin color and culture." Her vision refuses to "hide behind the mockeries of separations that have been imposed on us and which so often we accept as our own." It works to correct "cracks of misunderstanding among the many cultures in America."[57] Yet first we must experience the pain of stretching and extending ourselves beyond our own hurt to see another's—as well as our possible complicity in that suffering.

The Woman Warrior leaves us with the sense of an uneasy and painful connection, a reconciliation in which the pasted-up cracks still show, a togetherness that does not mask difference, and a unity that is diverse. It offers hope for a nation that has undergone the Cold War's tumult and change, but its vision of wholeness should not be mistaken for consensus or uniformity. It is a wholeness born out of differences. Kingston declares that even if the Frank Chins and the Allan Blooms of the world reject her work, they cannot remove the reality of their part in that work or her work's part in their America. She refuses either-ors and reaches for a both-and: "I don't want to become an American by wiping out all of my Chineseness. Nor do I want to stay Chinese and never participate in the wonderful American world that's out there. So instead of destroying part of myself or denying some of reality, to me there has to be a way to have it all and to do it all."[58] Kingston has written that, "like the people who carry them across oceans, the myths become American. The myths I write are new, American." Her recognition of the struggle and violence that this work entails distances her from more naïve movements of the 1980s—groups such as the "We are the World" singers and the National Rainbow Coalition. Yet it doesn't eliminate her hope: "In a time of destruction, create something. A poem. A parade. A friendship. A community. A place that is the commons. A school. A vow. A moral principle. One peaceful moment."[59]

Conclusion
"Reading Makes a Country Great"

When the planes hit the World Trade Center on 11 September 2001, President George W. Bush was seated in front of a poster that announced "Reading Makes a Country Great," reading *The Pet Goat* with students at Booker Elementary School. The now iconic image of the president holding a children's book while receiving word of the attacks occupied the media for days and foreshadowed the ways in which literacy, citizenship, and nationalism were destined to intersect once again. From that moment on, American literacy bore the weight of a nation in crisis as legislators, educators, and other invested parties passed laws, organized commissions, performed studies, and wrote guides to help combat the threat posed by "a huge population of citizens who are marginally literate, unable to self-govern intelligently, and easy prey to either demagogues or chaos."[1]

Former Cold Warriors in the Bush administration read the attacks in familiar terms: terrorism was the new totalitarian specter haunting America, extremists were the new demagogues threatening democracy, and terror was the new philosophy opposed to freedom.[2] In hopes of restoring order, certainty, unity, and national security, various post-9/11 reading initiatives also replicated battle-tested Cold War programs. Reports such as Ernest B. Fleishman's *Adolescent Literacy: A National Reading Crisis*, the National Council of Teachers of English's *Adolescent Literacy*, and the National Endowment of the Arts' *Reading at Risk* invoked the rhetoric of threat, attack, and destruction to communicate the urgency of the perceived literacy crisis among American youth and adults. According to the author of *Reading at Risk*, "anyone who loves literature or values the cultural, intellectual, and political importance

CONCLUSION   155

of active and engaged literacy in American society will respond to this report with grave concern."³

Like their postwar counterparts, some political figures advanced overtly nationalistic reading programs. Senator Ike Skelton, a Democrat from Missouri, published a "National Security Book List," which suggested texts to read to help keep America safe. Included were the U.S. Constitution, books about famous battles, memoirs of great leaders, and Sun Tzu's *The Art of War.* Second Lady Lynne Cheney helped establish the Defense of Western Civilization Fund, which subsequently released *Defending Civilization: How Our Universities Are Failing America and What Can Be Done about It* (2001). The high-profile report not only listed the names of purportedly unpatriotic university professors who opposed the War on Terror (or called for a more nuanced and informed discussion of terrorism) but also offered guidelines for using reading education to shore up national security. It called on citizen-readers to recommit to "patriotism," "rall[y] behind the President wholeheartedly," and read "the classics" and those "American histories" that did not emphasize "politically correct" ideas. Cheney herself published two children's reading primers, *America: A Patriotic Primer* (2002) and *A is for Abigail: An Almanac of Amazing American Women* (2003), for "at a time of national crisis," America must teach its "children and grandchildren—indeed, all of us . . . the ideas and ideals on which our nation has been built."⁴

Other government efforts to promote reading included the National Endowment for the Arts' initiative known as the Big Read. A national Great Books program of sorts, it "aim[ed] to address this crisis squarely and effectively" by giving "citizens . . . the opportunity to read and discuss a single book within their communities." Big Read books have included classics such as Mark Twain's *The Adventures of Tom Sawyer,* Henry James's *Washington Square,* F. Scott Fitzgerald's *The Great Gatsby,* Harper Lee's *To Kill a Mockingbird,* Ernest Hemingway's *A Farewell to Arms,* and the poetry of Henry Wadsworth Longfellow. The program has also promoted books by women and authors of color—for instance, Zora Neale Hurston's *Their Eyes Were Watching God,* Willa Cather's *My Ántonia,* Jhumpa Lahiri's *The Namesake,* Marilynne Robinson's *Housekeeping,* Edith Wharton's *The Age of Innocence,* Julie Otsuka's *When the Emperor Was Divine,* Ernest J. Gaines's *A Lesson Before Dying,* and the poetry of Emily Dickinson.⁵ Like so many postwar initiatives, the Big Read was meant to introduce readers to foundational American ideas, celebrate America's diverse culture and heritage, and help communities to unite to learn and grow.

America's post-9/11 turn toward reading was not just a political reaction but evidence of a larger cultural need for connection, community, and civic participation in the wake of national trauma. The popularity of book clubs soared, and Oprah Winfrey's Book Club played a particularly large role. Founded in 1996 as a pseudo-social club that emphasized affective reading, it was dismissed by many critics, who charged it with playing on "base sentiment," encouraging cheap overflows of emotion, and offering "healing-and-redemption packages" and "penny dreadfuls for the Therapy Age." After Oprah canceled her book club in 2002, several others sprang up in its place, including *The Today Show* Book Club, *USA Today*'s Book Club, *Good Morning America*'s Book Club, and Reading with Ripa. Though none was as successful as Winfrey's had been, all reflected a cultural need to read with a community. After a year's hiatus, Winfrey restarted her club, this time embracing the stability and security found in the classics and the established narratives and authors of the American tradition. Post-9/11, she embraced a more active role in guiding American citizen-readers, teaching her cohort how to read books such as John Steinbeck's *East of Eden* and Toni Morrison's *Paradise* and helping them find the "truth" in uncertain texts and contexts. The book club's makeover situated it squarely within the parameters of good citizen-readership, and her critics largely vanished.[6]

The post-9/11 marriage of reading and citizenship was visible in academic discussions of reading's role in American life. Like Adler's *How to Read a Book* and other postwar reading primers, Harold Bloom's *How to Read and Why* (2000), Cynthia Lee Katona's *Book Savvy* (2005), Terry Eagleton's *How to Read a Poem* (2007), and John Sutherland's *How to Read a Novel* (2007) worked to guide Americans' book selection and interpretation, offering security to those navigating not only the War on Terror but also the digital age.[7] As publishing formats and platforms multiplied, so did the number of texts; and experts addressed this proliferation with various lists, criteria, and methods of selection and interpretation. Books such as *What Should I Read Next?* (2008), published by the University of Virginia, responded to the insecurity of "even the most well-read among us," recommending titles based on a survey of seventy professors.[8] The comedian Wayne Turmel took a different tack in *A Philistine's Journal: An Average Guy Tackles the Classics* (2003), targeting a low- to middlebrow market as he claimed that collecting and reading the classics could help readers navigate or forestall midlife crises.[9]

Several authors who published literary works about 9/11 used reading to represent America's desire for stability in a chaotic and seemingly unknowable world. For instance, both Jonathan Safran Foer's *Extremely Loud and Incredibly Close* (2005) and Claire Messud's *The Emperor's Children* (2006) see reading as a possible means of ordering a fractured city and nation. The jeremiad of Foer's character Oskar Schell is prompted both literally and metaphorically by reading. How is he to interpret the word *black* written on the key he has found in his late father's belongings? And how will that word be a key to understanding his fallen world? Oskar struggles to impose interpretive order on disorder—to find the definite and to define his experience through knowable categories, not unlike the "yes" and "no" tattooed on his grandfather's hands. In so doing, he tries to commune with others and construct a community in the face of language and representation's inevitable failures. Messud's novel also follows a collection of New Yorkers—writers, critics, and intellectuals—as they attempt to read their world and author a place for themselves in 9/11's aftermath. The novel's epigraph is from Anthony Powell's *Books Do Furnish a Room* (1971), and the books written and read by the characters are the means through which they try to feel at home. Epistemology and ontology collide in their wanderings as their literary and citizen selves are linked to and by this violent event, troubling their ability to read and know both their selves and others. For all of these characters, reading, self, community, security, and knowledge are furtive and frantic bedfellows.[10]

Why do Americans turn to reading during times of real or perceived national crisis? One answer can be found in the fact that reading is an individual choice and act. Consequently, readers feel a degree of agency and authority as they perform its physical and cognitive work. In the face of the incomprehensible or uncertain, at moments when one feels helpless, reading is *something* one can do. It can provide a feeling of familiarity as one scans words, turns pages, identifies formal or generic conventions, and entertains familiar character types or themes. Attempts to read, know, and parse the world can offer a sense of security to those who feel unmoored. Reading also offers an escape from the chaos and disorder of the real world and from its restrictions and oppressions. Finally, it is an opportunity for creativity—whether that entails creating the story in one's hands, a world unmarred by hatred or fear, or a world rebuilt after crisis. Ultimately, the act demonstrates faith in the truism that "knowledge is power." Even as reading affirms individual citizen-readers' integrity, it provides the germ for community and coalition building. It allows individuals to be part of a larger whole—a reading group, a television- or web-based book club, a university cohort, a political constituency, an identity group, or a nation-state.

As we close this exploration of reading, let us return to where we began—*The Wonderful World of Books,* that epitome of Cold War liberal ideology. As a nurturer of citizen-readers, it sowed seeds that in later years produced a great variety of fruit. It celebrated the "reading of books" because "through them we have the privilege of exploring and finding out for ourselves"; "we can select what meets our needs, instead of having it selected for us."[11] Praising reading's power to facilitate "exploring" and "finding out for ourselves," the book advocated for reading and thinking skills that would move citizen-readers from all walks of life to examine, question, and challenge various systems and methods to determine their use-value to individuals and to Americans as a whole. Throughout the Cold War, readers asserted, "We can select what meets our needs," refining and revising received methods of readerly inquiry and interpretation and thus expanding the definitions of good reading and good readership. At times the definitions offered by various stakeholders lined up. At times they clashed. At times they were variations on a theme. But regardless of their political, social, or ideological position, all of America's citizen-readers believed that literacy was an essential component of democracy and freedom.

Cold War America's efforts to define good reading and good readers reveal democracy in action. As educators, librarians, politicians, editors, psychologists, writers, publishers, social activists, literary critics, public intellectuals, and book-club participants wrangled over how to read literature, self, nation, and others, they demonstrated their investment in authoring a more perfect union. All believed that individual citizen-readers had not only the responsibility but also the means to do such democratic work. As President Barack Obama said in his November 2015 interview with Marilynne Robinson:

> When I think about how I understand my role as citizen . . . and the most important set of understandings that I bring to that position of citizen, the most important stuff I've learned I think I've learned from novels. It has to do with empathy. It has to do with being comfortable with the notion that the world is complicated and full of grays, but there's still truth there to be found, and that you have to strive for that and work for that. And the notion that it's possible to connect with some[one] else even though they're very different from you.

In other words, the stories we encounter and the methods we use to interpret and understand them teach us "the most important stuff" about our world.[12]

If the United States is to have a functional democracy in the increasingly polarized twenty-first century, then its citizens must cultivate "understanding" and "empathy"; we must endeavor "to connect with some[one] else even though they're very different from [us]."[13] As Martha C. Nussbaum contends in *Not for Profit: Why Democracy Needs the Humanities* (2010), the reading and learning that are essential to humanistic study—whether in the classroom, the library, or the living room—provide "the faculties of thought and imagination that make us human and make our relationships rich human relationships, rather than relationships of mere use and manipulation." This requires Americans to read texts that expose them to new ideas as opposed to those that merely reinforce their "existing point of view." Reading introduces us to new individuals, experiences, and ideas and helps cultivate the imagination we need to breach the divide, engage difference, and make democracy work. Nussbaum warns, "If we have not learned to see both self and other in that way . . . [then] democracy is bound to fail, because democracy is built upon respect and concern, and these in turn are built upon the ability to see other people as human beings, not simply as objects." Whether or not America's citizen-readers are willing or able to do this work is uncertain. Time constraints, intellectual or ideological discomfort, and a lack of readerly self-consciousness will inhibit many. Nevertheless, as Mrs. Charles Slater reminded us in *The Wonderful World of Books,* "there is much to be gained by our reading" if we are ready to do the work of and for democracy.[14]

Notes

Introduction: "There Is Much to Be Gained by Our Reading"

1. Mrs. Charles Slater, "I Belong to a Discussion Group," *The Wonderful World of Books*, ed. Alfred Stefferud (Boston: Houghton Mifflin, 1953), 122. The U.S. Department of Education was created in 1980. Previously, various other government agencies had assumed education responsibilities. The U.S. Department of Agriculture housed the Extension Work program that spearheaded adult literacy programs and other reading initiatives. See the introduction to *The Wonderful World of Books* (13–16) for further discussion of the conference and book's genesis.
2. Slater, "I Belong to a Discussion Group," 122.
3. Carl Solberg, "You, Citizen-Reader in a Democracy," in Stefferud, *Wonderful World*, 125, 127.
4. Stefferud, *Wonderful World*, 15, 13.
5. On links between reading and the Cold War, see Louise Robbins, *Censorship and the American Library: The American Library Association's Response to Threats to Intellectual Freedom, 1939–1969* (Westport, Conn.: Greenwood, 1996); Leerom Medovoi, *Rebels: Youth and the Cold War Origins of Identity* (Durham, N.C.: Duke University Press, 2005); and Julia Mickenberg, *Learning from the Left: Children's Literature, the Cold War, and Radical Politics in the United States* (Oxford: Oxford University Press, 2006).
6. Cotton Mather, *Bonifacius*, in *Norton Anthology of American Literature*, 5th ed., gen. ed. Nina Baym (New York: Norton, 1998), 409; Benjamin Franklin, *Autobiography and Other Writings*, ed. Ormond Seavey (Oxford: Oxford University Press, 1993), 71–72; John Adams, *A Dissertation on the Canon and Feudal Law* (1765), quoted in *The Oxford Dictionary of Political Quotations*, ed. Antony Jay (Oxford University Press: New York, 1996), 3; Abraham Lincoln, "Address Before the Wisconsin State Historical Society, Milwaukee, Wisconsin," in *The Collected Works of Abraham Lincoln*, ed. Roy P. Basler (New Brunswick, N.J.: Rutgers University Press, 1953), 3:480; U.S. Office of War Information, "Books Are Weapons in the War of Ideas" (Washington, D.C.: General Printing Office, 1942); Benedict Anderson, *Imagined Communities*, rev. ed. (London: Verso, 1996), 65.
7. Geneva Hanna and Mariana McAllister, *Books, Young People, and Reading Guidance* (New York: Harper, 1960), 91; Lister Hill, "Freedom and Responsibility in Publishing," in Stefferud, *Wonderful World*, 214.
8. Steven Belletto, *No Accident, Comrade: Change and Design in Cold War American Narratives* (Oxford: Oxford University Press, 2011); Mickenberg, *Learning from the Left*; Medovoi, *Rebels*; Christina Klein, *Cold War Orientalism: Asia in the Middlebrow Imagination, 1945–1961* (Berkeley: University of California Press, 2003); Mary Dudziak, *Cold War Civil Rights* (Princeton, N.J.: Princeton University Press, 2000). See also Morris Dickstein, *Leopards in the Temple* (Cambridge: Harvard University Press, 2002); Lizabeth Cohen, *A Consumer's*

Republic: *The Politics of Mass Consumption in Postwar America* (New York: Vintage, 2003); and David Castronovo, *Beyond the Gray Flannel Suit: Books from the 1950s That Made American Culture* (New York: Continuum, 2004).
9. Dan Lacy and Paul Hill, "America, Democracy, and the Free World," in Stefferud, *Wonderful World*, 131.
10. Richard Wright, *An American Hunger* (New York: Perennial, 1977), 120, 135.
11. Ibid., 19; Saul Bellow, *The Adventures of Augie March* (New York: Crest, 1965), 203–204; Philip Roth, *Goodbye, Columbus* (New York: Vintage, 1993); J. D. Salinger, *The Catcher in the Rye* (Boston: Little, Brown, 1991); Ray Bradbury, *Fahrenheit 451* (New York: Ballantine, 1991), 72, 54.
12. Ralph Ellison, *Invisible Man* (1952; reprint, New York: Vintage, 1995), 581; Malcolm X, as told to Alex Haley, *The Autobiography of Malcolm X* (1964; reprint, New York: Ballantine, 1987), 179; Norman Mailer, *Armies of the Night* (New York: Plume, 1994), 117, 176, 53; Kurt Vonnegut, *Slaughterhouse Five* (New York: Dell, 1968), 206.
13. Marshall McLuhan, *The Medium Is the Message* (New York: Bantam, 1967); John Barth, *Lost in the Funhouse* (New York: Bantam, 1969), 123; Joan Didion, *Democracy* (1984; reprint, New York: Vintage, 1995), 188; Thomas Pynchon, *The Crying of Lot 49* (1966; reprint, New York: Perennial, 1990), 181; Joseph Heller, *Catch-22* (1961; reprint, New York: Laurel, 1994), 267.

1. America Reads: Literacy and Cold War Nationalism

1. Carl Solberg, "You, Citizen-Reader in a Democracy," in *The Wonderful World of Books*, ed. Alfred Stefferud (Boston: Houghton Mifflin, 1953), 125–127, *passim*.
2. Henry Steele Commager, *The American Mind* (New Haven: Yale University Press, 1950), 432–433; Howard Mumford Jones, *The Theory of American Literature* (Ithaca, N.Y.: Cornell University Press, 1965), 171; Raymond Daniell, "What the Europeans Think of Us," *New York Times*, 30 November 1947, 69.
3. Daniell, "What the Europeans Think," 7, 72, 68–69.
4. Tom Engelhardt, *The End of Victory Culture* (Amherst: University of Massachusetts Press, 1995), 99; George Kennan, "Long Telegram," National Security Agency Archive, 861.00/2-2246, http://www.trumanlibrary.org.
5. Dan M. Lacy, *Books and the Future: A Speculation* (New York: New York Public Library, 1956), 5.
6. Geneva Hanna and Mariana McAllister, *Books, Young People, and Reading Guidance* (New York: Harper, 1960), 32, 31; *Teachers for Our Times* (Washington, D.C.: National Association of Secondary School Principals, 1944), 114; Frank Jennings, *This Is Reading* (New York: Columbia University, Teacher's College, 1965), 190; Ruth Strang, *Exploration in Reading Patterns* (Chicago: University of Chicago Press, 1942), 1, 127; Jacques Barzun, *Teacher in America* (Boston: Little, Brown, 1945), 315.
7. Jean Grambs, *The Development of Lifetime Reading Habits: A Report of a Conference Called by the Committee on Reading Development in New York, June 25–26, 1954* (New York: Bowker, 1954), iv; *The Pursuit of Excellence: Education and the Future of America* (New York: Doubleday, 1958), 10–11; *P.T.A. Manual* (1952), quoted by Ruth Gagliardo, "Parents, Teachers, and Libraries," in Stefferud, *Wonderful World*, 231.
8. Jacob Price, *Reading for Life* (Ann Arbor: University of Michigan Press, 1959), viii; Robert Hutchins, *Education for Freedom* (Baton Rouge: Louisiana State University Press, 1947), 37; Paul B. Jacobson, *The American Secondary School* (New York: Prentice Hall, 1952), 427; Robert W. Iverson, *The Communists and the Schools* (New York: Harcourt, Brace, 1959), 3.
9. Mortimer J. Adler, *How to Read a Book* (New York: Simon and Schuster, 1940), ix.
10. Excellent examples include Greg Barnhisel, "Cold Warriors of the Book: American Book Programs in the 1950s," *Book History* 13 (2010), 185–217; Greg Barnhisel, *Cold War Modernists: Art, Literature, and American Cultural Diplomacy* (New York: Columbia University

Press, 2015); Amanda Laugesen, "Books for the World: American Book Programs in the Developing World, 1948–1968," and Martin Manning, "Impact of Propaganda Materials in Free World Countries," both in *Pressing the Fight: Print, Propaganda, and the Cold War*, ed. Catherine Turner and Greg Barnhisel (Amherst: University of Massachusetts Press, 2010); John B. Hench, *Books As Weapons: Propaganda, Publishing, and the Battle for Global Markets in the Era of World War* (Ithaca, N.Y.: Cornell University Press, 2010); Frances Stoner Saunders, *The Cultural Cold War: The CIA and the World of Arts and Letters* (New York: New Press, 1999); Kenneth Osgood, *Total Cold War: Eisenhower's Secret Propaganda Battle at Home and Abroad* (Lawrence: University of Kansas, 2006); Nicholas Cull, *The Cold War and the United States Information Agency: American Propaganda and Public Diplomacy, 1945–1989* (Cambridge: Cambridge University Press, 2009); Curtis G. Benjamin, *U.S. Books Abroad: Neglected Ambassadors* (Washington, D.C.: Library of Congress, 1984); Volker R. Berghahn, *America and the Intellectual Cold Wars in Europe* (Princeton: Princeton University Press, 2001); Walter L. Hixson, *Parting the Curtain: Propaganda, Culture, and the Cold War, 1945–1961* (New York: St. Martin's, 1997); *Books, Libraries, Reading, and Publishing in the Cold War*, ed. Hermina G. B. Anghelescu and Martine Poulain (Washington, D.C.: Library of Congress, 2001); and Penny M. Von Eschen, *Satchmo Blows up the World: Jazz Ambassadors Play the Cold War* (Cambridge: Harvard University Press, 2004). These studies map out systematic U.S. propaganda efforts to establish American cultural and military supremacy over the Soviets via books and reading, starting with Truman's Campaign of Truth, through Eisenhower's cultural battles, and into the late 1960s.

11. Lister Hill, "Freedom and Responsibility in Publishing," in Stefferud, *Wonderful World*, 214.
12. Dan M. Lacy and Paul Hill, "America, Democracy, and the Free World," in ibid., 131, 130; Laugesen, "Books for the World," 130; Lacy and Hill, "America, Democracy, and the Free World," 129.
13. Lacy and Hill, "America, Democracy, and the Free World," 128; Barzun, *Teacher in America*, 7, 9.
14. Their cause for trepidation is illustrated by my quotation from Stan Lee's *The Amazing Spider-Man*. While many people believe those words first came from a comic book, they actually originate with Voltaire. The massification, popularization, and subsequent blurring of canonical figures such as Voltaire is exactly the type of cultural degradation that postwar intellectuals, educators, and politicians feared.
15. Poll quoted in Alan Dutscher, "The Book Business in America," in *Mass Culture*, ed. David Manning White and Bernard Rosenberg (Glencoe, Ill.: Free Press and Falcon's Wing Press, 1957), 126. In the National Opinion Research Center's 1945 study "What . . . Where . . . Why . . . Do People Read?" conducted for the American Library Association, researchers reported that "reading is a favorite diversion for two out of every five adults in the 17 cities included in the survey" ([Denver: University of Denver, 1946], 3). The 1946 edition of *Books for Adult Beginners* cites census figures reporting that 13.5 percent of American are considered functionally illiterate and "there is no estimate as to how many are considered semiliterate, but we do know that the educational background of the average adult over twenty-five years of age consists of only a little over eight years of schooling" ([Chicago: American Library Association, 1946], 4). Grambs cites the Committee on Reading Development's finding that only "25% of Americans read as much as one book per month" (*Development*, iv). Also see Dutscher, "The Book Business," 127.
16. Rudolf Flesch, *Why Johnny Can't Read—And What You Can Do About It* (New York: Harper, 1955), 132. While debates over phonics versus word guessing existed before Flesch published his book, he became the poster boy for phonics, and the debates got fiercer. For a well-researched and methodical critique that debunks Flesch's central contention that the United States was behind Europe in reading proficiency, see Sam Duker and Thomas P. Nally, *The Truth about Your Child's Reading* (New York: Crown, 1956).

17. Arthur S. Trace, Jr., *What Ivan Knows That Johnny Doesn't* (New York: Random House, 1961), 187; Louis Menand, "Cat People: What Dr. Seuss Really Taught Us," *New Yorker*, 23 and 30 December 2002, 151; Ralph E. Ellsworth, "The University Library and the Lifetime Reader," *Reading for Life*, ed. Jacob Price (Ann Arbor: University of Michigan Press, 1960), 224; Jennings, *This Is Reading*, 112, 113.
18. Menand, "Cat People," 152; U.S. Senate Committee on Labor and Public Welfare, Subcommittee on Education, *National Defense Education Act of 1958, As Amended by the 88th Congress* (Washington, D.C.: Government Printing Office, 1964), 4; Martin Kling, "Background and Development of the Literature Search: Targeted Research and Development Program in Reading," *The Literature of Research in Reading with Emphasis on Models*, ed. Frederick B. Davis (New Brunswick, N.J.: Rutgers University, Graduate School of Education, 1971), sec. 1–1. For a summary of 1950s reading research, see Lester Asheim's "A Survey of Recent Research," in Price, *Reading for Life*, 3–26. For a discussion of various reading programs, institutions, and studies in the late 1950s and early 1960s, see Nelson B. Henry, ed., *Development in and through Reading: The Sixtieth Yearbook of the National Society of Education* (Chicago: University of Chicago Press, 1961); International Reading Association, "Research in Reading," in *Reading As an Intellectual Activity*, ed. J. Allen Figurel (New York: Scholastic, 1963), sec. G; Brewster Porcella, *A Summary of Research on the Reading Interests and Habits of College Graduates* (Chicago: American Library Association and University of Illinois Library Research Center, 1964); and Frederick B. Davis, ed., *The Literature of Research in Reading with Emphasis on Models* (New Brunswick, N.J.: Rutgers University, Graduate School of Education, 1971).
19. Kling, "Background and Development," sec. 1–9. Other reading programs were the U.S. Office of Education–supported Educational Resources Information Center/Clearinghouse on Retrieval of Information and Evaluation of Reading, funded by the U.S. Bureau of Research, the International Reading Association, and Indiana University; Project 1 at the Princeton University–based Educational Testing Service; and Project 3 at the University of California's Berkeley-based Educational Testing Service (secs. 1–3, 1–15).
20. Harry Singer, "Theories, Models, and Strategies for Learning to Read," in Davis, *Literature of Research*, secs. 7–116, 7–118, 7–123; John J. Geyer, "Comprehensive and Partial Models Related to the Reading Process," in ibid., sec. 5–3; Stanley F. Wanat, ed., *Graduate Programs and Faculty in Reading* (Newark, Del.: International Reading Association, 1973), 1; Walter Pauk, ed., *Reading for Success in College* (Oshkosh, Wisc.: Academia Press, 1968).
21. Joseph McCarthy, *McCarthyism: The Fight for America* (New York: Arno, 1952), 101.
22. Whittaker Chambers, *Witness* (1952; reprint, Washington, D.C.: Regnery, 1980), 79; Ellen Schrecker, *Many Are the Crimes: McCarthyism in America* (Princeton: Princeton University Press, 1998), 54, 132.
23. J. Edgar Hoover, *Masters of Deceit* (New York: Holt, 1958), 9. The book presents various scenarios that educate readers on how they may read and identify someone as an underground Communist.
24. Gregory Bern, *Behind the Red Mask* (Los Angeles: Bern, 1947), 3; Robert Stripling, *The Red Plot against America* (Drexel Hill, Pa.: Bell, 1949), 165–262. Also see W. Cleon Skousen, *The Naked Communist* (Salt Lake City: Ensign, 1961); Anthony Bouscaren, *Guide to Anti-Communist Action* (Chicago: Regnery, 1958); and Harry Overstreet and Bonaro Overstreet, *What We Must Know about Communism* (New York: Norton, 1958).
25. Skousen, *Naked Communist*, i. A major figure in anti-Communist circles, Skousen derived his credibility from his long-time post as the editor of the national police magazine, *Law and Order*, and his service as an American Security Council field director in Chicago.
26. Overstreet and Overstreet, *What We Must Know*, 9. The Overstreets were professors of philosophy and psychology, and Bonaro also wrote poetry. They made a name for themselves as proponents of adult education, and their books, which also included *The FBI in Our Open Society* (1969), were both bestsellers. (Some might argue that their true fame

resulted from an advantageous photo showing President Dwight D. Eisenhower reading one of their books.) Bonaro Overstreet offers explicit reading advice in "The Role of the Home," in *Development in and through Reading*, ed. Nelson B. Henry and Paul Witty (Chicago: University of Chicago Press, 1961), arguing that books serve as mediators, property, makers of an atmosphere, and builders of a person's inner source, thus strengthening the individual, the home, and the nation (79). The aims of her article resemble those of the Overstreets' anti-Communist primer: security on the home front.

27. "Technological, Business, and Government Foundations: Introduction," in *A History of the Book in America*, vol. 5, *The Enduring Book: Print Culture in Postwar America*, ed. David Paul Nord, Joan Shelley Rubin, and Michael Schudson (Chapel Hill: University of North Carolina Press, 2009), 25; Council on Books in Wartime, *A History of the Council on Books in Wartime, 1942–1946* (New York: Country Life Press, 1946), front matter; Trysh Travis, "Books As Weapons and 'The Smart Man's Peace,'" *Princeton University Library Chronicle* 60 (spring 1999), 353–99; Hench, *Books As Weapons*.

28. John Jamieson, *Editions for the Armed Services, Inc.: A History* (New York: Editions for the Armed Services, 1948), 3; "SRL Award," *Saturday Review of Literature*, 11 August 1945, 18.

29. David G. Wittels, "What the G.I. Reads," *Saturday Evening Post*, 23 June 1945, 11. For representative articles, see John L. Van Der Voort, "Armed Services Editions," *Saturday Review of Literature*, 26 May 1945, 19; "SRL Award," 18; "Armed Services Editions Well Received by Troops," *Publishers Weekly*, 12 February 1944, 777–779; "Quartermaster Procures Millions of Small Editions," *Publishers Weekly*, 15 April 1944: 1526; and "What the Armed Forces Read," *Publishers Weekly* 6 October 1945, 1647.

30. Wittels, "What the G.I. Reads," 11; Frank S. Adams, "As Popular As Pin-up Girls," *Senior Scholastic*, 2 October 1944, 21; Van Der Voort, "Armed Services Editions," 19.

31. Van Der Voort, "Armed Services Editions," 19; "What the Armed Forces Read," 1647.

32. Jason Epstein, *Book Business: Publishing Past Present and Future* (New York: Norton, 2001), 61; Beth Luey, *Expanding the American Mind: Books and the Popularization of Knowledge* (Boston: University of Massachusetts Press, 2010), 51; Alvin Johnson, *The Public Library—A People's University* (New York: American Association for Adult Education, 1938), 65.

33. For an excellent discussion of New Criticism's institutional contexts, see William J. Spurlin and Michael Fischer, eds. *The New Criticism and Contemporary Literary Theory: Connections and Continuities* (New York: Garland, 1995): xvii–xxix. Ransom, Tate, Warren, and other New Critics were originally known as the Fugitive Poets, part of the southern agrarian movement. Its manifesto was the anthology *I'll Take My Stand*, originally subtitled *A Stand against Marxism* (1930; reprint, New York: Harper and Brothers, 1962). In the postwar period, these poets, teachers, and critics offered "an anti-bourgeois ideology which had no taint of Soviet sympathies, and provided them with an image of an unalienated pre-capitalist culture of the past" that appealed to people on both sides of the American political spectrum (Mark Jancovich, *The Cultural Politics of the New Criticism* [Cambridge: Cambridge University Press, 1993], 18). For more about the diverse and divergent scholars known as the New Critics, also see Frank Lentricchia, *After the New Criticism* (Chicago: University of Chicago Press, 1980); and Frank Lentricchia and Andrew DuBois, eds., *Close Reading* (Durham, N.C.: Duke University Press, 2003).

34. John Crowe Ransom, *The New Criticism* (Westport, Conn.: Greenwood, 1941), 216; Spurlin and Fischer, *New Criticism*, xvii; Ransom, *The New Criticism*, 43–44; William J. Spurlin, "Afterword: An Interview with Cleanth Brooks," in ibid., 370.

35. Ransom, *New Criticism*, 281; Jancovich, *Cultural Politics*, 29–30; Jonathan Culler, *On Deconstruction: Theory and Criticism after Structuralism* (Ithaca, N.Y.: Cornell University Press, 1982), 19. For an excellent discussion of the ways in which New Critical terms and methodology reflected Cold War anxieties and ideologies, see Mark Walhout, "The New Criticism and the Crisis of American Liberalism: The Poetics of the Cold War," *College English* 49, no. 8 (1987): 861–871.

36. See Adler, *How to Read a Book;* Jennings, *This Is Reading;* Stefferud, *Wonderful World;* Price, *Reading for Life;* and Barzun, *Teacher in America.*
37. Cornelius Hirschberg, *The Priceless Gift* (New York: Simon and Schuster, 1960); Viola Wallace, ed., *Books for Adult Beginners: Grades I to VII* (Chicago: American Library Association, 1954), 3–4.
38. Linda M. Scott, "Markets and Audiences," in Nord et al., *Enduring Book,* 88.
39. Louise S. Robbins, *Censorship and the American Library: The American Library Association's Response to Threats to Intellectual Freedom, 1939–1969* (Westport, Conn.: Greenwood, 1996), 153; Julia L. Mickenberg, *Learning from the Left: Children's Literature, the Cold War, and Radical Politics in the United States* (Oxford: Oxford University Press, 2006), 101.
40. Robbins, *Censorship,* 189, 190, 162.
41. Christine Pawley, *Reading Places: Literacy, Democracy, and the Public Library in Cold War America* (Amherst: University of Massachusetts Press, 2010), 3, 7–8; Kenneth Cmiel, "Libraries, Books, and the Information Age," in Nord et al., *Enduring Book,* 330–331.
42. Lizabeth Cohen, *A Consumer's Republic* (New York: Vintage, 2003).
43. Epstein, *Book Business,* 61; Luey, *Expanding,* 54; Beth Luey, "The Organization of the Book Publishing Industry," in Nord et al., *Enduring Book,* 45.
44. Jay Satterfield, *The World's Best Books: Taste, Culture, and the Modern Library* (Amherst: University of Massachusetts Press, 2002), 162; Epstein, *Book Business,* 53–54; Laura J. Miller, "Selling the Product," in Nord et al., *Enduring Book,* 95, 97. For an extended discussion of this shift, also see Laura J. Miller, *Reluctant Capitalists: Bookselling and the Culture of Consumption* (Chicago: University of Chicago Press, 2006). As Satterfield discusses, middle-class book venues capitalized on the Modern Library's sometimes self-defeating department-store selling strategy, established in the 1930s.
45. Cover, *Life Special Issue: The Good Life* 47 (December 1958); "Leisure Could Mean a Better Civilization," ibid., 63.
46. Janice Radway, "The Library As Place, Collection, or Service," in *Institutions of Reading: The Social Life of Libraries in the United States,* ed. Thomas Augst and Kenneth Carpenter (Amherst: University of Massachusetts Press, 2007), 236; Samuel A. Schreiner, Jr., *The Condensed World of the "Reader's Digest"* (New York: Stein and Day, 1977), 93.
47. For a detailed discussion, see Christopher Lee, *Hidden Public: Story of the Book-of-the-Month Club* (New York: Doubleday, 1958). Adler's *How to Read a Book* established a foundation for the Great Books Program, proposing a rationale for how to study the great books and providing a list of them. Charles F. Strubbe, Jr., notes that, in 1953, there were operational discussion groups in more than "six hundred American communities." ("The Great Books Program," in Stefferud, *Wonderful World of Books,* 216). The success of Adler's text inspired many others to write books about how to read the classics and which texts were great. For instance, see Francis Hackett, *On Judging Books* (New York: Day, 1947); Stella S. Center, *The Art of Book Reading* (New York: Scribner's, 1952); and Clifton Fadiman, *The Lifetime Reading Plan* (New York: World, 1960).
48. Joan Shelley Rubin, "The Enduring Reader," in Nord et al., *Enduring Book,* 413; Robert Hutchins, *Great Books: The Foundation of a Liberal Education* (New York: Simon and Schuster, 1954), 28; Strubbe, "The Great Books Program," in Stefferud, *Wonderful World,* 217; Hutchins, *Great Books,* 14, 27.
49. Jennings, *Reading for Life,* 61, 147; Rubin, "The Enduring Reader," in Nord et al., *Enduring Book,* 413; Vance Packard, *Status Seekers* (New York: McKay, 1959).
50. Elizabeth Long, "The Chat-an-Hour Social and Cultural Club: African American Women Readers," in Nord et al., *Enduring Book,* 459.
51. "June 21, 1956: Arthur Miller," in *Thirty Years of Treason: Excerpts from Hearings before the House Committee on Un-American Activities, 1938–1968,* ed. Eric Bentley (New York: Viking, 1971), 824.
52. Erich Fromm, *The Sane Society* (New York: Rinehart, 1955), 172; Paul Boyer, *By the Bomb's*

Early Light: American Thought and Culture at the Dawn of the Atomic Age (Chapel Hill: University of North Carolina Press, 1994).
53. Duker and Nally, *Truth*, 10; Jennings, *This Is Reading*, 13.

2. Reading for Character, Community, and Country: J. D. Salinger's *The Catcher in the Rye*

1. J. D. Salinger, *The Catcher in the Rye* (1951; reprint, Boston: Little, Brown, 1991), 201. Further citations appear in the text.
2. See Donald M. Fiene, "From a Study of Salinger: Controversy in the *Catcher*," in *Salinger's "Catcher in the Rye": Clamor vs. Criticism*, ed. Harold P. Simonson and Philip E. Hager (Boston: Heath, 1963), 15–21; and W. P. Kinsella, *Shoeless Joe* (Boston: Houghton Mifflin, 1982). As Fiene points out, "only one word has been responsible for the removal of *Catcher* from so many libraries. . . . [W]hat seems to shock the conservatives into paralysis is the phrase which Holden Caulfield himself is shocked by: 'Fuck you.' . . . It is *the word itself* which librarians and teachers—and parents—object to" (17).
3. Pamela Hunt Steinle, *In Cold Fear* (Columbus: Ohio State University Press, 2000), 124–125.
4. Carl Solberg, "You, Citizen-Reader in a Democracy," in *The Wonderful World of Books*, ed. Alfred Stefferud (Boston: Houghton Mifflin, 1953), 125.
5. Juvenile delinquency, "the shame of America," was at the fore of both social science research and popular conversation (Richard Clendon and Herbert Beaser, "The Shame of America," *Saturday Evening Post*, 227 [January 1955]: 32). For examples, see U.S. Senate, Subcommittee on Juvenile Delinquency, *Juvenile Delinquency* (Washington, D.C.: Government Printing Office, 1954); Robert Lindner, *Rebel without a Cause: The Hypnoanalysis of a Criminal Psychopath* (New York: Grune and Stratton, 1944) ; Benjamin Fine, *1,000,000 Delinquents* (Cleveland: World, 1955); Albert Cohen, *Delinquent Boys: The Culture of the Gang* (Glencoe, Ill: Free Press, 1955); Bertram Beck, "The Nature of the Problem of Delinquency," *Religious Education* 50, no. 2 (1955): 83–87; Bertram Beck, "Crime and Delinquency," in *Search for America*, ed. Huston Smith, Richard T. Heffron, and Eleanor Wieman Smith (Englewood Cliffs, N.J., Prentice-Hall, 1959): 80–89.
6. The New Left radical Tom Hayden wrote, "There were several alternative cultural models beckoning to those of us who in a few years were to become activists: the fictional character Holden Caulfield, the actor James Dean, and the writer Jack Kerouac. The life crises they personified spawned not only political activism, but also the cultural revolution of rock and roll. . . . These characters, in their different ways, were responding to the human absurdity and emptiness of the secure material life parents of the fifties had built" (*Reunion: A Memoir* [New York: Collier /Macmillan, 1988], 17).
7. Thomas Schaub sees Cold War liberalism as a "spectrum of those interested in social reform" who share "a 'habit of mind' rather than a specific creed" (*American Fiction in the Cold War* [Madison: University of Wisconsin Press, 1991], 5). Like him, I recognize that liberalism was not a monolith and look to certain cultural narratives that connect its disparate persons and practices. The Cold War liberals I examine in this book run the gamut from radical communists, to moderate leftists, to centrists, to Republicans, to those on the right who embraced postwar policies of democracy spreading, nation securing, and individual advancement. One cultural connective was reading. Although their modes of argument and their rhetorical positions differed, these various thinkers all believed that reading is, should be, or can be democratizing and represents the best that America has to offer.
8. Mark Jancovich, *The Cultural Politics of the New Criticism* (Cambridge: Cambridge University Press, 2006), 19.
9. Alan Nadel, "Holden and the Cold War," in *Holden Caulfield*, ed. Harold Bloom (New York: Chelsea House, 1990); Leerom Medovoi, *Rebels: Youth and the Cold War Origins*

of Identity (Durham, N.C.: Duke University Press, 2005); Steinle, *In Cold Fear*; Abigail Cheever, *Real Phonies: Cultures of Authenticity in Post–World War II America* (Athens: University of Georgia Press, 2010).
10. Henry Steele Commager, *The American Mind: An Interpretation of American Thought and Character Since the 1880's* (New Haven: Yale University Press, 1950); David Riesman, Nathan Glazer, and Reuel Denny, *The Lonely Crowd: A Study of the Changing American Character* (1950; reprint, New Haven: Yale University Press, 1953); David Riesman and Nathan Glazer, *Faces in the Crowd: Individual Studies in Character and Politics* (New Haven: Yale University Press, 1952); C. Wright Mills, *White Collar* (New York: Oxford University Press, 1951); David M. Potter, *People of Plenty: Economic Abundance and the American Character* (Chicago: University of Chicago Press, 1954); Erich Fromm, *The Sane Society* (New York: Rinehart, 1955); William H. Whyte, Jr., *The Organization Man* (New York: Simon and Schuster, 1956); Vance Packard, *The Status Seekers* (New York: McKay, 1959); Warren Susman, *Culture As History: The Transformation of American Society in the Twentieth Century* (New York: Pantheon, 1984), 273–274; Robert J. Havighurst and Hilda Taba, *Adolescent Character and Personality* (New York: Wiley, 1949), 3.
11. Dale Carnegie, *How to Win Friends and Influence People* (1936; reprint, New York: Simon and Schuster, 1950); Erving Goffman, *The Presentation of Self in Everyday Life* (Garden City, N.Y.: Doubleday, 1959), 238, 251.
12. Mills, *White Collar*, 182–184, 187, passim; Fromm, *Sane Society*, 117, 142, 133, 188, 175.
13. Whyte, *Organization Man*, 201, 216; J. Edgar Hoover, *Masters of Deceit* (New York: Holt, 1958), 9. In *Real Phonies*, Cheever points out how postwar criticisms of conformity demonstrate a fear that all Americans are the same and that individuality does not actually exist. Whereas an individual (Cheever's focus) is a separate entity or essence, a character's moral or mental qualities and habits can be identified in and transferred to a whole. Character assumes that one is an individual and also part of a whole.
14. Commager, *American Mind*, 409; Edward Shils, "The Bookshop in America," in *The American Reading Public: What It Reads, Why It Reads*, ed. Roger H. Smith (New York: Bowker, 1962), 141; William S. Gray and Bernice Rogers, *Maturity in Reading* (Chicago: University of Chicago Press, 1956), 231.
15. Leslie Fiedler, "Adolescence, Maturity, and the American Novel," in *An End to Innocence* (Boston: Beacon, 1955), 200, 193. In *Rebels*, Medovoi emphasizes the ways in which *Catcher*'s rebel narrative works as an allegory for American identity. Focusing primarily on readings about and of *Catcher*, he spends little time examining the role of reading in the text. While he briefly recognizes and dismisses a conservative view of the novel as facile and limited to the concerns of a small group of New York intellectuals, I see Fiedler, Trilling, and Macdonald as part of a larger chorus of educators, politicians, and mass media mavens from across the political spectrum. Significantly, all of Holden's discussions about books, reading, and culture point toward a conservative narrative. The text, versus its reception, complicates Medovoi's reading and demands that we revisit the novel and its position within Cold War culture.
16. Leonard Shatzkin, "The Book in Search of a Reader," in Smith, *American Reading Public*, 129.
17. Jennings, *This Is Reading*, xi; Stefferud, *Wonderful World*; Jacob M. Price, *Reading for Life* (1959; reprint, Ann Arbor: University of Michigan Press, 1960); Jennings, *This Is Reading*; William S. Gray, ed., *Reading in an Age of Mass Communication* (New York: Appleton-Century-Crofts, 1949); Ruth Strang and Dorothy Kendall Bracken, *Making Better Readers* (Boston: Heath, 1957); Roy A. Kress, ed., *That All May Learn to Read: Papers Presented at the First Annual Reading Conference, the Reading Center, School of Education, University Division of Summer Sessions, Syracuse, University, 1959* (Syracuse, N.Y.: Syracuse University, School of Education, 1960); Mortimer J. Adler, *How to Read a Book* (1940; reprint, New York: Simon and Schuster, 1967); William S. Gray, ed., *Promoting Personal and Social*

Development through Reading: Conference on Reading (1947) (Chicago: University of Chicago Press, 1947); William S. Gray, ed., *Promoting Growth Toward Maturity in Interpreting What Is Read: Conference on Reading (1951)* (Chicago: University of Chicago Press, 1951); Gray and Rogers, *Maturity in Reading*.

18. American Library Association, "The Freedom to Read," in *Censorship and the American Library*, by Louise Robbins (Westport, Conn.: Greenwood, 1996), 189–190; Robert Maynard Hutchins, ed., *The Great Books of the Western World* (Chicago: Encyclopedia Britannica, 1952), 27, 25; Jacques Barzun, *Teacher in America* (Boston: Little, Brown, 1945), 134; William Elliott, "The Soviet Cultural Offensive against Freedom," in *Education and Freedom in a World of Conflict*, ed. Clarence Perry Oakes, Samuel M. Brownell, and William Y. Elliot, (Chicago: Regnery, 1963), 27.

19. Paul F. Lazarsfeld and Robert K. Merton, "Mass Communication, Popular Taste, and Organized Social Action," in Rosenberg and White, *Mass Culture*, 467.

20. William J. Spurlin, "An Interview with Cleanth Brooks," in *The New Criticism and Contemporary Literary Theory*, ed. William J. Spurlin and Michael Fischer (New York: Garland, 1995), 371; Jancovich, *Cultural Politics*, 42; Ransom, *New Criticism*, 95, 103, 295, 261; Spurlin, "An Interview with Cleanth Brooks," 375.

21. Steinle, *In Cold Fear*, 75, 135, 125.

22. Ibid., 125. Some saw these fears materialize in the person of Mark David Chapman, John Lennon's killer. In his trial, Chapman read from *Catcher* and cited Holden's desire to preserve innocence as his aim in shooting Lennon, a purported destroyer of innocence. More recently, books, music, and video games have been accused of turning kids into killers in Columbine, Aurora, and Newtown.

23. Geneva R. Hanna and Mariana K. McAllister, *Books, Young People, and Reading Guidance* (New York: Harper and Row, 1960), 31, 92.

24. On calls for censorship, see Edward P. J. Corbett, "Raise High the Barriers, Censors," in *Clamor vs. Criticism*, 5–9; Robert O. Bowen, "The Salinger Syndrome: Charity against Whom?" in ibid., 21–30; and William Wiegand, "The Knighthood of J. D. Salinger," in *Studies in J. D. Salinger*, ed. Marvin Laser and Norman Fruman (New York: Odyssey, 1963), 105–112. For other moral critiques, see Sanford Pinsker and Anna Pinsker, *Understanding "The Catcher in the Rye"* (Westport, Conn.: Greenwood, 1999); and Steinle, *In Cold Fear*. For personal attacks on Salinger, see George Steiner, "The Salinger Industry," in Laser and Fruman, *Studies*, 113–118; and Harvey Swados, "Must Writers Be Characters?" in Laser and Fruman, *Studies*, 119–212; and Paul Alexander, *Salinger: A Biography* (New York: Renaissance, 2010). Alexander repeatedly alleges improper sexual attraction and behavior in his descriptions of Salinger's limited interpersonal interactions. Though he does not critique Salinger's work implicitly, his autobiographical readings of the stories and the novel, coupled with his fixation on the writer's romantic relationships, suggest that improper sexual desire may be at the root of the protagonists' problems and the author's own struggle to be taken seriously in the publishing world. For articles that critique Salinger's style, see Mary McCarthy, "J. D. Salinger's Closed Circuit," in Laser and Fruman, *Studies*, 245–250; Frank Kermode, "Fit Audience," in *J. D. Salinger and the Critics*, ed. William Belcher and James Lee (Belmont, Calif.: Wadsworth, 1962), 40–43; and Michael Walzer, "In Place of a Hero," in Belcher and Lee, *Salinger and the Critics*, 129–137.

25. Robert Gutwillig, "Everybody's Caught *The Catcher in the Rye*," in Laser and Fruman, *Studies*, 2; Brian Way, "A Tight Three-Movement Structure," in ibid., 190; Arthur Mizener, "The Love Song of J. D. Salinger," in ibid., 210. Mizener associates Salinger's form with "the very American device of conveying meaning by describing object, gesture, action," again invoking American realism (203). See also Alfred Kazin, "J. D. Salinger: 'Everybody's Favorite,'" in ibid., 216–226. Kazin discusses the distinctly American qualities of Salinger's work but focuses on his short fiction. While he calls Salinger an accomplished writer, he sees the work as symptomatic of a general "immaturity" or "lack" in American literature (225).

26. See Belcher and Lee, *Salinger and the Critics;* Laser and Fruman, *Studies;* Malcolm M. Marsden, *If You Really Want to Know: A Catcher Casebook* (Chicago: Scott, Foresman, 1963); and Simonson and Hager, *Clamor vs. Criticism.*
27. The exception is Joyce Rowe, "Holden Caulfield and American Protest," in Jack Salzman, ed., *New Essays on "The Catcher in the Rye"* (Cambridge: Cambridge University Press, 1991): 77–95.
28. Richard Ohmann, "Teaching and Studying Literature at the End of Ideology," in Spurlin and Fischer, *New Criticism*, 83.
29. Jancovich, *Cultural Politics*, 16, 29.
30. Robert Pooley, *America Reads: Good Times through Literature* (Glenville, Ill.: Scott, Foresman, 1951), 402.
31. Examples include American Library Association, *By Way of Introduction: A Book List for Young People* (Chicago: American Library Association, 1947); Adler, *How to Read a Book*; Mortimer J. Adler, *The Great Ideas: A Syntopicon of Great Books of the Western World* (Chicago: Encyclopedia Britannica, 1952); Clifton Fadiman, *Reading I've Liked* (New York: Simon and Schuster, 1941); Clifton Fadiman, *The Lifetime Reading Plan* (1960; reprint, New York: Harper and Row, 1988); and Hutchins, *Great Books*.
32. Gerald Graff, *Literature against Itself: Literary Ideas in Modern Society* (Chicago: University of Chicago Press, 1979), 77.
33. Ransom, *New Criticism*, 184; Fadiman, *Reading I've Liked*, lvii; Harrison Smith, "Manhattan Ulysses, Junior," *Saturday Review of Literature*, 14 July 1951, 13.
34. Hartz, *The Liberal Tradition in America: An Interpretation of American Political Thought Since the Revolution* (New York: Harcourt, Brace, 1955); Emily Dickinson, Poem 1263, in *Final Harvest: Emily Dickinson's Poems*, ed. Thomas H. Johnson (Boston: Little, Brown, 1961), 248, 249.
35. Fadiman, *Reading I've Liked*, xiv; Mark Walhout, "The New Criticism and the Crisis of American Liberalism: The Poetics of the Cold War," *College English* 49, no. 8 (1987): 861–871; Nadel, "Holden and the Cold War." Walhout argues that New Critics manifest "Cold War anxiety and self-doubt" in their efforts to unearth "tension," "ambiguity," and "paradox" (868). Nadel links Holden's struggle for authenticity with Cold War rhetoric and the sociopolitical pressure to search for "phonies," require loyalty oaths, and name names (155, 157–158, 159). Because all truth claims are seen as phony in Cold War discourse, Holden gains credibility by claiming fraudulence, therein attaining what is perceived as authenticity (159).
36. On how museums create nation and national imagination, see Benedict Anderson, "Census, Map, Museum," in *Imagined Communities: Reflections on the Origin and Spread of Nationalism* (New York: Verso, 1998): 163–185.
37. John Higham, "Cult of the 'American Consensus,'" *Commentary* 27 (February 1959): 95.
38. J. D. Salinger, "Teddy," in *Nine Stories* (Boston: Little, Brown, 1991). The story introduces a precocious boy who, like Phoebe, writes in notebooks, reads "poetry books," and quotes verse verbatim (179–180, 185). Even more fascinating is his ability to read people, their lives, and their impending deaths. Like the Caulfields and the Glasses, Teddy is not interested in people who "stay too right on the surface" and privileges those who acknowledge "the real ways of looking at things" (196).
39. Allie is another of Salinger's wise children; and like many Cold War political, social, and literary theorists, the writer places the burden of future social order and niceness on the shoulders of such children.
40. Philip Roth, *The Great American Novel* (New York: Vintage, 1973). Writers from Walt Whitman to Thomas Wolfe have spoken of the Americanness of baseball. See also National Geographic Society, *Baseball As America: Seeing Ourselves through Our National Game* (Washington, D.C.: National Geographic Society, 2002); David Q. Voigt, *America through Baseball* (Chicago: Nelson-Hall, 1976); Jules Tygiel, *Past Time: Baseball As History* (Oxford: Oxford University Press, 2000); Lawrence Baldassaro and Richard Johnson, eds.,

The American Game: Baseball and Ethnicity (Carbondale: Southern Illinois University Press, 2002); Adrian Burgos, Jr., *Playing America's Game: Baseball, Latinos, and the Color Line* (Berkeley: University of California Press, 2007); Mitchell Nathanson, *A People's History of Baseball* (Urbana: University of Illinois Press, 2012); Michael Butterworth, *Baseball and the Rhetoric of Purity* (Tuscaloosa: University of Alabama Press, 2010); Robert Elias, *The Empire Strikes Out: How Baseball Sold U.S. Foreign Policy and Promoted the American Way Abroad* (New York: New Press, 2010); and Carol J. Pierman, "Scorecards, Scrapbooks, and Stats: Girls, Women, and the Game of Baseball," in *The Cooperstown Symposium on Baseball and American Culture, 1998*, ed. Alvin Hall (Jefferson, N.C.: McFarland, 2002): 210–220.

41. Richard Skolnik, *Baseball and the Pursuit of Innocence* (College Station: Texas A&M Press, 1994), 3. Scholars of the game also note that this ideal of Americanness was largely white and male. In the early twentieth century, black and ethnic baseball stars were celebrated as role models and cultural heroes; but the history of the sport was whitewashed into a generalized national narrative until Jackie Robinson joined the Brooklyn Dodgers in 1947.

42. Brower, "Humanities," 75; Bernard Rosenberg, "Mass Culture in America," in Rosenberg and Manning, *Mass Culture*, 5; Cleanth Brooks, "My Credo—The Formalist Critics," in Spurlin and Fischer, *New Criticism*, 49, 50. Even though *Catcher* was a Book of the Month Club selection, his biographical record, Salinger's chosen publishing venues (the *New Yorker*, *Collier's*, and the *Saturday Evening Post*), and his writings themselves suggest that his target audience was not the collective reader. On how mass production influenced the reception of *Catcher*, see Medovoi, *Rebels*.

43. Barzun, *Teacher in America*, 77.

44. A similar deception appears in Salinger's story "Uncle Wiggily in Connecticut," included in *Nine Stories*. The character Eloise cites her husband Lew's "unintelligence" as one cause of her lackluster marriage. When pressed as to why she married him, she responds, "He told me he loved Jane Austen. He told me her books meant a great deal to him. That's exactly what he said. I found out after we were married that he hadn't even read *one* of her books." Lew lies to mask his love of popular fiction—for instance, a book "about four guys that starved to death in an igloo or something" (32). Like Holden, Eloise feels betrayed to discover that her husband is a phony.

45. J. D. Salinger, "Franny," in *Franny and Zooey* (Boston: Little, Brown, 1991). The character Lane exemplifies readers who, according to Franny Glass, "monopoliz[e] conversation" with inane readings, associate with superficial types who insist on "*name*-dropping in a terribly quiet, *casual* voice," and ultimately "*ruin*" novels for other people (11, 25, 15). Like the emblematic type in Whyte's *Organization Man*, Franny's "section man," Lane, is instrumental to consensus creation (14).

46. Macdonald, "Theory of Mass Culture," 72.

47. Holden's condemnation of D.B. parallels Fiedler's well-known critique of Hemingway. Whereas Holden sees D.B. as a shell of his former reader/writer self, Fiedler criticizes Hemingway for imitating "the marvelous spare style that was once a revelation" and becoming "irrelevant, a little boring." He, like Holden, suggests that Hemingway's characters are "playing war"; and he groups the writer into a category of authors who have become "intolerable parodies of their own best work." Fiedler notes that "the youngsters of today are disgusted not only by the dated and ridiculous role which Hemingway, more and more frantically, plays in his own life, but also by his failure to project an adult love, an adult commitment, and adult courage—from which they might at least revolt with dignity" ("Adolescence," 193–194). Interestingly, in 1962, Mary McCarthy identified Salinger as the best candidate "to inherit the mantle of Papa Hemingway" ("J. D. Salinger's Closed Circuit," 245).

48. R. W. B. Lewis, *The American Adam: Innocence, Tragedy, and Tradition in the Nineteenth Century* (Chicago: University of Chicago Press, 1955), 196; Fromm, *Sane Society*, 5.

49. T. Morris Longstreth, "New Novels in the News," in Bloom, *Holden Caulfield*, 6.

50. J. D. Salinger, *Raise High the Roof Beam, Carpenters and Seymour: An Introduction* (1965; reprint, Boston: Little, Brown, 1991). Like Holden, Buddy Glass is haunted by his dead brother, Seymour, who becomes the central character in Buddy's literal and literary world. Their connection typifies the Kierkegaard quotation that Buddy cites: "No. I will not be erased" (95). Seymour is both Buddy's subject and internal audience; consequently, he drives Buddy and, by extension, Salinger.
51. Rowe suggests that readers' silent allegiance with Holden is a token of an ideal communion in which the character's authority and subjectivity are confirmed ("Holden Caulfield," 110).
52. "New Reading Standards Aim to Prep Kids For College—but at What Cost?," *All Things Considered*, 19 January 2013, http://www.npr.org; Ihab Hassan, "The Idea of Adolescence in American Fiction," *American Quarterly* 10, no. 3 (1958): 312–324.
53. "New Reading Standards."
54. Kevin Smokler, *Practical Classics: 50 Reasons to Reread 50 Books You Haven't Touched Since High School* (Amherst, N.Y.: Prometheus, 2013), 233; National Public Radio, "Rereading the Classics: Lessons Learned the Second Time Around," *Talk of the Nation*, 19 January 2013, http://www.npr.org; Harold Bloom, *How to Read and Why* (New York: Scribner, 2001).
55. Smokler, like many critics who write about *Catcher*, slips into a Holdenesque voice when discussing the character and text; even his introduction takes on that quality: "I saw these teachers as criminals who had stolen books I would have enjoyed. . . . Just leave my damn books alone and don't spoil them with . . . with . . . education! The jerks" (*Practical Classics*, 11).

3. Reading to Outmaneuver: Ralph Ellison's *Invisible Man* and African American Literacy in Cold War America

1. Robert Stepto, *From behind the Veil: A Study of Afro-American Narrative* (Urbana: University of Illinois Press, 1979), ix. In the foreword to his anthology *The Classic Slave Narratives*, Henry Louis Gates, Jr., argues that a primary purpose of slave narratives was to assert the slave's desire to be "free and literate" (New York: New American Library, 1987), ix.
2. Elizabeth McHenry notes this erasure of alternate stories of black literacy in *Forgotten Readers: Recovering the Lost History of African American Literary Societies* (Durham, N.C.: Duke University Press, 2002). For literary criticism that clings to the slave narrative myth, see Reggie Young, "On Stepping into Footprints Which Feel Like Your Own: Literacy, Empowerment, and the African-American Literary Tradition," in *Literary Influence and African-American Writers: Collected Essays*, ed. Tracy Mishkin (New York: Garland, 1996): 359–389; Marilyn J. Atlas, "The Issue of Literacy in America: Slave Narratives and Toni Morrison's *The Bluest Eye*," *Midamerica* 27 (2000): 106–118; Henry Louis Gates, Jr., *Figures in Black* (Oxford: Oxford University Press, 1987); Brian Norman, *Neo-Segregation Narratives* (Athens: University of Georgia Press, 2010); Suzanne M. Miller and Barbara McCaskill, *Multicultural Literature and Literacies: Making Space for Difference* (Albany: SUNY Press, 1993); and Valerie Smith, "The Meaning of Narration in *Invisible Man*," in *New Essays on "Invisible Man*," ed. Robert O'Meally (Cambridge: Cambridge University Press, 1988): 189–220. A search of the MLA database will yield many more examples.
3. Anne Meis Knupfer, *Toward a Tenderer Humanity and a Nobler Womanhood* (New York: New York University Press, 1996); Anne Meis Knupfer, *The Chicago Black Renaissance and Women's Activism* (Urbana: University of Illinois Press, 2006); Jacqueline Jones Royster, *Traces of a Stream: Literacy and Social Change among African American Women* (Pittsburgh: University of Pittsburgh Press, 2000); Todd Vogel, ed., *The Black Press: New Literary and Historical Essays* (New Brunswick, N.J.: Rutgers University Press, 2001); McHenry, *Forgotten Readers*; Lara Langer Cohen and Jordan Alexander Stein, eds., *Early African American Print Culture* (Philadelphia: University of Pennsylvania Press, 2012). See also James P.

Danky and Wayne A. Wiegand, eds., *Print Culture in a Diverse America* (Urbana: University of Illinois Press, 1998); and Donald Franklin Joyce, *Black Book Publishers in the United States: A Historical Dictionary of the Presses, 1817–1990* (New York: Greenwood, 1991).
4. Mary Dudziak, *Cold War Civil Rights: Race and the Image of American Democracy* (Princeton: Princeton University Press, 2000).
5. Geneva Smitherman, *Talkin and Testifyin: The Language of Black America* (Boston: Houghton Mifflin, 1977); Geneva Smitherman, *Black Talk: Words and Phrases from the Hood to the Amen Corner* (Boston: Houghton Mifflin, 1994); Geneva Smitherman, *talkin that talk: Language, Culture and Education in African America* (New York: Routledge, 2000); Sonja L. Lanehart, *Sista, Speak! Black Women Kinfolk Talk about Language and Literacy* (Austin: University of Texas Press, 2002); Sonja L. Lanehart, ed., *Sociocultural and Historical Contexts of African American English* (Philadelphia: Benjamin, 2001); Carmen Kynard, *Vernacular Insurrections: Race, Black Protest, and the New Century in Composition-Literacies Studies* (Albany: SUNY Press, 2013).
6. Literacy narratives appear in the autobiographies of Richard Wright, Langston Hughes, Lorraine Hansberry, James Baldwin, Eldridge Cleaver, Malcolm X, Audre Lorde, Samuel R. Delany, Nikki Giovanni, Rita Dove, Maya Angelou, Ralph Ellison, and many other African American writers. In *BookMarks: Reading in Black and White,* Karla FC Holloway points out that most African American writers and thinkers have shared lists of the books that first opened their eyes to the power and potential of reading (New Brunswick, N.J.: Rutgers University Press, 2006). Their literacy autobiographies underscore the complex emotional, social, and political process that reading became for them.
7. James Baldwin, *Go Tell It on the Mountain* (New York: Dell, 1953); Lorraine Hansberry, *A Raisin in the Sun* (1958; reprint, New York: Vintage, 1994); Richard Wright, *Black Boy (American Hunger)* (1944; reprint, New York: HarperCollins, 1993); *The Autobiography of Malcolm X,* with Alex Haley (New York: Ballantine, 1964); Eldridge Cleaver, *Soul on Ice* (New York: Dell, 1968); Toni Morrison, *The Bluest Eye* (New York: Washington Square, 1970); Toni Morrison, *Song of Solomon* (New York: Signet, 1977). Holloway's *BookMarks* is an important source for my thoughts on the ways in which twentieth century African American writers and writings relied on books to narrate who they are and from whence they have come, and to author themselves as individuals, community members, and American citizens.
8. Ralph Ellison, *Invisible Man* (1952; reprint, New York: Vintage International, 1995). Subsequent citations appear in the text.
9. For instance, see Smith, "Meaning of Narration"; Abby Arthur Johnson, "From Ranter to Writer: Ralph Ellison's 'Invisible Man,'" *South Atlantic Bulletin* 42, no. 2 (1977): 35–44; and John Callahan, "Frequencies of Eloquence: The Performance and Composition of *Invisible Man,*" in O'Meally, *New Essays,* 55–94.
10. Exceptions include Robert Stepto and Thomas H. Schaub. Stepto reads *Invisible Man*'s literacy narrative as a break from slave narratives and the "lockstep imposed by the tradition's dominant and prefiguring narrative patterns." Yet even as he analyzes the novel alongside Du Bois rather than Douglass, he continues to read the various papers that the invisible man collects through the lens of the slave narrative tradition, seeing them as failed "protections." Still, he rightfully identifies the invisible man as a poor reader, who "thinks he knows how to read" but "only knows or reads in a very limited way." He is illiterate about "his tribe" and "the non-tribal social structures besetting him" (*From Behind the Veil,* 164, 173). Schaub identifies the invisible man as a reader but only insofar as the narrator's reading informs his writing style and its place within a formal tradition of nineteenth-century realism ("Ellison's Masks and the Novel of Reality," in O'Meally, *New Essays,* 133–141).
11. Addison Gayle, Jr., ed., *The Black Aesthetic* (Garden City, N.Y.: Doubleday, 1971).
12. John Baugh, "Coming Full Circle: Some Circumstances Pertaining to Low Literacy Achievement among African Americans," in *Literacy in African American Communities,*

ed. Joyce L. Harris, Alan G. Kahmi, and Karen E. Pollock (Mahwah, N.J.: Erlbaum, 2001), 279; Patterson Toby Graham, *A Right to Read: Segregation and Civil Rights in Alabama's Public Libraries, 1900–1965* (Tuscaloosa: University of Alabama Press, 2002), 11, 4; A. D. Beittel, "Some Effects of the 'Separate but Equal' Doctrine of Education," *Journal of Negro Education* 20, no. 2 (1951): 141; Eliza Atkins Gleason, *The Southern Negro and the Public Library: A Study of the Government and Administration of Public Library Services to Negroes in the South* (Chicago: University of Chicago Press, 1941), 76–77.

13. Beverly Moss, "From the Pews to the Classrooms: Influences of the African American Church on Academic Literacy," in Harris et al., *Literacy,* 196; Jacqueline Bacon, "The History of *Freedom's Journal*: A Study in Empowerment and Community," *Journal of African American History* 88, no. 1 (2003): 8; Robert S. Levine, "Circulating the Nation: David Walker, the Missouri Compromise and the Rise of the Black Press," in Vogel, *Black Press,* 27.

14. Dudley Taylor Cornish, "The Union Army As a School for Negroes," *Journal of Negro History* 37, no. 4 (1952): 369, 381; Michael Goldhaber, "A Mission Unfulfilled: Freedmen's Education in North Carolina, 1865–1870," *Journal of Negro History* 77, no. 4 (1992): 199; Graham, *Right to Read,* 11; Mary White Ovington, "Selling Race Pride," *Publishers Weekly* 10 January 1925, 112. The hunger for literature and art was apparent in the sell-out crowds attending Langston Hughes's poetry barnstorming tour in 1931; people not only devoured his free pamphlets and broadsides but also bought large quantities of his inexpensive reading materials. See Elizabeth Davey, "Building a Black Audience in the 1930s: Langston Hughes, Poetry Readings, and the Golden Stair Press," in Danky and Wiegand, *Print Culture,* 224–225.

15. Dan R. Lee, "Faith Cabin Libraries: A Study of an Alternative Library Service in the Segregated South, 1932–1960," *Libraries and Culture* 26, no. 1 (1991): 179. Spearheaded by the white minister and educator Willie Lee Buffington, scores of black communities in the South implemented the Faith Cabin program in the early twentieth century. At first Buffington solicited book donations from his religious connections, but eventually the communities themselves banded together to build, organize, and run the libraries: "the success of the program rest[ed] with the communities themselves" (Willie Lee Buffington, "What a Dime and Faith Can Do," in *The Wonderful World of Books,* ed. Alfred Stefferud [Boston: Houghton Mifflin, 1953], 221). The library historian Dan Lee notes that, in the space of ten years, communities in South Carolina had founded twenty-nine Faith Cabin libraries. By March 1960, there was a total of 107 of them in South Carolina and Georgia alone (Lee, "Faith Cabin Libraries," 173, 180).

16. Stephen Schneider, "The Sea Island Citizenship Schools: Literacy, Community Organization, and the Civil Rights Movement," *College English* 70, no. 2 (2007): 155.

17. McHenry, *Forgotten Readers,* 3, 17; Dorothy B. Porter, "The Organized Educational Activities of Negro Literary Societies, 1828–1846," *Journal of Negro Education* 5, no. 4 (1936): 574; Rosie Albritton, "The Founding and Prevalence of African-American Social Libraries and Historical Societies, 1828–1918: Gatekeepers of Early Black History, Collections, and Literature," in *Untold Stories: Civil Rights, Libraries, and Black Librarianship,* ed. John Mark Tucker (Urbana: University of Illinois Press, 1998): 23, 28; Royster, *Traces of a Stream,* 8; and McHenry, *Forgotten Readers,* 18. Circulation numbers for these periodicals were impressive, with *Freedom's Journal* subscription rates reaching "at least 800," a number that does not account for the practice of passing along papers from person to person or purchasing them for reading rooms and Sunday schools. See Bacon, "History," 6, 7.

18. Carter G. Woodson, *The Mis-Education of the Negro* (1933; reprint, Trenton, N.J.: Africa World Press, 1990), 194, 205, xii; Porter, "Organized Educational Activities," 557, 560; Holloway, *BookMarks,* 30; J. Saunders Redding, "American Negro Literature," *American Scholar* 18, no. 2 (1949): 143, 144, 148.

19. Alfred J. Brophy, "*Invisible Man* As Literary Analog to *Brown v. Board of Education,*" in

Ralph Ellison and the Raft of Hope: A Political Companion to Invisible Man, ed. Lucas Morel (Lexington: University Press of Kentucky, 2004), 126.
20. Chas. H. Thompson, "The Negro Child in the American Social Order," *Journal of Negro Education* 19, no. 3 (1950): 216, 217.
21. Beittel, "Some Effects," 146; Frank A. DeCosta, "The Relative Enrollment of Negroes in the Common Schools in the United States," *Journal of Negro Education* 22, no. 3 (1953): 418; American Library Association, *Access to Public Libraries* (Chicago: American Library Association, 1963), xxi.
22. Ralph Ellison, "Brave Words for a Startling Occasion," in *The Collected Essays of Ralph Ellison*, ed. John F. Callahan (New York: Modern Library, 2003), 153.
23. Davey, "Building a Black Audience," 238; Ambrose Caliver, "Certain Significant Developments in the Education of Negroes during the Past Generation," *Journal of Negro History* 35, no. 2 (1950): 112, 134; Carroll L. Miller, "The Relative Educational Attainment of the Negro Population in the United States," *Journal of Negro Education* 22, no. 3 (1953): 388, 390.
24. Augusta Baker, "Reading for Democracy," *Wilson Library Bulletin* 18, no. 2 (1943): 141; E. J. Josey, "Reading Is What's Happening," *Negro History Bulletin* 30, no. 5 (1967): 17, 16; DeCosta, "Relative Enrollment," 429; A. Scott Powell, "Group Identity and Book Interests of College Students," *Journal of Negro Education* 21, no. 4 (1952): 540.
25. "New Negro Book Club to Issue First Book in September," *Publishers Weekly*, 8 June 1946, 3025; Lavinia Lowery Johnson, "Publication of Negro Literature Has a Bright Outlook," *Library Journal* 73 (1948): 182–84; "Negro Press Sees Steady Expansion of Book News," *Publishers Weekly*, 16 November 1946, 2801; Joyce, *Black Book Publishers*; Nancy Larrick, "The All-White World of Children's Books" (1965), reprinted in *Journal of African Children's and Youth Literature* 3 (1991–1992): 1–10.
26. Josey, "Reading and the Disadvantaged," 156. On the American Library Association's failures in the face of Cold War racism, see Louise Robbins, *The Dismissal of Miss Ruth Brown: Civil Rights, Censorship, and the American Library* (Norman: University of Oklahoma Press, 2001). The book describes the campaign against and ultimate firing of a long-time librarian in Bartlesville, Oklahoma, for attempting to integrate the library and forward the cause of civil rights. While the library association "was publicly opposed to library segregation and . . . would attempt to determine the extent of the problem," it refused to "directly participate in the movement to end segregation in libraries" (Graham, *Right to Read*, 123).
27. See "The Read-In," *Newsweek*, 10 April 1961, 27–28; and "'Read-in' Demonstration at Jackson (Miss.) Public Library," *Library Journal* 86 (1961): 1751.
28. Henry G. Badger, "Negro Colleges and Universities: 1900–1950," *Journal of Negro Education* 21, no. 1 (1952): 92.
29. Martin D. Jenkins, "Enrollment in Institutions of Higher Education of Negroes, 1949–1950," *Journal of Negro Education* 19, no. 2 (1950): 204, 205. Jenkins is quick to point out that the numbers were higher than reported because his study did not include integrated schools in the North, summer school or extension courses, or information from non-responding institutions (197).
30. Miller, "Relative Educational Attainment," 400; Chas. H. Thompson, "The Relative Enrollment of Negroes in Higher Educational Institutions in the United States," *Journal of Negro Education* 22, no. 3 (1953): 434. On common school attendance, see DeCosta, "Relative Enrollment," 427–428. On high school attendance, see Miller, "Relative Educational Attainment." On postsecondary attendance, see Joseph S. Himes and A. E. Manley, "The Success of Students in a Negro Liberal Arts College," *Journal of Negro Education* 19, no. 4 (1950): 466–473. On reading ability, see Leander Boykin, "A Summary of Reading Investigations among Negro College Students, 1940–1954," *Journal of Educational Research* 51, no. 6 (1958): 471–475; and Powell, "Group Identity," 183–185.

31. Katherine Clay Bassard, "Gender and Genre: Black Women's Autobiography and the Ideology of Literacy," *African American Review* 26, no. 1 (1992): 120.
32. George Hutchinson and John K. Young, "Introduction," in *Publishing Blackness*, eds. George Hutchinson and John K. Young (Ann Arbor: University of Michigan Press, 2013), 5; Ralph Ellison, "Commencement Address at the College of William and Mary," in *Collected Essays*, 415.
33. Ruth Finnegan, "Literacy As Mythical Charter," in *Literacy: Interdisciplinary Conversations*, ed. Deborah Keller-Cohen (Creskill, N.J.: Hampton, 1994), 35; J. Elspeth Stuckey, *The Violence of Literacy* (Portsmouth, N.H.: Boynton/Cook, 1991), 64, 123.
34. According to Norma R. LeMoine, "[the] *deficient perspective* dates back to the early 1900s, when the language of the descendents of enslaved Africans was viewed as substandard or inferior speech resulting from mental feebleness, inherent anatomical deviations, and, in general, the product of deficient language learners" ("Language Variation and Literacy Acquisition in African American Students," in Harris et al., *Literacy*, 172).
35. LeMoine, "Language Variation," 172; Keith Gilyard, *Let's Flip the Script: An African American Discourse on Language, Literature, and Learning* (Detroit: Wayne State University Press, 1996), 23. During the past thirty years, literacy studies have shown that African American English is a systematic linguistic system with a complex array of rules and patterns "that have been in existence for generations" (William A. Stewart, "Continuity and Change in American Negro Dialects," in *Contemporary English*, ed. David L. Shores [Philadelphia: Lippincott, 1972]: 97). They have also noted ways in which the oral performance of African American English is more complicated than that of standard English. However, such practices continue to be denigrated, thereby maintaining the "power and privileges of the high-prestige groups" (Jerrie Scott and Cheryl Marcus, "Emergent Literacy: Home-School Connections," in Harris et al., *Literacy*, 84).
36. James Baldwin, "Talk to Teachers," *Saturday Review*, 21 December 1963, 42; National Association for the Advancement of Colored People, "An Appeal to the World," reprinted in W.E.B. Du Bois, "Three Centuries of Discrimination," *Crisis* 54 (December 1947): 380; Brophy, "*Invisible Man*," 126; Caliver, "Certain Significant Developments," 111; Charles Morgan, "The Freedom to Read and Racial Problems," *ALA Bulletin* 59, no. 6 (1965): 485; Virginia Lacy Jones, "'How long? Oh, How long?,'" *Library Journal* 87, no. 22 (1962): 4513; "'Read-in' Demonstration," 1751; Dudziak, *Cold War Civil Rights*, 3.
37. James Baldwin, *The Fire Next Time* (1963; reprint, New York: Vintage International, 1993), 87.
38. Beittel, "Some Effects," 147; Ralph Bunche, "Democracy: A World Issue," *Journal of Negro Education* 19, no. 4 (1950): 436–437.
39. Dudziak, *Cold War Civil Rights*, 11, 29; Doug McAdam, *Freedom Summer* (New York: Oxford University Press, 1988), 257–282; Elizabeth Martinez, ed., *Letters from Mississippi* (Brookline, Mass.: Zephyr, 2007), 90. Martinez's book includes a letter from Barb, a Freedom Summer volunteer in Greenville, Mississippi: "The old Negro leaders threatened to put an ad in the paper branding us as Communists. It's a bad situation. A lot of the poor Negroes who are just beginning to get active accuse the old leaders of being directly under the thumb of the white power structure" (90).
40. William J. Maxwell, "Editorial Federalism: The Hoover Raids, the New Negro Renaissance, and the Origins of FBI Literary Surveillance," in Hutchinson and Young, *Publishing Blackness*, 137, 138. For primary documentation of such attacks, see Ward Churchill and Jim Vander Wall, *The COINTELPRO Papers* (Cambridge, Mass.: South End, 2002), chap. 5.
41. Miriam Braverman, "Mississippi Summer," *Library Journal* 90, no. 2 (1965): 5045; Josey, "Reading and the Disadvantaged," 157, 157, 159; Morgan, "Freedom to Read," 487, 485.
42. Martinez, *Letters*, 152; Ralph Ellison, "Roscoe Dunjee and the American Language," in *Collected Essays*, 464. Both Barbara Foley's *Wrestling with the Left: The Making of Ralph Ellison's Invisible Man* (Durham: Duke University Press 2010) and Lucas Morel's edited

volume *Ralph Ellison and the Raft of Hope: A Political Companion to Invisible Man* (Lexington: University Press of Kentucky, 2004) examine Ellison's complicated politics, and many other texts have been written about Ellison as either a radical, a liberal, a conservative, or an "Uncle Tom." My purpose in this chapter is not to nail down his politics but to demonstrate the ways in which *Invisible Man* participated in the postwar conversation about reading and race and articulated particular demands for and of African American citizen-readers in Cold War America.

43. Ralph Ellison, "The Little Man at Cheehaw Station," in *Collected Essays*, 518.
44. Lesley Larkin, "Postwar Liberalism, Close Reading, and 'You': Ralph Ellison's *Invisible Man*," *Lit* 19, no. 3 (2008): 268–304; Alan Nadel, *Invisible Criticism: Ralph Ellison and the American Canon* (Iowa City: University of Iowa Press, 1988), 55; Gates, *Figures in Black*, 243–247.
45. Roderick A. Ferguson, *Aberrations in Black: Toward a Queer of Color Critique* (Minneapolis: University of Minnesota Press, 2003), 59; Smith, "Meaning of Narration," 34. Recalling his own experience, Ellison writes, "At Tuskegee, I couldn't go to a theater without being discriminated against, and in Birmingham, I couldn't move around the streets without worrying about Bull Connor (oh yes, Bull Connor was there even then)." However, he is quick to distinguish between his history and his narrator's, stressing that his own experiences took place while "I was reading T.S. Eliot. I was concerned with the nature of power; I was trying to find a way of relating myself to the major concerns of our society"—a consciousness the invisible man has yet to develop ("On Initiation Rites and Power," in *Collected Essays*, 534–535).
46. In "Letter from Birmingham Jail," Martin Luther King, Jr., wrote, "For years now I have heard the word 'Wait!' It rings in the ear of every Negro with piercing familiarity. This 'Wait' has almost always meant 'Never.' We must come to see, with one of our distinguished jurists, that 'justice too long delayed is justice denied.' We have waited for more than 340 years for our constitutional and God given rights" (in *Why We Can't Wait* [New York: New American Library, 1943], 80–81).
47. Beittel, "Some Effects," 141; E. L. Josey, "Reading: Negro Youths Quest for Certainty," *Negro History Bulletin* 27, no. 7 (1964): 172.
48. Addison Gayle, Jr., "The Literature of Protest," *Negro History Bulletin* 29, no. 3 (1965): 62.
49. Harvey J. Graff, *The Literacy Myth* (New York: Academic Press, 1979); Finnegan, "Literacy As Mythical Charter"; Gates, *Figures in Black*, 21.
50. Stephen Henderson, *Understanding the New Black Poetry: Black Speech and Black Music As Poetic References* (New York: Morrow, 1973), 16.
51. Woodson, *Mis-Education*, xiii, 3, 22, 23, 2.
52. Kenneth Clark, *Prejudice and Your Child* (Boston: Beacon, 1955), 86; Lerone Bennett, Jr., "The Negro in Textbooks: Reading, 'Riting and Racism'," *Ebony* 22 (1967): 134.
53. Morris Dickstein "Ralph Ellison, Race, and American Culture," *Raritan* 18, no. 4 (1999): 44.
54. For an excellent discussion of the principle, see James Seaton, "Affirming the Principle," in Morel, *Raft of Hope*, 22–36.
55. Ibid., 33; Ron Karenga, "Black Cultural Nationalism," and Larry P. Neal, "The Black Arts Movement," both in Gayle, *The Black Aesthetic*, 32, 257. Ellison rejected the separationist philosophy of postwar black nationalism and the Black Arts Movement, which dismisses all European or white art and embraces only black art, as another form of segregation. "For all their talk of black separatism—really another version of secessionism, an old American illusion which arises whenever groups reach an explosive point of frustration—and for all their stance of alienation, they are really acting out a state of despair" brought about by persistent white opposition to black self-determination ("Haverford Statement," in *Collected Essays*, 436). Likewise, those involved in the Black Arts Movement found no common ground or value in Ellison's work, labeling him an Uncle Tom and an assimilationist and calling him emasculated and inhuman. On the younger generation's reception

of Ellison, see Myler Weber, *Consuming Silences* (Athens: University of Georgia Press, 2005), chap. 5.
56. Even though he ends with a claim that could be read as reinscribing him and his readers into yet another a lock-step program—"Who knows but that, on the lower frequencies, I speak for you?" (581)—the words "who knows" speaks to his uncertainty and his unwillingness to dictate "the" way "for" readers to read his words. He suggests a possibility and a possible connection, not unlike Walt Whitman's "Crossing Brooklyn Ferry" to which he alludes, and in which he sees promise.
57. LeRoi Jones, "Problems of the Negro Writer," *Saturday Review*, 20 April 1963, 21.
58. The subtitle of this section quotes from Ralph Ellison, "Hidden Name and Complex Fate," in *Collected Essays*, 199.
59. Ibid., 198–199.
60. Ibid., 200.
61. Ibid., 202, 203; Ralph Ellison, "The World and the Jug," in *Collected Essays*, 164, 185; Ellison, "Hidden Name," 208.
62. Ellison, "The World and the Jug," 169; Ralph Ellison, "Harlem Is Nowhere," in *Collected Essays*, 326; Ellison, "The World and the Jug," 169, 171.
63. Ellison, "The World and the Jug," 178.
64. For representative documents, see Students for a Democratic Society, *The Port Huron Statement* (1962; reprint, New York: Students for a Democratic Society, 1964); and Gayle, *Black Aesthetic*.
65. Robert E. Cushman, "Our Civil Rights Become a World Issue," *New York Times Magazine*, 11 January 1948; Ellison, "The World and the Jug," 169. By representing the invisible man's education as a mis-education, Ellison's text parallels the arguments in *Brown v. Board of Education*. As Brophy writes, "both the novel and the decision stem from a similar moral vision and both reject moral evasions" (*"Invisible Man,"* 129).
66. Ralph Ellison, "What These Children Are Like," in *Collected Essays*, 546–547.
67. Ibid., 549, 551.
68. Ibid., 553–554.

4. Reading against the Machine: Oedipa Maas and the Quest for Democracy in Thomas Pynchon's *The Crying of Lot 49*

1. Thomas Pynchon, *The Crying of Lot 49* (1966; reprint, New York: Perennial Fiction Library, 1990). Further citations appear in the text.
2. Pynchon scholars primarily focus on readings of *Lot 49* and rarely on reading in the novel. Representative essays include Thomas H. Schaub, "'A Gentle Chill, an Ambiguity': *The Crying of Lot 49*," in *Critical Essays on Thomas Pynchon*, ed. Richard Pearce (Boston: Hall, 1981): 51–68; Edward Mendelson, "The Sacred, the Profane, and *The Crying of Lot 49*," in *Individual and Community: Variations on a Theme in American Fiction*, ed. Kenneth H. Baldwin and David K. Kirby (Durham, N.C.: Duke University Press, 1975): 182–222; Kashihara Toshiki, "The Subject Given to/by the Other: Reading *The Crying of Lot 49* through Optical Metaphors," *Studies in American Literature* 38 (2001): 113–133; Frank Kermode, "The Use of Codes in *The Crying of Lot 49*," in *Thomas Pynchon: Modern Critical Views*, ed. Harold Bloom (New York: Chelsea House, 1986): 11–14; Richard Poirier, "The Importance of Thomas Pynchon," in Bloom, *Thomas Pynchon*, 47–58; George Levine, "Risking the Moment," in Bloom, *Thomas Pynchon*, 59–77; Maureen Quilligan, "Thomas Pynchon and the Language of Allegory," in Bloom, *Thomas Pynchon*, 111–137; Peter Cooper, *Signs and Symptoms: Thomas Pynchon and the Contemporary World* (Berkeley: University of California Press, 1983); C. E. Nicholson and R. W. Stevenson, "'Words You Never Wanted to Hear': Fiction, History, and Narratology in *The Crying of Lot 49*," in *Tropic Crucible: Self and Theory in Language and Literature*, ed. Ranjit Chatterjee and Colin Nicholson (Singapore: Singapore University Press, 1984): 297–315; and Debra Moddelmog, "The Oedipus

Myth and Reader Response in Pynchon's *The Crying of Lot 49*," *Papers on Language and Literature* 23, no. 3 (1987): 240–249.
3. Nicholson and Stevenson correctly argue that Pynchon's text works to "decondition" conventional modes of meaning making and "conventional assumptions about the relation between fiction and the wider world in which it is written." Yet like many other Pynchon scholars, they reduce the historical to events in the text and do not recognize the text itself as an event in or part of history ("Words," 313–314). An exception is Chris Hall, who asserts that *Lot 49* represents the postmodern text and Oedipa the postmodern reader. He criticizes other Pynchon scholars for not grounding Oedipa-as-reader within the larger critical context of postmodernism. Nonetheless, he does little to situate Pynchon in relation to the political and cultural discourses of reading that existed outside the Cold War academy and treats postmodernism in the abstract rather than historically ("'Behind the Hieroglyphic Streets': Pynchon's Oedipa Maas and the Dialectics of Reading," *Critique* 33, no. 1 [1991]: 63–77).
4. Jacques Barzun, *Teacher in America* (Boston: Little, Brown, 1945), 287.
5. Deborah Madsen argues that, within *Lot 49*'s romantic narrative, Oedipa experiences a "clash of conservativism and innovation, old and new, the past and present." I agree but see those clashes as representative of a shift in postwar reading and readership ("Pynchon's Quest Narratives and the Tradition of American Romance," in *Approaches to Teaching Pynchon's "The Crying of Lot 49" and Other Works*, ed. Thomas H. Schaub [New York: Modern Language Association, 2008], 30).
6. Barzun, *Teacher in America,* 277, 281; Tom Engelhardt, *The End of Victory Culture* (Amherst: University of Massachusetts Press, 1995), 113; Winston Churchill, "The Sinews of Peace," in *Winston S. Churchill: His Complete Speeches, 1897–1963,* ed. Robert Rhodes James (New York: Chelsea House, 1974), 7290.
7. Dwight D. Eisenhower, "First Inaugural Address" (20 January 1953), "Atoms for Peace" (8 December 1953), "Annual Message to the Congress on the State of the Union" (2 February 1953), all available at http://www.eisenhower.archives.gov; George Kennan, "Long Telegram" (22 February 1946), http://nsarchive.gwu.edu.
8. Kennan, "Long Telegram."
9. John Foster Dulles, "Thoughts on Soviet Foreign Policy and What to Do about It: Part 1," *Life,* 3 June 1946, 113. Dulles scholars note his rigorous research, study, and learning in their discussions of his person and practices. For example, see Richard J. Immerman, *John Foster Dulles: Piety, Pragmatism, and Power in U.S. Foreign Policy* (Wilmington, Del.: SR Books, 1999), 28; and Chris Tudda, *The Truth Is Our Weapon* (Baton Rouge: Louisiana State University Press, 2006), 19.
10. Dulles, "Thoughts: Part 1," 113; Tudda, *Truth,* 19.
11. Dulles, "Thoughts: Part 1," 113, 126, 114; John Foster Dulles, "Thoughts on Soviet Foreign Policy and What to Do about It: Part 2," *Life,* 10 June 1946, 120.
12. Kennan, "Long Telegram."
13. Ibid.; J. Edgar Hoover, *Masters of Deceit* (New York: Holt, 1958), viii.
14. Seth Rosenfeld, *Subversives: The FBI's War on Student Radicals and Reagan's Rise to Power* (New York: Farrar, Straus, and Giroux, 2012), 29, 71.
15. Joseph McCarthy, "Enemies from Within" (9 February 1950), http://historymatters.gmu.edu.
16. Ibid.; Joseph McCarthy, *McCarthyism: The Fight for America* (1952; reprint, New York: Arno, 1977), 7. In his Wheeling speech, McCarthy announced that he had a list of 205 Communists who were working in the U.S. government. Later he changed that total to 57, 81, 10, and other numbers. He also employed facts creatively in other public speeches and in the House Committee on Un-American Activities sessions he chaired. The 1962 film *The Manchurian Candidate* parodied McCarthy's shifting numbers, and both Edward R. Murrow's CBS newsmagazine *See It Now* and the televised Army-McCarthy hearings exposed the senator's misuse of facts, deliberate falsifications, and

misinformation campaigns. On his rhetoric, methods, and attacks, see Ellen Schrecker, *Many Are the Crimes: McCarthyism in America* (Princeton: Princeton University Press, 1998).
17. Jack Beall, "The Community Program—What to Do at Local Levels," in *Red Exposure* (Indianapolis: American Legion, 1948), 223.
18. These guides call to mind the many "how to read *The Crying of Lot 49*" texts that have emerged since the novel's publication, most recently Schaub's *Approaches*.
19. Robert C. Pooley, Irvin C. Poley, Jean Cravens Leyda, and Lillian Zellhoefer, *Good Times through Literature* (Chicago: Scott, Foresman, 1951), 5.
20. John Gassner, "Plays: A Vast Territory of Enjoyment," in *The Wonderful World of Books*, ed. Alfred Stefferud (Boston: Houghton Mifflin, 1953), 47–48; Leo Marx, *The Machine in the Garden* (Oxford: Oxford University Press, 2000), 205, 187, 185, 181; Thomas Riggs, Jr., "What Good Are Poems?" in Stefferud, *Wonderful World*, 44.
21. Advertisement for the Mid-Century Book Society (1962), reproduced in Mark Krupnick, *Lionel Trilling and the Fate of Cultural Criticism* (Evanston, Ill.: Northwestern University Press, 1985), n.p.; Charles F. Strubbe, Jr., "The Great Books Program," in Stefferud, *Wonderful World*, 216; Frank Jennings, *This Is Reading* (New York: Dell, 1965), 147; Charles Lee, *The Hidden Public: The Story of the Book-of-the-Month Club* (Garden City, N.Y.: Doubleday, 1958), 29. For more on the Book of the Month Club, see Joan Shelley Rubin, "Between Culture and Consumption: The Mediations of the Middlebrow" in *The Power of Culture*, ed. Richard Wightman Fox and T. J. Jackson Lears (Chicago: University of Chicago Press, 1993), 162–191; Janice Radway, "The Book-of-the-Month Club and the General Reader," in *Reading in America: Literature and Social History*, ed. Cathy N. Davidson (Baltimore: Johns Hopkins University Press, 1989), 259–284; and Janice Radway, *A Feeling for Books* (Chapel Hill: University of North Carolina Press, 1999).
22. "*Mad* Looks at Book Clubs," *Mad* 49 (September 1959): 10–13; Krupnick, *Lionel Trilling*, 134. Nonetheless, while Trilling criticized this culture industry, his essays and position as board member for both the Mid-Century and Readers' book clubs make him guilty of a similar crime. He believed he was offering a higher standard of books and reading experience, but the clubs for which he worked were commercial ventures that commodified reading and relied on readers' desire to sit in "this chair" with great thinkers and men (advertisement for the Mid-Century Book Society).
23. John Crowe Ransom, *The New Criticism* (Westport, Conn.: Greenwood, 1941), 41, 44; René Wellek, "The New Criticism: Pro and Contra," in *The New Criticism and Contemporary Literary Theory: Connections and Continuities*, ed. William J. Spurlin and Michael Fischer (New York: Garland, 1995), 64.
24. William J. Spurlin, "Introduction," in Spurlin and Fischer, *New Criticism*, xvii; Gerald Graff, *Literature against Itself: Literary Ideas in Modern Society* (Chicago: University of Chicago Press, 1979), 133; Krupnick, *Lionel Trilling*, 144–145. Christopher Norris also recognizes that both New Criticism and structuralism were "subject to various domesticating pressures which effectively sealed off its more disturbing implications" (*Deconstruction: Theory and Practice* [New York: Methuen, 1982], 15).
25. Reuben A. Brower and Richard Poirier, eds., *In Defense of Reading: A Reader's Approach to Literary Criticism* (New York: Dutton, 1962), vii, viii, ix.
26. Ibid., vii, x; Frank Lentricchia, *After the New Criticism* (Chicago: University of Chicago Press, 1980), 110. Notably, Lentricchia neglects to account for Ransom's idea of texture and the locality of reader-author vis-à-vis the text.
27. Vance Packard, *The Status Seekers* (New York: McKay, 1959), 152, 151; Hellmut Lehmann-Haupt, *The Life of the Book* (London: Abelard-Schuman, 1957), 218; Jennings, *This Is Reading*, 7; Helen E. Haines, *Living with Books: The Art of Book Selection* (1935; reprint, New York: Columbia University Press, 1950), 9.
28. Postwar men also read magazines and were criticized for doing so. However, mass-market

magazines were more often gendered toward females whereas newspapers were gendered toward males.

29. William S. Gray and Bernice Rogers, *Maturity in Reading* (Chicago: University of Chicago Press, 1956), 149; Lester Asheim, "A Survey of Recent Research," in *Reading for Life*, ed. Jacob M. Price (Ann Arbor: University of Michigan Press, 1959), 15.

30. On comparative enrollment and its change during the second half of the twentieth century, see Claudia Goldin, Lawrence F. Katz, and Ilyana Kuziemko, "The Homecoming of American College Women: The Reversal of the College Gender Gap," *Journal of Economic Perspectives*, 20, no. 4 (2006): 139. In *When Men Were the Only Models We Had*, Carolyn G. Heilbrun recalls studying with Barzun, Fadiman, and Trilling at Columbia University immediately after World War II. The book describes a general cultural environment in which women readers and scholars were either not considered or were trained to "wr[i]te about guys, and [think] about guys, and read as a guy: what else was possible?" (Philadelphia: University of Pennsylvania Press, 2002), 3.

31. Krupnick, *Lionel Trilling*, 49–50; Barzun, *Teacher in America*, 250; Clifton Fadiman, *Reading I've Liked* (New York: Simon and Schuster, 1943), xxviii.

32. Betty Friedan, *The Feminine Mystique* (New York: Norton, 1997), 157. For examples of sex-directed curricula, see George W. Norvell, *The Reading Interests of Young People* (Boston: Heath, 1950); and Geneva R. Hanna and Mariana K. McAllister, *Books, Young People, and Reading Guidance* (New York: Harper, 1960). Both books see sex and gender as central to what and how reading is taught, appeal to gender stereotypes in discussing interests, recognize the role that books play in socialization, and recommend appropriate books for girls and boys.

33. Mary S. Switzer, "Is a Woman's Work Never Done?," in Stefferud, *Wonderful World*, 131; Bernard Berelson, "Who Reads What Books and Why?," in *Mass Culture*, ed. Bernard Rosenberg and David Manning White (Glencoe, Ill.: Free Press, 1957), 119. There were only two female contributors to *Mass Culture*, although the collection featured the work of more than fifty scholars.

34. Friedan, *Feminine Mystique*, 180.

35. Ibid., 15; Barzun, *Teacher in America*, 4; Fadiman, *Reading I've Liked*, xxviii.

36. Gray and Rogers, *Maturity in Reading*, 129, 115, 114, 152, 156, 150.

37. Barzun, *Teacher in America*, 250.

38. Krupnick, *Lionel Trilling*, 115; Thomas Pynchon, "Introduction," in *Slow Learner: Early Stories* (Boston: Little, Brown, 1985), 6, 22; Henry Steele Commager, *The American Mind* (New Haven: Yale University Press, 1950), 413. Commager claimed that those leading the charge to neutralize American ideas were themselves poor readers and scholars, even by their own definition of good reading: "they were dogmatic about traditional economic virtues without familiarizing themselves with the most elementary facts of American economic history" (414).

39. Robert W. Iversen, *The Communists and the Schools* (New York: Harcourt, Brace, 1959), 345. For in-depth discussions of Cold War attacks on intellectuals, academics, and universities, see Iversen's book and Ellen Schrecker, *No Ivory Tower: McCarthyism and the Universities* (Oxford: Oxford University Press, 1986).

40. Hanna and McAllister, *Books*, 120.

41. Iversen, *Communists and the Schools*, 344.

42. On Oedipa as a New Critical reader, see Nicholson and Stevenson, "Words"; and Carolyn Brown, "Waste, Death, and Destiny: Heterotopic Scenarios in *The Crying of Lot 49*," in *Thomas Pynchon: Reading from the Margins*, ed. Niran Abbas (Madison, N.J.: Fairleigh Dickinson University Press, 2003), 154–161.

43. Schrecker, *Many Are the Crimes*, 225.

44. Graff has noted that postmodern critics of New Critics called them "Puritans" and accused them of being close-minded (*Literature*, 82).

45. John Farrell, "The Romance of the '60s: Self, Community and the Ethical in *The Crying of Lot 49*," *Pynchon Notes* 30–31 (1992): 144.
46. Kai Bird and Martin J. Sherwin, *American Prometheus: The Triumph and Tragedy of Robert J. Oppenheimer* (New York: Vintage, 2006); Rosenfeld, *Subversives*.
47. J. Edgar Hoover, "'A Nation's Call to Duty': Commencement Address, St. John's University Law School, 11 June 1942," quoted in Richard Gid Powers, *Secrecy and Power: The Life of J. Edgar Hoover* (New York: Free Press, 1987), 263; Leon F. Litwack, "Preface," in *The Free Speech Movement: Reflections on Berkeley in the 1960s*, ed. Robert Cohen and Reginald E. Zelnik (Berkeley: University of California Press, 2002), xvi–xvii.
48. J. Edgar Hoover, "Excerpts from an Address by J. Edgar Hoover to Catholic University Alumni" (13 November 1954), quoted in Anthony Bouscaren, *A Guide to Anti-Communist Action* (Chicago: Regnery, 1958), 226.
49. Michael V. Miller and Susan Gilmore, ed., *Revolution at Berkeley* (New York: Dial, 1965); Irving Howe, "Introduction," in ibid., xvi, xvii; Clark Kerr, "Selections from *The Uses of the University*," in *The Berkeley Student Revolt: Facts and Interpretations*, ed. Seymour Martin Lipset and Sheldon S. Wolin (Garden City, N.Y.: Anchor, 1965), 47.
50. Richard Fallenbaum, "University Abdicates Social Responsibility," in Lipset and Wolin, *Berkeley Student Revolt*, 65; Robert Cohen, "The Many Meanings of the FSM," in Cohen and Zelnik, *Free Speech Movement*, 21.
51. Oedipa also encounters students on the political right, including the Young Americans for Freedom, a popular 1960s coalition of conservatives and libertarians with ties to William F. Buckley, Jr. The group focused on individual liberties and thus, like students in the burgeoning New Left, was invested in the ideas of individual integrity outlined by the Free Speech Movement.
52. The idea that reading could be democraticizing, pluralistic, and uncertain was a governing idea in the New Criticism before it became institutionalized and domesticated.
53. Oedipa's changing mode of reading is foreshadowed in the novel's earlier scenes. For instance, while watching *The Courier's Tragedy*, she notes that "a gentle chill, an ambiguity, begins to creep in among the words" as mute actors indicate that they have "become aware of a possibility" different from the mode of interpretation hitherto presented in the play (71–72). Another early harbinger is the visit from the Shadow, whose many voices anticipate and thematize the "metaphor of God knew how many parts" (109). Likewise, her early phone conversation with Pierce is marked by a "quiet ambiguity" (12).
54. Pynchon, "Introduction," in *Slow Learner*, 6.
55. For a discussion of this terminology, see Schrecker, *Many Are the Crimes*, 169, 377. Examples are fairly common in postwar reading guides. While most authors hoped to promote reading, they often contrasted good Cold War readers with those who were "bookish" or "egg head[ed]" (Jennings, *This Is Reading*, 100, 119).
56. Hall calls this Pynchon's "ambivalent personification of the postmodern reader" ("Behind the Hieroglyphic Streets," 64).
57. Michael Harrington, *The Other America* (1962; reprint, New York: Scribner, 1997).
58. Thomas Pynchon, *Gravity's Rainbow* (1973; reprint, New York: Penguin, 1995), 740.
59. In "Reconsideration—The New Critics," New Criticism defector Murray Kreiger reexamines both the theory and its interpretations, which were said to bring about a wholly new way of reading. He notes (as do many who have followed him) that structuralism and poststructuralism are predicated on ideas about the centrality of language, ideas that are at "the very heart of New-Critical doctrine." Yet he argues that postmodern critics are "narcissistic" because they make all interpretation about themselves, and he accuses them of equalizing and therein reducing everything under the mantle of *écriture* (in *Poetic Presence and Illusion* [Baltimore: Johns Hopkins University Press, 1979], 111, 113, 113). William E. Cain also claims that deconstruction limits itself because it does not see anything as being intrinsic ("Robert Penn Warren, Paul de Man, and the Fate of Criticism" in Spurlin and Fischer, *New Criticism*, 315).

60. Graff, *Literature*, 58.
61. Jacques Derrida, "Structure, Sign and Play in the Discourse of the Human Sciences," in *Writing and Difference*, trans. Alan Bass (Chicago: University of Chicago Press, 1978), 292, 289, 293. As I will discuss in chapter 5, his characterization of structuralism as limited and exhausted is informed in part by his desire to be new, or post-. William J. Spurlin demonstrates that postmodern theories of reading falsely claim to "have (supposedly) liberated the reader from the tyranny of the text by considering the reader's role in textual understanding" ("New Critical and Reader-Oriented Theories of Reading: Shared Views on the Role of the Reader," in Spurlin and Fischer, *New Criticism*, 229).
62. Norman Mailer, *The Armies of the Night* (1968; reprint, New York: Plume, 1994), 288.

5. Metafiction and Radical Democracy: Getting at the Heart of John Barth's *Lost in the Funhouse*

1. John Barth, "The Literature of Exhaustion," in *The Friday Book* (New York: Putnam, 1984), 63.
2. Kenneth J. Heineman, *Campus Wars* (New York: New York University Press, 1993), 35. Events in Buffalo in 1968 included an antiwar Strike for Knowledge; a faculty senate resolution condemning the Vietnam War; a student protest of a Nixon visit, resulting in the arrest of the Buffalo Nine; a confrontation between draft resisters and police, FBI officials, and federal marshals inside the Elmwood Unitarian Church; protests against Dow Chemical; the destruction of a ROTC construction site; a 1,000 person all-night sit-in at SUNY-Buffalo's Norton Union; and a weeklong protest involving Yippie leader Jerry Rubin. During and after these actions, the city police department, with the cooperation of campus security and disgruntled university administration officials, began "wire tapping activists' telephones, photographing peace demonstrations, and tailing prominent faculty antiwar leaders" (209–210, 212–215, 35). In a 1981 interview, Barth commented that "1968 was even more extraordinary and turbulent [than 1969]; it's the one that is most commonly considered the 'Big Bang' year. . . . the cultural watershed year in that decade" (Charlie Reilley, "An Interview with John Barth," *Contemporary Literature* 22, no.1 [1981]: 15).
3. Barth, "Literature of Exhaustion," 64.
4. Reilley, "Interview," 16, 6–8. In 1982, Barth remarked that "as a writer I'm glad to have sniffed the tear gas and to have heard—if only like Odysseus tied to the mast—the siren songs of Marshall McLuhan and my friend Leslie Fiedler" ("Some Reasons Why I Tell the Stories I Tell the Way I Tell Them Rather Than Some Other Sort of Stories Some Other Way," in *The Friday Book*, 11–12).
5. John Barth, "Muse, Spare Me," in *The Friday Book*, 55; John Carlos Rowe, "Postmodernist Studies," *Redrawing the Boundaries*, ed. Stephen Greenblatt and Giles Gunn (New York: Modern Language Association, 1992), 187.
6. John Barth, *Lost in the Funhouse* (1968; reprint, New York: Bantam, 1969), 92. Further citations appear in the text. An exception to this critical trend is Thom Seymour, who suggests that the seeming de-contextualization of the title story is a "joke." Despite Ambrose's self-conscious attempts to remove details of name, time, and place in the title story, the tale is full of hints that draw readers' attention to the World War II context ("One Small Joke and a Packed Paragraph in John Barth's 'Lost in the Funhouse,'" *Studies in Short Fiction* 16, no. 3 [1979]: 190).
7. Barth, "Literature of Exhaustion," 70; Students for a Democratic Society (SDS), *The Port Huron Statement* (1962; reprint, New York: Students for a Democratic Society, 1964), 2.
8. Edgar H. Knapp, "Found in the the Barthhouse: Novelist As Savior," in *Critical Essays on John Barth*, ed. Joseph J. Waldmeir (Boston: Hall, 1980), 187; Beth A. Boehm, "Educating Readers: Creating New Expectations in *Lost in the Funhouse*," in *Reading Narrative: Form, Ethics, Ideology*, ed. James Phelan (Columbus: Ohio State University Press, 1989),

118; Michael Carey, "Barth's *Lost in the Funhouse*," *Explicator* 52, no. 2 (1994): 122; Brian Edwards, "Deconstructing the Artist and the Art: Barth and Calvino at Play in the Funhouse of Language," *Canadian Review of Comparative Literature* 12, no. 2 (1985): 268.

9. The New Left was comprised of many loosely affiliated groups that only sometimes worked together: SDS, the Yippies, the Diggers, the Weathermen, the Young Lords, the Black Panthers, the Asian American Political Alliance, the Third World Liberation Front, the American Indian Movement, the Progressive Labor Party, the Gay Liberation Front, anti-nuke activists, women's liberation organizations, and many others. For an excellent study, see Van Gosse, *Rethinking the New Left: An Interpretive History* (New York: Palgrave, 2005). In this chapter, I focus predominantly on Students for a Democratic Society (before its split into multiple factions) because it "[became] known, among other things, as the '*writingest*' organization around" (Kirkpatrick Sale, *SDS: The Rise and Development of Students for a Democratic Society* [New York: Random House, 1973], 125). Importantly, the period also saw the rise of the New Right, a movement comprised of student organizations, conservative single-issue groups, and conservative evangelicalism (see chap. 6).

10. Thomas Pynchon, *The Crying of Lot 49* (1966; reprint, New York: Perennial, 1990), 103.

11. SDS, *Port Huron*, 3; Alvin Johnson, *The Public Library—A People's University* (New York: American Association for Adult Education, 1938), 68; Mario Savio, "An End to History," in *The Politics and Anti-Politics of the Young*, ed. Michael Brown (1964; reprint, London: Glencoe, 1969), 35; Norman Mailer, *The Armies of the Night* (1968; reprint, New York: Plume, 1994), 86; David M. Potter, *People of Plenty* (Chicago: University of Chicago Press, 1954).

12. Geneva R. Hanna and Mariana K. McAllister, *Books, Young People, and Reading Guidance* (New York: Harper, 1960), 31; *Teachers for Our Times: A Statement of Purposes by the Commission on Teacher Education* (Washington, D.C.: American Council on Education, 1944), 114; SDS, *Port Huron*, 4, 4–5; E. L. Doctorow, *The Book of Daniel* (New York: Plume, 1971), 301; Larry D. Spence, "Berkeley: What It Demonstrates," in Brown, *Politics and Anti-Politics*, 41; Mailer, *Armies*, 92.

13. Edward Bloomberg, *Student Violence* (Washington, D.C.: Public Affairs Press, 1970), 45; Brown, *Politics and Anti-Politics*, 129; William L. O'Neill, *Coming Apart: An Informal History of America in the 1960's* (Chicago: Quadrangle, 1971), 291. Some faculty and administrators did get involved—for example, Leslie Fiedler in Buffalo or faculty members at Columbia who were working to find a peaceable solution to the campus takeover. For more examples, see Heineman, *Campus Wars*.

14. U.S. Congress, House Committee on Internal Security, "SDS Plans for America's High Schools" (Washington, D.C.: U.S. Government Printing Office, 1969), 1. Other targeted organizations included Martin Luther King, Jr.'s, Southern Christian Leadership Coalition, the Student Nonviolent Coordinating Committee, the Black Panthers, and the American Indian Movement. For more on these repressive efforts, see Ward Churchill and Jim Vander Wall, *The COINTELPRO Papers: Documents from the FBI's Secret Wars against Dissent in the United States* (Boston: South End, 2001).

15. Kristin L. Matthews, "The Medium, the Message, the Movement: Print Culture and New Left Politics," in *Pressing the Fight: Print, Propaganda, and the Cold War*, ed. Greg Barnhisel and Catherine Turner (Amherst: University of Massachusetts Press, 2010), 31–49.

16. For documentation, see Churchill and Vander Wall, *COINTELPRO PAPERS*.

17. U.S. Congress, House Committee on Internal Security, "Investigation of Students for a Democratic Society. Part 7-B: SDS Activities at Fort Dix, N.J." (Washington, D.C.: U.S. Government Printing Office, 1969), 2435; U.S. Congress, "SDS Plans," 6, 9, 11, 12.

18. Mailer, *Armies*, 91.

19. SDS, *Port Huron*, 4; Students for a Democratic Society (SDS), *America and the New Era* (New York: Students for a Democratic Society, 1963), 13, 15.

20. SDS, *Port Huron*, 58; O'Neill, *Coming Apart*, 279; SDS, *America*, 18; SDS, *Port Huron*, 5, 5, 4.

21. SDS, *America*, 18; Thomas Hayden, "A Letter to the New (Young) Left," in *The New Student Left*, ed. Mitchell Cohen and Dennis Hale (Boston: Bean, 1966), 8; SDS, *Port Huron*, 61.
22. Seth Rosenfeld, *Subversives: The FBI's War on Student Radicals and Reagan's Rise to Power* (New York: Farrar, Straus, and Giroux, 2012), 22; SDS, *Port Huron*, 61.
23. John McDermott, "Knowledge Is Power," in *The Movement toward a New America*, ed. Mitchell Goodman (New York: Knopf, 1970), 343; SDS, *Port Huron*, 9; Thomas Hayden, "Student Social Action," in Cohen and Hale, *New Student Left*, 286; James Miller, *"Democracy Is in the Streets": From Port Huron to the Siege of Chicago* (New York: Simon and Schuster, 1987), 80.
24. SDS, *Port Huron*, 50; Hayden, "Letter," 2, 3; Steven V. Roberts, "Why Students Want Power," in Brown, *Politics and Anti-Politics*, 47.
25. SDS, *Port Huron*, 2, 7; Matthews, "The Medium," 32, 37; Kenneth Keniston, "Young Radicals and the Fear of Power," in Brown, *Politics and Anti-Politics*, 51.
26. Sale, *SDS*, 125, 255; Louis Menashe and Ronald Radosh, *Teach-Ins: U.S.A.* (New York: Praeger, 1967), 343; Alan Adelson, *SDS* (New York: Scribner, 1972), 177.
27. Hayden, "Letter," 5.
28. Ibid., 6.
29. SDS, *Port Huron*, 6, 6–7.
30. Ibid., 6; Miller, *Democracy*, 143. In interrogating possible meanings of participatory democracy, Miller likens the term to a "labyrinth" that is "remarkable" for its "*resonance*—its multiple layers of implied meaning, . . . its *elasticity*—the ease with which it could be stretched to cover a wide variety of different political situations; and its *instability*—a volatility caused, in part, by its range of different possible meanings and the implicit contradictions they contained" (142).
31. SDS, *America*, 26.
32. Arguably, SDS saw itself and its project in terms of Jean-Jacques Rousseau's proposition: that there are times when citizens must "be forced to be free; for such is the condition which, giving each citizen to his country, guarantees that he will not depend on any person" (*The Social Contract*, trans. Christopher Betts [Oxford: Oxford University Press, 1994], 58). As the organization's materials make clear, members believed Americans had been brainwashed by Cold War reading programs and rhetorics that aimed to circumscribe their means of interpreting the world. They saw it as their duty to de-program and open citizen-readers' minds to new interpretive modes (see chap. 4).
33. SDS, *Port Huron*, 62; Students for a Democratic Society (SDS), "We've Got to Reach Our Own People," in *Don't Mourn—Organize* (Chicago: Students for a Democratic Society, 1967), 2–9; Mike James, *Getting Ready for the Firing Line* (Oberlin, Ohio: Students for a Democratic Society, 1968), 1–8; Richard Flacks, "Chicago: Organizing the Unemployed" (New York: Students for a Democratic Society/Economic Research and Action Project, 1964), 8; Miller, *Democracy*, 150.
34. Sara Evans, *Personal Politics* (New York: Knopf, 1979), 116, 76, 86; Michelle Wallace, "A Black Feminist's Search for Sisterhood," in *All the Women Are White, All the Blacks Are Men, but Some of Us Are Brave*, ed. Gloria T. Hull, Patricia Bell Scott, and Barbara Smith (Old Westbury, N.Y.: Feminist Press, 1982), 6; Evans, *Personal Politics*, 192.
35. Julie Rivkin and Michael Ryan, *Literary Theory: An Anthology* (London: Blackwell, 1998), 335; Frank Lentricchia, "History or the Abyss: Poststructuralism," in *After the New Criticism* (Chicago: University of Chicago Press, 1980), 157–158. See also Rowe, "Postmodernist Studies."
36. Terry Eagleton, *Literary Theory: An Introduction* (Minneapolis: University of Minnesota Press, 2008), 123; Astra Taylor, "Post-'68: Theory Is in the Streets," in *Growing Up Postmodern*, ed. Ronald Strickland (New York: Rowman and Littlefield, 2002), 207; Miller, *Democracy*, 158.

37. Taylor, "Post-'68," 208–210; Eagleton, *Literary Theory,* 123; Mark Rudd, "Columbia: Notes on the Spring Rebellion," in *The New Left Reader,* ed. Carl Oglesby (New York: Grove, 1969), 294; Rowe, "Postmodernist Studies," 184.
38. Hayden, "Letter," 6.
39. Jacques Derrida, "Structure, Sign and Play in the Discourse of the Human Sciences," in *Writing and Difference,* trans. Alan Bass (Chicago: University of Chicago Press, 1978), 281, 288. Derrida participated in the May 1968 demonstrations but was not fully committed to them. As part of the old Communist left, he did not consider himself "what they call a *soixant-huitard.*" He noted: "I was on my guard, even worried in the face of a certain cult of spontaneity, a fusionist, anti-trades-union euphoria, in the face of the finally 'freed' speech. . . . I was not against it, but I have always had trouble vibrating in unison." Though he was skeptical of claims of transparency and liberated language/ speech, his philosophical propositions and readerly methods did work to free readers from interpretive structures. Thus, his work is tied to this movement and its moment, even if he was somewhat unsettled by the connection (Benoit Peeters, *Derrida: A Biography,* trans. Andrew Brown [Cambridge: Polity, 2013]: 197).
40. Geoffrey Hartman, *Beyond Formalism* (New Haven: Yale University Press, 1970), 56.
41. William J. Spurlin, "New Criticism and Reader-Oriented Theories of Reading and Shared Views on the Role of the Reader," in *The New Criticism and Contemporary Literary Theory: Connections and Continuities,* ed. William J. Spurlin and Michael Fischer (New York: Garland, 1995), 229; Michael Fischer, "The New Criticism in the New Historicism: The Recent Work of Jerome J. McGann," in Spurlin and Fischer, *New Criticism,* 321. Spurlin challenges what he sees as the "easy opposition of New Criticism and postmodern" theories of reading (ibid.). Geoffrey Hartman also notes the bias against the New Criticism "found not only in counterecultural students but also in such theorists as Kristéva, Sollers, and Deleuze" (*The Fate of Reading* [Chicago: University of Chicago Press, 1975], 272).
42. John Crowe Ransom, *The New Criticism* (Westport, Conn.: Greenwood, 1941), 335; Frank Lentricchia and Andrew DuBois, "Preface," in *Close Reading: The Reader,* ed. Frank Lentricchia and Andrew DuBois (Durham, N.C.: Duke University Press, 2003), n.p. Gerald Graff goes so far to argue that deconstruction is a conservative interpretive philosophy because it fails to contest the authority and privilege of standard authors and works ("Who Killed Criticism?," in Spurlin and Fischer, *New Criticism,* 119).
43. Paul A. Bové, "Variations on Authority: Some Deconstructive Transformations of the New Criticism," in Spurlin and Fischer, *New Criticism,* 171; William J. Spurlin, "New Critical and Reader-Oriented Theories of Reading: Shared Views on the Role of the Reader," in Spurlin and Fischer, *New Criticism,* 238; William E. Cain, "Robert Penn Warren, Paul de Man, and the Fate of Criticism," in Spurlin and Fischer, *New Criticism,* 307; Graff, *Literature against Itself,* 51, 312, 129; Jonathan Culler, *On Deconstruction: Theory and Criticism after Structuralism* (Ithaca, N.Y.: Cornell University Press, 1982), 220. The New Criticism and postmodernism were radical responses to what their theorists saw as elitist interpretive modes. Yet once they won respectability, they themselves were seen as elitist, and both became somewhat formulaic in practice. As Christopher Norris contends, "in the hands of less subtle and resourceful readers deconstruction can become—it is all too clear—a theoretical vogue as uniform and cramping as the worst New Critical dogma" (*Deconstruction: Theory and Practice* [London: Methuen, 1982], 17).
44. Graff, *Literature against Itself,* 6. Also see Spurlin and Fischer, *New Criticism*; Mark Jancovich, *The Cultural Politics of the New Criticism* (Cambridge: Cambridge University Press, 1993); Thomas Young, ed., *The New Criticism and After: John Crowe Ransom Memorial Lectures, 1975* (Charlottesville: University Press of Virginia, 1976); Lentricchia, *After the New Criticism*; Lentricchia and DuBois, *Close Reading*; and Hartman, *Beyond Formalism.*
45. Roland Barthes, *The Pleasure of the Text,* trans. Richard Miller (New York: Hill and Wang, 1975), 53. Eagleton has remarked, "That reference to the Political Father is not fortuitous.

The Pleasure of the Text was published five years after a social eruption that rocked France's political fathers to their roots. In 1968 the student movement had swept across Europe, striking against the authoritarianism of the educational institutions" (*Literary Theory*, 122–123). The student movements of the late 1960s charged authorities with manipulating language, normalizing convention, and universalizing interpretation in efforts to control others. See Jacques Derrida, "The End of the Book and the Beginning of Writing," in *Of Grammatology*, trans. Gayatri Chakravorty Spivak (Baltimore: Johns Hopkins University Press, 1998), 19.

46. Barthes's proposed methods of reading and interpretation are similar to those originally theorized by the New Critics. In that way, he returns to the root of modern critical theory. See also Derrida, "The End of the Book," in *Of Grammatology*, 6–26.
47. Roland Barthes, "From Work to Text," in *Image Music Text*, trans. and ed. Stephen Heath (New York: Hill and Wang, 1977), 160, 161–163. For those who are well versed in New Critical theory, the word *text* recalls Ransom's use of *texture*—the idea that a literary text has multiple layers of meaning that interact through the process of reading (*New Criticism*, 25, 101,130, 175).
48. Wolfgang Iser, *Implied Reader* (Baltimore: Johns Hopkins University Press, 1974), 275. In Iser's theories of reading, *work* is akin to Barthes's *text*.
49. According to Hayden, "every new act is preceded by . . . the writing of books that somebody has read and passed on" (Tim Findley, "Tom Hayden: *Rolling Stone* Interview, Part 2," *Rolling Stone*, 9 November 1972, 30).
50. Iser, *Implied Reader*, 275; Derrida, "Structure, Sign and Play," 292.
51. Detractors charge postmodernism and the New Criticism with being ahistorical, asocial, and apolitical, condemning them for appealing to idealism and "the purest of pieties." For instance, Lentricchia criticizes them for "pure subjectivism" and their denial of "ontological supports and cultural goals," and he alleges that they claim there is "nothing outside of the text" (*After the New Criticism*, 207, 169, 170). Graff argues that both see texts and language as "unaccountable to external reality" (*Literature against Itself*, 21). Culler contends that deconstruction, like the New Criticism, demonstrates great "concern for purity" among its defenders (*On Deconstruction*, 228). While I read discourse as a social act, I recognize that that it was predominantly reserved for the elite. Postwar Americans most in need of the postmodernism's possibility—the poor, people of color, women, and so on—did not have access to it.
52. The subtitle of *Giles Goat-Boy—The Revised New Syllabus of George Giles Our Grand Tutor*—hints at Barth's move toward examining reading and institutionalized learning itself. In the novel's extended allegory and satire of the Cold War, the university is the world.
53. "Fables for People Who Can Hear with Their Eyes," *Time*, 27 September 1968, 100; Guy Davenport, "Like Nothing Nameable," *New York Times Book Review*, 20 October 1968, 63; Jack Richardson, "Amusement and Revelation," *New Republic*, 23 November 1968, 30; Pete Axthelm, "Tiny Odyssey," *Newsweek*, 30 September 1968, 108.
54. Barth, "Literature of Exhaustion," 69–70, 69; Joe David Bellamy, "Having It Both Ways," *New American Review* 15 (1972): 139.
55. Barth, "Literature of Exhaustion," 68, 70; John Barth, "Literature of Replenishment," in *The Friday Book*, 205. In that collection, Barth asserts that "The Literature of Exhaustion" "has been frequently reprinted and as frequently misread as one more Death of the Novel or Swan-Song of Literature piece. It isn't" (64). Similarly, in "The Literature of Replenishment," he reiterates that people have misunderstood his theory of narrative fiction and his use of conventions "against themselves to generate new and lively work. I would have thought that point unexceptionable. But a great many people . . . mistook me to mean that literature, at least fiction, is *kaput*; that it has all been done already; that there is nothing left for contemporary writers but to parody and travesty our great predecessors in our exhausted medium" (205). For an argument against such nihilism charges, see Steven

M. Bell, "Literature, Self-Consciousness, and Writing: The Example of Barth's *Lost in the Funhouse*," *International Fiction Review* 11, no. 1 (1984): 84–89.

56. Carol Schloss and Khachig Tololyan, "The Siren in the Funhouse: Barth's Courting of the Reader," *Journal of Narrative Technique* 11, no.1 (1981): 65.

57. Beverly Gray Bienstock notes a unity in the text of *Funhouse* ("Lingering in the Autognostic Verge: John Barth's *Lost in the Funhouse*," *Modern Fiction Studies* 19 [1973]: 69–78.) See also Zack Bowen, "Funhouse Reflexes: *Lost in the Funhouse*," in *A Reader's Guide to John Barth* (Westport, Conn.: Greenwood, 1994): 51–65; Carey, "Barth's *Lost in the Funhouse*," 119–122; Gerald Gillespie, "Barth's 'Lost in the Funhouse': Short Story Text in Its Cyclic Context," *Studies in Short Fiction* 12, no. 3 (1975): 223–230; Carol Kyle, "The Unity of Anatomy: Structure of Barth's *Lost in the Funhouse*," *Critique* 13, no. 3 (1972): 31–43; Victor J. Vitanza, "The Novelist As Topologist: John Barth's *Lost in the Funhouse*," *Texas Studies in Literature and Language* 2, no. 1 (1977): 83–97; and Michael Hinden, "*Lost in the Funhouse*: Barth's Use of the Recent Past," *Twentieth-Century Literature* 19, no. 2 (1973): 107–118.

58. Loretta M. Lampkin, "An Interview with John Barth," *Contemporary Literature* 29, no.4 (1988): 489. Oedipa Maas also refers to reading as a process of exfoliation (Pynchon, *Lot 49*, 163).

59. Bové, "Variations,"167; Barth, "Literature of Exhaustion," 70.

60. Bellamy, "Having It Both Ways,"148.

61. Charles Harris, *Passionate Virtuosity: The Fiction of John Barth* (Urbana: University of Illinois Press, 1983), 116; Bell, "Literature," 8; Hayden, "Letter," 8.

62. Hinden, "*Lost in the Funhouse*," 196; Bellamy, "Having It Both Ways," 141.

63. Edwards, "Deconstructing the Artist," 265. Likewise, Linda Westervelt suggests that "Barth on the one hand educates his reader to confront the problem of self-consciousness, at the same time that he challenges himself to play an exemplary game with such a created reader." She proposes that reader, text, and author participate in a mutual creation ("Teller, Tale, Told: Relationships in John Barth's Latest Fiction," *Journal of Narrative Technique* 8, no. 1 [1978]: 42).

64. Knapp, "Found in the Barthhouse," 189.

65. Carey, "Barth's *Lost in the Funhouse*," 122.

66. Robert Liebert, *Radical and Militant Youth: A Psychoanalytic Inquiry* (New York: Praeger, 1971), 20; Spence, "Berkeley," 40.

67. Edwards, "Deconstructing the Artist," 268.

68. Carol Booth Olsen, "Lost in the Madhouse," *Review of Contemporary Fiction* 10, no. 2 (1990): 57; Hayden, "Letter," 6.

69. Westervelt, "Teller," 44; Marjorie Worthington, "Done with Mirrors: Restoring the Authority Lost in John Barth's Funhouse," *Twentieth-Century Literature* 47, no.1 (2001): 114, 116; Boehm, "Educating Readers," 104. At the 2014 Modern Language Association conference in Chicago, an agitated audience member chided me for demoting Barth's artistry and authority in my reading, asserting instead that his central aim was to create malleable readers. Many scholars share this person's point of view.

70. Hayden, "Letter," 6.

71. In "Life-Story," the author-narrator directly addresses the reader, arguing that he has "ruthlessly set about not to win you over but to turn you away[.] Because your own author bless and damn you his life is in your hands! He writes and reads himself; don't you think he knows who gives his creatures their lives and deaths? Do they exist except as he or others read their words?" (124).

72. Hayden, "Letter," 6.

73. Lampkin, "Interview," 489–490; Barthes, "From Work to Text," 164.

74. Nils Clausson argues, "Perhaps the most serious misrepresentation of deconstruction is that it is essentially a negative or nihilist project that condemns us to relativism, anarchy, conservatism, meaninglessness, paralysing undecidability, along with a host of other terrible things" ("Practicing Deconstruction, Again: Blindness, Insight and the Lovely

Treachery of Words in D. H. Lawrence's 'The Blind Man,'" *College Literature* 34, no. 1 [2007], 108). Befuddled observers often called SDS and other New Left groups nihilistic. In an open letter to President Grayson Kirk of Columbia University, Mark Rudd replied, "Your cry of 'nihilism' represents your inability to understand our positive values. . . . We do have a vision of the way things could be: . . . how men could be free to keep what they produce, to enjoy peaceful lives, to create. These are positive values, but since they mean the destruction of your order, you call them 'nihilism'" (Jerry L. Avorn, Andrew Crane, Mark Jaffe, Oren Root, Jr., Paul Starr, Michael Stern, and Robert Stultberg, *Up against the Ivy Wall: A History of the Columbia Crisis*, ed. Robert Friedman [New York: Atheneum, 1969], 26).

75. SDS, *Port Huron*, 6, 7, 42.
76. Mailer, *Armies*, 288.
77. Barthes, "From Work to Text," 164.

6. Confronting Difference, Confronting Difficulty: Culture Wars, Canon Wars, and Maxine Hong Kingston's *The Woman Warrior*

1. Paul Skenazy, "Coming Home," in *Conversations with Maxine Hong Kingston*, ed. Paul Skenazy and Tera Martin (Jackson: University of Mississippi Press, 1998), 108–109.
2. Todd Gitlin, *The Twilight of Common Dreams* (New York: Holt, 1995), 78; Ronald Reagan, *A Time for Choosing: The Speeches of Ronald Reagan, 1961–1982*, ed. Alfred A. Balitzer and Gerald M. Bonetto (Chicago: Regnery Gateway, 1983), 195.
3. Maxine Hong Kingston, *The Woman Warrior* (1976; reprint, New York: Vintage International, 1989). Further citations appear in the text.
4. Eric J. Schroeder, "As Truthful As Possible: An Interview with Maxine Hong Kingston," in Skenazy and Martin, *Conversations*, 220.
5. For scholarly discussions, see Lisa Plummer Crafton, " 'We Are Going to Carve Revenge on Your Back': Language, Culture, and the Female Body in Kingston's *The Woman Warrior*," in *Women As Sites of Culture*, ed. Susan Shifrin (Burlington, Vt.: Ashgate, 2002), 51–63; Lothar Bredella, "Involvement and Detachment: How to Read and Teach Maxine Hong Kingston's *The Woman Warrior*," in *Emotion in Postmodernism*, ed. Gerhard Hoffmann and Alfred Hornung (Heidelberg: Universitätsverlag C. Winter, 1997), 421–439; J. Kim, "Anger, Temporality, and the Politics of Reading *The Woman Warrior*," in *Analyzing World Fiction: New Horizons in Narrative Theory*, ed. Frederick Luis Aldama (Austin: University of Texas Press, 2011), 93–108; Aleksandra Izgarjan, "Language As a Means of Shaping New Cultural Identity in Maxine Hong Kingston's *The Woman Warrior*," *Gender Studies* 1, no. 7 (2008): 7–16; Bradley John Monsma, " 'Active Readers . . . Observe Tricksters': Trickster Texts and Cross-Cultural Reading," *Modern Language Studies* 26, no. 4 (1996): 83–98; and Bonnie TuSmith, "Literary Tricksterism: Maxine Hong Kingston's *The Woman Warrior: Memoirs of a Girlhood among Ghosts*," in *Anxious Power: Reading, Writing, and Ambivalence in Narrative by Women*, ed. Carol J. Singley and Susan Elizabeth Sweeney (Albany: State University of New York, 1993), 279–294.
6. For discussions of reading or interpretation, see Patricia Chu, " 'The Invisible World the Emigrants Built': Cultural Self-Inscription and the Antiromantic Plots of *The Woman Warrior*," *Diaspora* 2, no. 1 (1992): 95–115; Joanne S. Frye, "*The Woman Warrior*: Claiming Narrative Power, Recreating Female Selfhood," in *Faith of a (Woman) Writer*, ed. Alice Kessler-Harris and William McBrien (New York: Greenwood, 1988), 293–301; Jeehyun Lim, "Cutting the Tongue: Language and the Body in Kingston's *The Woman Warrior*," *MELUS* 31, no. 3 (2006): 49–65; Margaret Miller, "Threads of Identity in Maxine Hong Kingston's *Woman Warrior*," *biography* 6, no. 1 (1983): 13–33; and Karoline Krauss, "Identity As Textual Event," *Utah Foreign Language Review* (1993): 147–158.
7. Rachel Lee claims that the power of Kingston's text comes from its refusal to be read into the canon and its claim to marginalization ("Claiming Land, Claiming Voice, Claiming

Canon: Institutionalized Challenges in Kingston's *China Men* and *The Woman Warrior*," in *ReViewing Asian America*, ed. Wendy L. Ng, Soo-Young Chin, James S. Moy, and Gary Y. Okihiro [Pullman: Washington State University Press, 1995], 157). I counter that the text rejects definitions of *margin* and *center* and attempts to expand the idea of Americanness to include all.

8. Maxine Hong Kingston, "Cultural Mis-readings by American Reviewers," in *Asian and Western Writers in Dialogue*, ed. Guy Amirthanayagam (New York: Macmillan, 1982), 64; Maxine Hong Kingston, *I Love a Broad Margin to My Life* (New York: Vintage International, 2011), 221.

9. Sara Evans, *Personal Politics: The Root of Women's Liberation in the Civil Rights Movement and the New Left* (New York: Knopf, 1979), 76–77; Toni Cade Bambara, "The Pill: Genocide or Liberation," in *The Black Woman: An Anthology*, ed. Toni Cade Bambara (New York: Penguin, 1970), 162–163.

10. Charlotte Bunch, "Beyond Either/Or: Feminist Options," in *Building Feminist Theory: Essays from "Quest*," ed. Charlotte Bunch, Jane Flax, Alexa Freeman, Nancy Hartsock, and Mary-Helen Mautner (New York: Longman, 1981), 48; Kate Millett, *Sexual Politics* (Garden City, N.Y.: Doubleday, 1970), 24, 25; Kay Bonetti, "An Interview with Maxine Hong Kingston," in Skenazy and Martin, *Conversations*, 40.

11. Charlotte Bunch, *Passionate Politics: Feminist Theory in Action* (New York: St. Martin's, 1987), 219, 222, 218; Charlotte Bunch and Sandra Pollack, eds., *Learning Our Way: Essays in Feminist Education* (Trumansburg, N.Y.: Crossing, 1983), xv; Junko R. Onosaka, *Feminist Revolution in Literacy: Women's Bookstores in the United States* (New York: Routledge, 2006), 192–193.

12. Kay Lindsey, "The Black Woman As a Woman," in Bambara, *Black Woman*, 85; doris davenport, "The Pathology of Racism: A Conversation with Third World Wimmin," in *This Bridge Called My Back: Writings by Radical Women of Color*, ed. Gloria Anzaldúa and Cherríe Moraga (New York: Kitchen Table, 1981), 89; Mitsuye Yamada, "Invisibility Is an Unnatural Disaster: Reflections of an Asian American Woman," in Anzaldúa and Moraga, *This Bridge*, 37, 40; Skenazy, "Coming Home," 116; bell hooks, *Feminist Theory: From Margin to Center* (Boston: South End, 1984), 47; Audre Lorde, "Eye to Eye," in *Sister Outsider: Essays and Speeches* (Freedom, Calif.: Crossing, 1984), 173.

13. Gloria Anzaldúa, "Haciendo caras, una entrada," in *Making Face/Making Soul: Creative and Critical Perspectives by Feminists of Color*, ed. Gloria Anzaldúa (San Francisco: Aunt Lute, 1990), xxv; hooks, "Preface," *Feminist Theory*, n.p.; *The Combahee River Collective Statement: Black Feminist Organizing in the Seventies and Eighties* (Albany: Kitchen Table/Women of Color Press, 1986), 17; Anzaldúa, "Haciendo caras," xviii.

14. Alice Walker, "Women," in *All the Women Are White, All the Blacks Are Men, But Some of Us Are Brave: Black Women's Studies*, ed. Gloria T. Hull, Patricia Bell Scott, and Barbara Smith (Old Westbury, N.Y.: Feminist Press, 1982), xiii; Gloria Anzaldúa, *Borderlands/La Frontera: The New Mestiza*, 2nd ed. (1987; reprint, San Francisco: Aunt Lute, 1999), i; Merle Woo, "Letter to Ma," in Anzaldúa and Moraga, *This Bridge*, 147; Skenazy, "Kingston at the University," in Skenazy and Martin, *Conversations*, 144; Toni Cade Bambara, "Foreword," in Anzaldúa and Moraga, *This Bridge*, viii; bell hooks, *Talking Back* (Boston: South End, 1989), 46. Many of these anthologies also recommend additional readings from, of, by, and for feminists of color.

15. hooks, *Talking Back*, 24; hooks, *Feminist Theory*, 108, 107; Anzaldúa, "Haciendo caras," xxiii; Bunch, *Passionate*, 221.

16. Kit Yuen Quan, "The Girl Who Wouldn't Sing," in Anzaldúa, *Making Face/Making Soul*, 215, 217; Skenazy, "Kingston at the University," in Skenazy and Martin, *Conversations*, 127.

17. hooks, *Talking Back*, 31; Robert C. Smith, *Conservatism and Racism and Why in America They Are the Same* (Albany: SUNY Press, 2010), 80; Seymour Lipset and Earl Raab, *The Politics of Unreason* (New York: Harper and Row, 1970), 3.

18. Peter Steinfels, *The Neoconservatives* (New York: Simon and Schuster, 1979), 3; Mark Gerson, *The Neoconservative Vision: From the Cold War to the Culture Wars* (Lanham, Md.: Madison, 1996), 133, 144, 87.
19. James Q. Wilson, *The Moral Sense* (New York: Free Press, 1993), xi; Steinfels, *The Neoconservatives*, 4, 7, 11, 9.
20. Wilson, *Moral Sense*, 8; William Simon, *A Time for Truth* (New York: Reader's Digest Press, 1978), 42, 43.
21. Jerry Falwell, *Listen, America!* (New York: Doubleday, 1980), 12.
22. For examples of these campaigns, see Richard Viguerie, *The New Right: We're Ready to Lead* (Falls Church, Va.: Viguerie Company, 1981); and Alan Crawford, *Thunder on the Right* (New York: Pantheon, 1980), 5.
23. James Davison Hunter, *Culture Wars: The Struggle to Define America* (New York: Basic Books, 1991); Jonathan Zimmerman, *Whose America? Culture Wars in the Public Schools* (Cambridge: Harvard University Press, 2002); Richard Bolton, "Introduction," in *Culture Wars: Documents from the Recent Controversies in the Arts*, ed. Richard Bolton (New York: New Press, 1992), 3; Paul Lauter, *Canons and Contexts* (New York: Oxford University Press, 1991), x, 226.
24. Lauter, *Canons and Contexts*, 112; Skenazy, "Kingston at the University," 145; Kingston, *I Love a Broad Margin*, 221; Lauter, *Canons and Contexts*, xii; Sheila Ruth, ed., *Issues in Feminism: A First Course in Women's Studies* (Boston: Houghton Mifflin, 1980); Paul Lauter, ed., *Reconstructing American Literature* (New York: Feminist Press, 1983); Anzaldúa, *Borderlands*, 90.
25. Task Force on Education for Economic Growth, *Action for Excellence* (Denver: Education Commission of the United States, 1983), 3 and inside back cover; D. Richard Little, "Legacy of the '60s—Declining Quality," *Christian Science Monitor*, 17 January 1977, B12.
26. Ira Shor, *Culture Wars* (Boston: Routledge and Kegan Paul, 1986), 68; Merrill Sheils, "Why Johnny Can't Write," *Newsweek*, 8 December 1975, par. 17; Ellie McGrath, "The Bold Quest for Quality," *Time*, 10 October 1983, 58, 61; Donna Woolfolk Cross, *Word Abuse* (New York: Coward, McCann, and Geoghegan, 1979), 224; Allan Bloom, *The Closing of the American Mind* (New York: Simon and Schuster, 1987), 50.
27. Richard Ohmann, "The Decline in Literacy Is a Fiction, If Not a Hoax," *Chronicle of Higher Education*, 2 October 1976, 32; Cross, *Word Abuse*, 217; John Goodland, *A Place Called School* (New York: McGraw-Hill, 1984), 6; E. D. Hirsch, Jr., *Cultural Literacy: What Every American Needs to Know* (Boston: Houghton Mifflin, 1987), 4; Sheils, "Why Johnny Can't Write," par. 8; Bloom, *Closing*, 86, 140, 373, 32, 129. See also Roger Kimball, *Tenured Radicals: How Politics Has Corrupted Our Higher Education* (1990; reprint, Chicago: Dee, 2008), 7; and Richard Bernstein, *Dictatorship of Virtue: Multiculturalism and the Battle for America's Future* (New York: Knopf, 1994). On the conversations and controversies swirling around Bloom's infamous book, see Robert Stone, ed., *Essays on "The Closing of the American Mind"* (Chicago: Chicago Review Press, 1989); and James Seaton and William K. Buckley, eds., *Beyond Cheering and Bashing: New Perspectives on "The Closing of the American Mind"* (Bowling Green, Ohio: Bowling Green State University Popular Press, 1992).
28. Reagan appointed William J. Bennett to report on the humanities in American universities; the result was *To Reclaim a Legacy: Report on the Humanities in Higher Education* (Washington, D.C.: National Endowment for the Humanities, 1984). According to Shor, the rhetoric of "excellence, . . . a key word in the lexicon of traditionalism," associating multicultural and other texts with lesser quality (*Culture Wars*, 107). Also see National Education Association, *Excellence in Our Schools* (Washington, D.C.: National Education Association, 1982), 7; Lynne V. Cheney, *50 Hours: A Core Curriculum for College Students* (Washington, D.C.: National Endowment for the Humanities, 1989), 11, 12, 13; and Mortimer J. Adler, *The Paideia Proposal: An Educational Manifesto* (New York: Collier, 1982).

29. Hirsch, *Cultural Literacy*; E. D. Hirsch, Jr., *A First Dictionary of Cultural Literacy: What Our Children Need to Know* (Boston: Houghton Mifflin, 1989); Bloom, *Closing*, 344, 51, 48; "The Heath Travesty of American Literature," *New Criterion* 9 (October 1990): 4. Bennett condemned multicultural programs and curricula for using the humanities "as if they were the handmaiden of ideology, subordinated to particular prejudices and valued or rejected on the basis of their relationship to a certain social stance" (*To Reclaim a Legacy*, 16). See also Bloom, *Closing*, 91–96; and Kimball's discussion of academic interest groups in *Tenured Radicals*, 9.

30. Bloom, *Closing*, 51; Lauter, *Canons and Contexts*, xiii; Henry Louis Gates, Jr., *Loose Canons* (New York: Oxford University Press, 1992), 17; Arnold Krupat, *The Voice in the Margin: Native American Literature and the Canon* (Berkeley: University of California Press, 1989), 49; Gates, *Loose Canons*, 174.

31. Lauter's *Reconstructing American Literature* lists *The Woman Warrior* in nine of twenty-four relevant courses—that is, almost 38 percent of them (16, 61, 125, 133, 145, 168, 171, 183, 210). See also Paul Skenazy and Tera Martin, "Introduction," in Skenazy and Martin, *Conversations*, vii; Uyen Cao, "Renowned Writer and Novelist Maxine Hong Kingston to Speak in 'Conversations with Writers Series,'" *California Aggie* (24 February 2011), https://theaggie.org; Lim, "Cutting the Tongue," 49; and David Leiwei Li, "The Naming of a Chinese American 'I': Cross-Cultural Sign/ifications in *The Woman Warrior*," *Criticism* 30, no. 4 (1988): 497.

32. Sau-ling Cynthia Wong, "Staying Alive: Kingston's *Woman Warrior* Afterlife and Marilyn Chin's *Revenge of the Mooncake Vixen*," in *On the Legacy of Maxine Hong Kingston: The Mulhouse Book*, ed. Sämi Ludwig and Nicoleta Alexoae-Zagni (Zurich: LIT Verlag, 2014), 313; Marilyn Chin, "Writing the Other: A Conversation with Maxine Hong Kingston," in Skenazy and Martin, *Conversations*, 97; Shirley Geok-Lin Lim, "'Growing with Stories': Chinese American Identities, Textual Identities (Maxine Hong Kingston)," in *Teaching American Ethnic Literatures*, ed. John R. Maitino and David R. Peck (Albuquerque: University of New Mexico Press, 1996), 279.

33. Paula Rabinowitz, "Eccentric Memories: A Conversation with Maxine Hong Kingston," in Skenazy and Martin, *Conversations*, 73. For examples of Chin's critique, see Frank Chin, "Come All Ye Asian American Writers of the Real and the Fake," in *The Big Aeeeiiiii! An Anthology of Chinese American and Japanese American Literature*, ed. Frank Chin, Jeffrey Paul Chan, Lawson Fusao Inada, and Shawn Hsu Wong (New York: Meridian, 1991), 24–52; and Frank Chin, "The Most Popular Book in China," in *Maxine Hong Kingston's "The Woman Warrior": A Casebook*, ed. Sau-ling Cynthia Wong (New York: Oxford University Press, 1999), 27–28. Kingston has repeatedly reiterated that she bears no ill will toward Chin but thinks his accusations are ridiculous. She asserts that she writes stories, not history, and therefore is not beholden to others for representational accuracy. For an excellent take on Chin's essentialism, see Paul Outka, "Publish or Perish: Food, Hunger, and Self-Construction in Maxine Hong Kingston's *The Woman Warrior*," *Contemporary Literature* 38, no. 3 (1997): 447–482.

34. See Kingston's "Cultural Mis-readings." Khani Begum makes a similar claim about literary scholars and asserts the text's Americanness as opposed to marginality ("Confirming the Place of 'The Other': Gender and Ethnic Identity in Maxine Hong Kingston's *The Woman Warrior*," in *New Perspectives on Women and Comedy*, ed. Regina Barreca [Storrs: University of Connecticut, 1992], 143).

35. Shirley Geok-lin Lim, ed., *Approaches to Teaching Kingston's "The Woman Warrior"* (New York: Modern Language Association, 1991), 21. On Kingston's transnational import, see Sau-ling Cynthia Wong, "Staying Alive," in *On the Legacy of Maxine Hong Kingston*, 313–342.

36. Ralph Ellison, *Invisible Man* (1952; reprint, New York: Vintage International, 1995), 3; Mitsuye Yamada, "Asian Pacific American Women and Feminism," in Anzaldúa and Moraga, *This Bridge*, 71; Yamada, "Invisibility," 40; Krauss, "Identity," 151.

37. Kingston has commented that, like most Americans, her understanding of Chinese culture is drawn from popular culture—for example, the misrepresentations in Louisa May Alcott's novels (Jody Hoy, "To Be Able to See the Tao," in Skenazy and Martin, 62) or the kung-fu films Maxine watched every Sunday at "the Confucius Church," where she "saw swordswomen jump over houses from a standstill; they didn't even need a running start" (*Woman Warrior*, 19). She has also noted that her understanding of Chinese culture has been filtered through her understanding of western culture: for instance, the television show *I Love Lucy* was a reference for Moon Orchid's story, and Daniel Defoe's *Robinson Crusoe* was the foundation of the tale of Lo Bun Sun. See Chin, "Writing the Other," 87; and Maxine Hong Kingston, *China Men* (New York: Vintage International, 1989), 224–233.

38. Reed Way Dasenbrock, "Intelligibility and Meaningfulness in Multicultural Literature in English," in Wong, *Maxine Hong Kingston's "The Woman Warrior": A Casebook*, 165.

39. Lorraine Bethel, "'This Infinity of Conscious Pain': Zora Neale Hurston and the Black Female Literary Tradition," in Hull et al., *All the Women Are White*, 177; Dexter Fisher, ed., "Introduction," in *The Third Woman: Minority Women Writers of the United States* (Boston: Houghton Mifflin, 1980), xxvii; and Barbara Christian, "Race for Theory," in *Making Face, Making Soul*, 337. On Maxine's quest to find words and herself, see Agieszka Wróblewska, "Aspects of Female Identity in Maxine Hong Kingston's *The Woman Warrior*," *American Studies* 19 (2001): 81–87.

40. Kingston has since reiterated that she wishes she had focused on Fa Mu Lan's work as a weaver. See Skenazy, "Coming Home," 131; and Donna Perry, "Interview with Maxine Hong Kingston," in Skenazy and Martin, *Conversations*, 175.

41. Silvia Schultermandl, "The Politics of Transnational Identity in and of Maxine Hong Kingston's *The Woman Warrior*," in Ludwig and Alexoae-Zagni, *On the Legacy*, 36. Later Schultermandl sort of acknowledges Maxine's interpretive power, but attributes it less to her reading and more to her "quest for truth" (41). Margaret Miller also sees Maxine as a reader in "No Name Woman" but likewise privileges the "act of writing" as "the most important element in her self-affirmation" ("Threads," 25, 27).

42. Frye, "*The Woman Warrior*," 298, 297; Aleksandra Izgarjan, "Language As a Means of Shaping New Cultural Identity in Maxine Hong Kingston's *The Woman Warrior*," *Gender Studies* 1, no.7 (2008): 7.

43. Walt Whitman, "Song of Myself," in *Leaves of Grass* (1855; reprint, New York: New American Library, 1980), 96. Kingston named her protagonist in *Tripmaster Monkey* after Whitman (1987; reprint, New York: Vintage International, 1990).

44. Dasenbrock, "Intelligibility," 160. Marlene Goldman also reads the woman warrior's body as a communal text and weapon yet suggests that it is an object belonging to others (parents, community, and so on). The text itself refuses this either-or binary. See Goldman's "Naming the Unspeakable: The Mapping of Female Identity in Maxine Hong Kingston's *The Woman Warrior*," in *International Women's Writing: New Landscapes of Identity*, ed. Anne Brown and Marjanne Goozé (Westport, Conn.: Greenwood, 1995), 227–228.

45. For criticism that views sexism as wholly Chinese, see Linda Hunt, "'I Could Not Figure Out What Was My Village': Gender vs. Ethnicity in Maxine Hong Kingston's *The Woman Warrior*," *MELUS* 12, no. 3 (1985): 5–12.

46. The book as a whole adopts a contrastive structure, contrasting stories about apparent victims with those about apparent heroes: No Name Woman is followed by Fa Mu Lan (sections 1 and 2), Moon Orchid is followed by Brave Orchid (sections 4 and 3). Although the section titled "At the Western Palace" appears to break this structure, it really extends it: because Maxine's response to or interpretation of the Moon Orchid tale comes at the start of the final section, the section break seems to signal the break with reality, family, nation, and community that Moon Orchid experiences in her madness.

47. According to Kim, "*Woman Warrior* enables readers to work through the contradiction between ideologies of individuality and collectivity at a historical moment when racial and

ethnic collectives were invested anew with political and cultural significance" ("Anger," 106).
48. Lauter, *Canons and Contexts*, 283.
49. According to Chu, Kingston puts Chinese America and America into a dialogic, collaborative, and competitive conversation ("Invisible World," 106–107).
50. Pfaff, "Talk with Mrs. Kingston," 18.
51. Malini Schueller, "Questioning Race and Gender Definitions: Dialogic Subversions in *The Woman Warrior*," *Criticism* 31, no. 4 (1989): 422, 428. Nonetheless, Schueller's argument relies on two huge and problematic binaries: unified/propaganda texts versus diverse/political texts. *The Woman Warrior* clearly challenges such limiting distinctions.
52. Kingston, *I Love a Broad Margin*, 10, 7, 8, 9, 24, 29, 46, 47, 141, 162, 186, 205, 129, 12.
53. Ibid., 104, 199, 32, 127, 186–189, 168–171.
54. Gary Kubota, "Maxine Hong Kingston: Something Comes from Outside onto the Paper," in Skenazy and Martin, *Conversations*, 3.
55. Skenazy, "Coming Home," 110; Skenazy, "Kingston at the University," 114; Maxine Hong Kingston, "The Novel's Next Step," *Mother Jones* 14, no. 10 (1989): 39; Skenazy, "Kingston at the University," 142; Schroeder, "As Truthful As Possible," 225.
56. Skenazy, "Kingston at the University," 152; Kingston, "Novel's Next Step," 38, 39, 40.
57. Kingston, "Novel's Next Step," 41; Neila C. Seshachari, "Reinventing Peace: Conversations with Tripmaster Maxine Hong Kingston," in Skenazy and Martin, *Conversations*, 199; June Jordan, "Report from the Bahamas," in *On Call: Political Essays* (Boston: South End, 1985), 35; Lynet Uttal, "In Alliance, in Solidarity," in Anzaldúa, *Making Face/Making Soul*, 319; Perry, "Interview," 185; Seshachari, "Reinventing Peace," 213; Shelley Fisher Fishkin, "Interview with Maxine Hong Kingston," in Skenazy and Martin, *Conversations*, 163; Lorde, *Sister Outsider*, 43; Fay Chiang, Helen Wong Huie, Jason Hwang, Richard Oyama, and Susan L. Yung, eds., *American Born and Foreign: An Anthology of Asian American Poetry* (Bronx, N.Y.: Sunbury, 1979), xiv.
58. Skenazy, "Kingston at the University," 156.
59. Maxine Hong Kingston, "Personal Statement," in Lim, *Approaches*, 24; Maxine Hong Kingston, *The Fifth Book of Peace* (New York: Vintage International, 2004), 402.

Conclusion: "Reading Makes a Country Great"

1. Cynthia Lee Katona, *Book Savvy* (Lanham, Md.: Scarecrow, 2005), 11.
2. For example, in a speech before Congress on 20 September 2001, President Bush posed and answered a series of questions purporting to be from the American people: "Americans are asking 'Why do they hate us?' . . . They hate what they see right here in this chamber: a democratically elected government. Their leaders are self-appointed. They hate our freedoms: our freedom of religion, our freedom of speech, our freedom to vote and assemble and disagree with each other" (http://www.washingtonpost.com). Such post-9/11 rhetoric resurrected what Tom Engelhardt calls "victory culture"—a way of thinking that relies simultaneously on victimization and triumphalism (*The End of Victory Culture* [Amherst: University of Massachusetts Press, 1997]).
3. Ernest B. Fleishman, *Adolescent Literacy: A National Reading Crisis* (New York: Scholastic, 2004); National Council of Teachers of English, *Adolescent Literacy* (Ann Arbor, Mich.: National Council of Teachers of English, 2007); National Endowment for the Arts, *Reading at Risk: A Survey of Literary Reading in America* (Washington, D.C.: National Endowment for the Arts, 2004), vii.
4. "Congressman Ike Skelton's National Security Book List with Reviews," http://www.cgsc.edu; Defense of Civilization Fund, *Defending Civilization: How Our Universities Are Failing America and What Can Be Done about It* (Washington, D.C.: American Council of Trustees and Alumni, 2001), 1, 7–8, 5, cover. The fund was associated with the conservative nonprofit American Council of Trustees and Alumni, and its report bemoans the fact that,

instead of survey courses in western civilization, students are faced with "a smorgasbord of often narrow and trendy classes and incoherent requirements that do not convey the great heritage of human civilization" (5).
5. National Endowment for the Arts, "The Big Read," http://www.neabigread.org.
6. Gavin McNett, "Reaching to the Converted," *Salon* (12 November 1999), http://www.salon.com; Susan Wise Bauer, "Oprah's Misery Index," *Christianity Today* 42, no. 14 (1998): 70–74; Tom Shone, "The Last Time They Met," *New York Times Book Review*, 22 April 2001, 34. For scholarly reactions to Oprah's Book Club, see Cecilia Konchar Farr, ed., *The Oprah Effect* (Albany: SUNY Press, 2008); Cecilia Konchar Farr, *Reading with Oprah: How Oprah's Book Club Changed How America Reads* (Albany: SUNY Press, 2005); Kathleen Rooney, *Reading with Oprah: The Book Club That Changed America* (Fayetteville: University of Arkansas Press, 2005); and Trysh Travis, "'It Will Change the World If Everyone Reads This Book': New Thought Religion in Oprah's Book Club," *American Quarterly* 53, no. 3 (2007): 1017–1041.
7. Harold Bloom, *How to Read and Why* (New York: Scribner, 2000). Bloom published his book before 9/11. While he could not have foreseen those events, the urgency in his text was crystallized and magnified by them, and his book gained popularity in the years after they occurred.
8. Jessica Feldman and Robert Stilling, eds., *What Should I Read Next?* (Charlottesville: University of Virginia Press, 2008), back cover.
9. Wayne Turmel claims that a crisis and embarrassment about his literary ignorance moved him to "get me an education" (*A Philistine's Journal: An Average Guy Tackles the Classics* [Villa Park, Ill.: New Leaf, 2003], 13).
10. Jonathan Safran Foer, *Extremely Loud and Incredibly Close* (New York: Mariner, 2005); Claire Messud, *The Emperor's Children* (New York: Knopf, 2006).
11. Alfred Stefferud, ed., *The Wonderful World of Books* (Boston: Houghton Mifflin, 1953), 13.
12. "President Barack Obama and Marilynne Robinson: A Conversation, II," *New York Review of Books*, 62, no. 18 (2015): 6.
13. Ibid.
14. Martha C. Nussbaum, *Not for Profit: Why Democracy Needs the Humanities* (Princeton: Princeton University Press, 2010), 6; "President Barack Obama"; Mrs. Charles Slater, "I Belong to a Discussion Group," in Stefferud, *Wonderful World*, 122.

Index

activism: canon wars and, 139; civil rights movement, 8, 62–65, 66, 137; conservative, 138; feminist, 133–36; reading methods and, 109. *See also* student radicalism
Adams, John, 3
Adler, Mortimer J., 29
aesthetics: canon wars and, 141, 147; politics and, 108, 109, 129; student radicalism and, 109; Western, 139
African Americans: Black Arts Movement, 71, 75, 177n55; black feminism, 134–36; Black Power, 78; black studies, 139; civil rights movement, 8, 62–65, 66, 137; culture of, 70–71, 75–77; speech of, 62, 176n35. *See also* literacy, African American
A is for Abigail (Cheney), 155
Alabama, 56
alienation: in *Catcher*, 39, 42; New Criticism and, 38, 42; postmodernism and, 100–101; reading education and, 81; universities and, 96
Alien Registration Act, 19
All the Women Are White, All the Blacks Are Men, But Some of Us Are Brave, 135
All Things Considered, 50
America: A Patriotic Primer (Cheney), 155
America and the New Era, 111–12
American Adam (Lewis), 48
American Association of University Professors, 92–93
American Book Publisher's Council, 14
American Born and Foreign, 138
American Legion, 86
American Library Association, 14, 25, 26, 60, 65
American Mind (Commager), 34

Americanness, 5, 11; facts and, 84; Hoover and, 85; minorities and, 132; order and, 86; reading and, 2; stability of, 12, 143; student radicals and, 110, 133; success and, 149. *See also* character, American; values, American
American Subscription Library, 3
"An Appeal to the World" (Du Bois), 62
Anderson, Benedict, 3
Anzald, Gloria, 135
Appeal (Walker), 56
Approaches to Teaching "Woman Warrior" (Lim), 142
Armies of the Night (Mailer), 7, 103, 111, 129
Asheim, Lester, 90
Augie March (Bellow), 7
Aunt Lute Books, 134
authenticity, 42, 170n35
authorial intent, 118, 119, 122, 124, 127–28
authority: of author, 118, 119, 122, 124, 127–28; vs. democracy, 111; displacement of, 124; limitations of, 125; metafiction and, 129; postmodernism and, 118, 121–22; of reader, 7–8, 124, 127. *See also* power
Autobiography (Franklin), 3
Autobiography of Malcolm X, 7
autonomy, 88

Baldwin, James, 54, 62, 63
Bambara, Toni Cade, 136
Baraka, Amiri, 75
Barth, John, 106–7; on fiction, 121, 187n55; on history, 129; on literary devices/conventions, 123. *See also Lost in the Funhouse* (Barth)
Barthes, Roland, 116, 118
Barzun, Jacques, 15–16, 37, 81–82, 90, 92

baseball, 45–46, 171n41
Baseball and the Pursuit of Innocence (Skolnik), 45–46
Beall, Jack, 86
Beittel, A. D., 64
Bell, Steven, 123
Bellow, Saul, 6
Bennett, William J., 140, 141
Bennett Jr., Lerone, 73
Berelson, Bernard, 91
Bethel Historical and Literary Association, 56–57
Big Read, 155
Black Aesthetic (Gayle), 55
Black Arts Movement, 71, 75, 177n55
Black Boy (Wright), 55
Black-Eyed Susans, 138
Black Power, 78
black studies, 139
Bloom, Allan, 140, 141
Bloom, Harold, 51
Bloomberg, Edward, 109
Bluest Eye, The (Morrison), 55, 138
Boehm, Beth A., 107, 128
Bonifacius (Mather), 3
book clubs/literary societies, 28–30; African American, 54, 56–57, 60, 135; community and, 156; criticism of, 46, 87–88, 156, 180n22; feminist, 135; post-9/11, 156
books. *See* literature/books
Books, Young People, and Reading Guidance (Hanna, McAllister), 4, 93
Book Savvy (Katona), 156
Books for Adult Beginners (Wallace), 25, 163n15
bookstores, 27–28, 134
Borderlands/La Frontera (Anzaldúa), 135
Bradbury, Ray, 7
Braverman, Miriam, 65
Brooks, Cleanth, 24, 34
Brower, Reuben, 46, 88
Brown v. Board of Education, 62, 63, 178n65
Buchanan, Scott, 109–10
Bulletin, 65
Bunch, Charlotte, 133
Bunche, Ralph, 64
Bush, George W., 154

Caliver, Ambrose, 59–60, 62
Calvino, Italo, 108
Calyx Press, 134
canonicity/canon wars, 132, 163n14; conservatism about, 139–41; diversity and, 138–39, 147–48, 150–51. *See also* multiculturalism
Catcher in the Rye (Salinger), 7, 8, 32–34, 40–50, 167n2; American character and, 34–39, 45–46, 49–50, 168n15, 170n35; cult of personality in, 46–47; good vs. bad books in, 47–48; reading guides and, 40–41; reading methods in, 41–45. *See also* character, American
Catch-22 (Heller), 7
censorship, 26, 32–33, 34, 38–39, 93, 167n2
Center for the Study of Democratic Institutions, 109–10
Central America, 131
certainty/uncertainty, 2–3, 11–12, 30–31; agency and, 112; conservatism and, 136; creativity and, 149–50; reader participation and, 127; reading lists and, 156; student radicals and, 111–12, 115
Chamber of Commerce, 86
Chambers, Whittaker, 19
character, American, 34–39; baseball and, 45–46, 171n41; censorship and, 38–39; cult of personality and, 46–47; vs. European, 36–37; instability of, 49–50; reading methods and, 37–38, 44–45. *See also* Americanness; morality/ethics; values, American
Cheever, Abigail, 34
Cheney, Lynne, 155
"Chicago: Organizing the Unemployed" (Flacks), 116
Chicanas, 135
Chin, Fran, 142
Chin, Marilyn, 142
China, 143, 150
China Men (Kingston), 152
Chinese Americans, 135, 142, 142–44, 146, 148, 149, 153, 193n37
Christianity. *See* religion
Christian Science Monitor, 48
Cisneros, Sandra, 138
citizen-readers. *See* citizenship; democracy; reading initiatives
citizenship, 5, 10; as conformity, 74, 75; definition of, 141; feminism and, 134; of minorities, 12, 53, 56, 70, 75; as readership, 46, 113
civil rights movement, 8, 62–65, 66, 137
Civil War, 56, 57
Clark, Kenneth, 73
class: baseball and, 45–46; bookstores and, 27–28; canon wars and, 141; character and, 44; classism, 115–16, 146; education access

and, 23; facts and, 82; feminism and, 134; knowledge and, 112; language and, 136; literacy and, 62, 140; postmodernism and, 120, 187n51; reading guides and, 25; social stability and, 12
Clausen, Christopher, 141
Cleis Press, 134
Closing of the American Mind, The (Bloom), 140, 141
COINTELPRO, 85, 110
Cold War, 7; definition of, 4–5. *See also* communism; democracy; Soviet Union
Cold War Civil Rights (Dudziak), 54
College of William and Mary, 61
colonialism, 135
Colored American, 56
Color Purple, The (Walker), 139
Columbia University, 13, 117
Combahee River Collective, 135
Coming Apart (O'Neill), 110
Commager, Henry Steele, 34, 36, 92
commodification, 35, 39, 47, 87
Common Core, 50
communism, 3, 4–5, 13; anti-Communist literature, 15, 19–20; anti-Communist programs, 20, 85; *Catcher in the Rye* and, 38; civil rights movement and, 64–65; conservatism and, 137; education and, 20, 92–93; markers of, 12; objectivity and, 82–83; personality of communists, 36; philosophical basis of, 86; race and, 54, 62; student radicalism and, 110; surveillance of, 94, 95–96; U.S foreign policy and, 131. *See also* democracy
Communists and the Schools (Iverson), 92–93
community: book clubs as, 87, 156; collective body, 145–46, 193n44; global, 151–52; inclusivity of, 146; intertexuality and, 127; New Criticism and, 42; postmodernism and, 119; of readers, 115, 129; reading education and, 103; student radicals and, 133
conformity: book clubs and, 87–88; to gender roles, 91; individualism and, 144, 168n13; vs. nonconformity, 74; pluralism and, 75; universities and, 92
conservatism: canon wars and, 139–41; neoconservatism, 136–37; New Right, 101, 137–38, 184n9; at universities, 137, 182n51
consumerism/consumption, 15, 27, 34, 46, 109
Council for Books in Wartime, 21–23, 27
creativity: democracy and, 112; hope and, 153; reading and, 119, 157; uncertainty/instability and, 115, 149–50
Crisis, 57
Cross, Donna Woolfork, 140
"Crossing Brooklyn Ferry" (Whitman), 151
Crucial Decade: America, 1945–1955 (Goldman), 34
Crying of Lot 49, The (Pynchon), 7, 8, 89–105, 179n3; gender in, 89–92, 98, 182n53; reading education in, 92–94, 98; universities in, 95–98. *See also* facts/truth
cult of personality, 35–36, 46–47
"Cultural Mis-readings by American Reviewers" (Kingston), 142
culture wars, 131–32, 137
Culture Wars: The Struggle to Define America (Hunter), 138

Daniell, Raymond, 11
Dasenbrock, Reed Way, 143
Davenport, Guy, 120
David Copperfield (Dickens), 40
"Decline in Literacy Is a Fiction, If Not a Hoax" (Ohmann), 141
deconstruction, 122, 186nn42, 43, 187n51, 188n74. *See also* postmodernism
Defending Civilization, 155
Defense of Western Civilization Fund, 155
democracy, 1–2, 10–11, 158–59; vs. authority, 111; book clubs and, 87–88; vs. communism, 85; creativity and, 112; cult of personality and, 35; knowledge and, 112–13; literary diversity and, 139; love and, 129; meaning of, 83; openness of, 111; participatory, 114, 116, 119, 129, 185n30; race and, 54, 60, 64, 76; reading method and, 20; segregation and, 73; social justice and, 78; student radicalism and, 110–11; terrorism and, 154, 194n2. *See also* communism
Democracy (Didion), 7
Derrida, Jacques, 103, 116, 118–19, 186n39
Dickens, Charles, 40
Dickinson, Emily, 42, 46
Dickstein, Morris, 74
direct-mail, 138
Donato, Eugenio, 116
Douglass, Frederick, 53
Dragnet, 81–82
drama, 93–94
Du Bois, W. E. B., 62
Dudziak, Mary, 54, 64
Duker, Sam, 31
Dulles, John Foster, 81, 83

Eagleton, Terry, 117
Ebony, 60
education: access to, 23–25, 60–61, 90, 133, 134; communism and, 20, 92–93; conservatism and, 137–38; ideals, 140; imagination and, 78–79; liberal education, 29–30; liberatory, 136; race and, 57, 60–61, 79. *See also* reading education; universities
"Education for Culturally Different Youth" (Ellison), 79
Edwards, Brian, 108, 124
Eisenhower, Dwight D., 81, 82
Eliot, T. S., 151
Ellison, Ralph, 177nn42, 45, 55; autobiography of, 76–77; on racism, 61; on reading education, 77–79. See also *Invisible Man* (Ellison)
Ellsworth, Ralph E., 18
Emerson, Ralph Waldo, 151
Engelhardt, Tom, 12
epistemology. *See* knowledge/epistemology
Epstein, Jason, 24
Equiano, Olaudah, 53
ethics. *See* morality/ethics
ethnicity, 12, 24, 139
ethnocentrism, 139
Europe, 36–37, 42
Excellence in Our Schools, 140
existentialism, 116–17, 120
Extremely Loud and Incredibly Close (Foer), 156

Faces in the Crowd (Riesman), 34
facts/truth: alternatives to, 99–101; authority, vulnerability to, and, 94–95; Cold War rhetoric and, 81–87; contingency of, 98–99, 127, 179n16; reading for, 156; women readers and, 91–92. *See also* knowledge/epistemology
Fadiman, Clifton, 40, 42, 51, 90
Fahrenheit 451 (Bradbury), 7
Falwell, Jerry, 137–38
Farewell to Arms (Hemingway), 42, 47
fascism, 110
FBI (Federal Bureau of Investigation), 64, 85, 86, 94, 95, 106, 110
Fellowship of Reconciliation, 64
Feminine Mystique (Friedan), 90–91
feminism, 8; collective body and, 145–46; ideal feminist reader, 149; literacy and, 134–36; patriarchy and, 133–34; student radicalism and, 133; women of color and, 134–36

Feminist Press, 134
Ferguson, Roderick, 67
Fiedler, Leslie, 36
Fight for America (McCarthy), 85
Fitzgerald, F. Scott, 49
Flacks, Richard, 116, 117
Flesch, Rudolf, 16, 17
Foer, Jonathan Safran, 156
foreign policy, 12, 83, 131
Franklin, Benjamin, 3
freedom, 73, 82, 104, 108, 111, 127
Freedom's Journal, 56, 174n17
Friedan, Betty, 90, 91
Fromm, Erich, 31, 34, 35, 48
"From Work to Text" (Barthes), 118–19, 129
Frye, Joanne, 144

Gassner, John, 86
Gates Jr., Henry Louis, 66
Gayle Jr., Addison, 55, 71
gender: canon wars and, 141; education and, 24, 90–91, 98, 181n32; facts and, 82; gendered texts, 25–26; gender roles, 3, 143, 146, 147, 148; masculinity, 142, 144; postmodernism and, 120; reading ability and, 90–92; reading guides and, 90, 92, 181n32; social stability and, 12; student radicals and, 116, 133–34; violence and, 145. *See also* feminism; sex/sexuality; women
Geyer, John J., 18–19
G.I. Bill, 23–24
Goffman, Erving, 35
Goldman, Eric F., 34
Goodland, John, 140
Good Times through Literature, 86
Go Tell It on the Mountain (Baldwin), 54–55
Graff, Gerald, 103
Gray, William S., 36, 86, 89–90, 91
Great American Novel (Roth), 45
Great Books program, 87, 119, 141, 166n47. *See also* canonicity / canon wars

Haines, Helen, 89
Hanna, Geneva, 4
Hansberry, Lorraine, 54
Harris, Charles, 123
Hartz, Louis, 34, 42
Hassan, Ihab, 50
Hayden, Casey, 116
Hayden, Tom, 113
Heath Anthology of American Literature (Lauter), 141
Heller, Joseph, 7

Hemingway, 42, 47, 171n47
Hench, John B., 21
Henderson, Stephen, 73
HerBooks Feminist Press, 134
Higham, John, 44
Hill, Lister, 4, 15
Hinden, Michael, 123
Hirschberg, Cornelius, 25
Hirsch Jr., E. D., 140, 141
history: character and, 44; family, 146, 151; immigration and, 143; of literature, 122–23, 129; of U.S. literacy, 3
Home Girls, 138
homemaking, 91
hooks, bell, 135, 136
Hoover, J. Edgar, 19, 36, 64–65, 81, 84, 85, 94, 95, 96
House Committee on Internal Security, 110, 111
House Committee on Un-American Activities, 85, 86
House on Mango Street, The (Cisneros), 139
Howard University, 59, 60
Howe, Irving, 77, 78, 96
How to Read a Book (Adler), 166n47
How to Read and Why (Bloom), 51, 156, 195n7
How to Read a Novel (Sutherland), 156
How to Read a Poem (Eagleton), 156
Hunter, James Davison, 138
Hutchins, Robert, 29–30, 37

Ichord, Richard H., 110
identity/selfhood: marginalized, 142–43; multiple, 125; national, 3–4; reading method and, 126, 146–47, 149–50; rejection of, 149; self-definition, 11
I Love a Broad Margin to My Life (Kingston), 151
Imagined Communities (Anderson), 3–4
immigration: baseball and, 45–46; identity and, 142–43, 149; uncertainty and, 3, 12
Implied Reader (Iser), 119
inclusivity, 130, 138, 139, 146, 151. *See also* canonicity / canon wars; multiculturalism
In Defense of Reading (Brower, Poirier), 88–89
individualism, 34, 40
instability. *See* certainty/uncertainty
International Bibliography, 142
interpretation. *See* reading / interpretive methods
intertextuality, 119, 125, 127
Invisible Man (Ellison), 7, 8, 66–79; reading education in, 66–69; reading / interpretive methods in, 69–76, 173n10
"Is a Woman's Work Never Done?" (Switzer), 91
Iser, Wolfgang, 119
Iversen, Robert W., 92, 93
Izgarjan, Aleksandra, 145

Jacobs, Harriet, 53
Jamieson, John, 21
Jennings, Frank, 18, 31, 87
Jim Crow laws, 3, 53–54, 56, 59–60, 78, 109
Johns Hopkins University, 116, 116–17
Johnson, Alvin, 24
Johnson, Kathryn M., 56
Jones, Howard Mumford, 11
Jones, LeRoi, 75
Jordan, June, 152
Josey, E. J., 65
Journal of Negro Education, 54, 57, 59
juvenile delinquency, 3, 33, 38, 167n5

Keniston, Kenneth, 114
Kennan, George, 12, 81, 82–83, 84
Kerr, Clark, 96
King, Mary, 116
Kingston, Maxine Hong: on Chinese culture, 193n37; on colonialism, 135; on ethical literacy, 131–32; on feminism, 134; on language, 136; on political writing, 151; on reading, 135. *See also Woman Warrior, The* (Kingston)
Knapp, Edgar H., 107
knowledge/epistemology: access to, 114; American vs. Communist, 86; class and, 112–13; freedom and, 127; postmodernism and, 80, 101, 104; as power, 157; power and, 71–73; responsibility and, 131; self-knowledge, 73, 157. *See also* facts/truth
Korean Americans, 135
Krauss, Karoline, 143
Kreuger, Karen, 26
Krupat, Arnold, 141
Krupnick, Mark, 90

language: academic, 136; African American speech, 62, 176n35; confrontation and, 150; fixity of, 123; as illogical, 149; postmodernism on, 117; power and, 34, 111; texts and, 129. *See also* rhetoric
"Languages of Criticism and the Sciences of Man: The Structuralist Controversy," 116–17

Lardner, Ring, 49
Larkin, Lesley, 66
Laugesen, Amy, 15
Lauter, Paul, 139, 141
law, 62–64, 137
Lazarsfeld, Paul, 37
leisure, 26–27, 27–28
Lentricchia, Frank, 116
"Letter to Ma" (Woo), 135
Levin, Harry, 18
Lewis, R.W.B., 48
liberalism, 34–35, 43, 108, 112, 137, 157, 167n7
Liberal Tradition in America (Hartz), 34, 42
libraries: censorship and, 39; growth of, 26–27; importance of, 3; race and, 54, 56, 57, 65, 76, 174n15, 175n26; surveillance of, 94
Library Services Act, 27
Life magazine, 28, 83
Lifetime Reading Plan (Fadiman), 51
Lim, Shirley Geok-Lin, 142
Lincoln, Abraham, 3
Lindsey, Kay, 134
literacy: canon wars and, 139; ethical, 131; feminism and, 134–36; gender and, 90–92; as oppressive, 61–62; rate of, 36, 56, 60, 163n15; as social construction, 54; terrorism and, 154; value of, 148, 158. *See also* literacy, African American; literature/books; reading education; reading / interpretive methods
literacy, African American, 8, 53–65; civil rights movement and, 62–65; freedom and, 57, 61–62, 72, 73, 172n1; improvement of, 59–61; reading practices and, 56–57; slavery and, 53, 55–56. *See also* literacy
literary devices/conventions: artificiality of, 126; Barth on, 123; expectations about, 125–26; metaphor, 100–102; New Criticism and, 38; puns, 121
literature/books: accessibility of, 136; access to, 60, 108; African American, 77–78, 135–36; bookstores, 27–28, 134; censorship of, 26, 32–33, 34, 38–39, 93, 167n2; cultural diversity of, 138–39; death of, 121, 187n55; definition of, 119, 132; history of, 122–23, 129; metafiction, 107–8, 120, 122; oral, 76–77; publishing of, 21, 27, 28, 36–37, 60, 134, 142, 156; purpose of, 128; quality of, 47–48, 86, 139, 147, 191n28; social dimension of, 139; themes of, 37; universality of, 144. *See also* book clubs / literary societies; canonicity / canon wars; drama; libraries; literacy; reading, purpose of
"Literature of Exhaustion" (Barth), 121
"Literature of Protest" (Gayle), 71
"Little Man at Chehaw Station" (Ellison), 66
Little Rock, Arkansas, 62
Litwack, Leon F., 95
living documents, 107, 114, 117, 124, 129
Living with Books (Haines), 89
Lonely Crowd (Riesman), 34
Longstreth, T. Morris, 48
Lorde, Audre, 135
Lost in the Funhouse (Barth), 7, 8, 106–30; categorization of, 122; criticism of, 127–28; effect of, on readers, 121–22; reader's role in, 123–30; success of, 120–21. *See also* postmodernism; student radicalism

Macdonald, Dwight, 47
Mad magazine, 26, 87–88, 180n22
mail, 138
Mailer, Norman, 7, 103, 111
Making Face, Making Soul, 135, 138
marketing, 28
masculinity, 142, 144
Mass Culture, 91
mass media, 38, 46–48, 137–38
Mass Media Program, 85
Masters of Deceit (Hoover), 19
Mather, Cotton, 3
Maturity in Reading (Gray, Rogers), 36, 91–92
McAllister, Marianne, 4
McCarthy, Joseph, 19, 34, 36, 81, 84–86, 94, 98, 179n16
McKelway, Bill, 63
McLuhan, Marshall, 7
meaning. *See* reading / interpretive methods
media, 137–38
Medovoi, Leerom, 34
Menand, Louis, 18
Merton, Robert, 37
Messud, Claire, 156
metafiction, 107–8, 120, 122
metaphor, 100–102
Mickenberg, Julia L., 26
Miller, Arthur, 30
Miller, Carroll, 60
Miller, James, 115
Millett, Kate, 133–34
Mills, C. Wright, 34, 35, 112–13
mimetic function of reading, 32–33, 37, 39, 44
Mis-Education of the Negro (Woodson), 73

Mississippi, 109
modernism, 88, 108, 118. *See also* postmodernism
Modern Language Association, 142
morality/ethics: community and, 119; conservatism and, 137–38, 140; metafiction and, 129; as performance, 35; reading and, 8, 114, 126, 127, 128, 131. *See also* character, American
Moral Majority, 137
Morgan, Charles, 65
Morrison, Toni, 55, 138, 147
multiculturalism, 8, 132; criticism of, 141, 191n28, 192n29; value of, 139, 150–51. *See also* canonicity / canon wars
"Muse, Spare Me" (Barth), 107
Museum of Natural History (New York City), 43–44
Music-Image-Text (Barthes), 129
Myth of a 'Negro Literature' (Baraka), 75
mythology: American, 143, 153; as collective imagination, 123; family, 144, 146, 147; postmodernism and, 128; pregeneric, 53

NAACP (National Association for the Advancement of Colored People), 62, 64
Nadel, Alan, 34, 66
Naked Communist (Skousen), 20
Nally, Thomas P., 31
narratives: about African American literature, 77–78; authoritative, 7, 95; binaries, 148; colonialism and, 135; of conservatism, 137; disruption of, 126–27; exclusion from, 80; facts and, 84; inclusivity of, 139; of progress, 14, 88; of racial inferiority, 73–74; reshaping of, 144, 147; as weapons, 134. *See also* rhetoric
National Book Committee, 14
National Council of Juvenile Court Judges, 38
National Defense Education Act, 18
National Education Association, 140
National Endowment for the Arts, 155
National Institute of Arts and Literature, 120
nationalism, 6, 19, 86, 155
National Public Radio, 50, 51
national security, 10–11, 111, 140, 155
National Security Book List, 155
"National Vietnam Examination," 114
Negro in Textbooks: Reading, 'Riting and Racism (Bennett), 73
neoconservatism, 136–37
New Criticism, 38, 165n33; criticism of, 93–94, 187n51; institutionalization of, 88–89, 182n52; on order, 40; postmodernism and, 118, 122, 182n59, 186n41, 186n43; reading method and, 41–42, 88–89
New Criticism (Ransom), 41
New Left, 78, 101, 108, 110, 116, 133, 184n9, 189n74. *See also* student radicalism; Students for a Democratic Society (SDS)
New Left Notes, 116
New Republic, 120–21
New Right, 101, 137, 137–38, 184n9
newspapers, 60
Newsweek, 121
New York City, 43–44
New Yorker, 18
New York Times, 11, 29, 93, 120
nihilism, 121, 129, 140, 188n74
No Ivory Tower (Schrecker), 92–93
Not for Profit (Nussbaum), 158–59
NPR (National Public Radio), 50, 51
nuclear weapons, 131
Nussbaum, Martha C., 158

Obama, Barack, 158
Oglesby, Carl, 117
Ohmann, Richard, 140
Olson, Carol Booth, 127
Omaha, 134
O'Neill, William, 110
Oppenheimer, Robert, 95
oppression: diversity and, 139; intellectuals and, 117; patriarchy, 133–34; reading guides and, 72; resistance to, 77–78, 133; slavery, 53, 55–56, 172n1, 173n10. *See also* race/racism
Ordinary Women, 138
Organization Man (Whyte), 34
orientalization, 142

Packard, Vance, 30, 34, 89
Pas, Justine, 38
patriarchy, 133–34
patriotism, 49
Pawley, Christine, 26
people of color. *See* African Americans; Chinese Americans; race/racism
People of Plenty (Potter), 34
phenomenology, 116–17
Philistine's Journal (Turmel), 156
philosophy: nihilism, 121, 129, 140, 188n74; phenomenology, 116–17. *See also* knowledge/epistemology; morality/ethics; postmodernism

Pleasure of the Text (Barthes), 118–19, 187n45
pluralism. *See* multiculturalism
Poirier, Richard, 88
police, 106, 109, 110
politics: aesthetics and, 108, 109, 129; defining culture as, 141; fascism, 110; law, 62–64, 137; liberalism, 34–35, 43, 108, 112, 137, 157, 167n7; nationalism, 6, 19, 49, 86, 155; neoconservatism, 136–37. *See also* citizenship; conservatism; student radicalism
Pooley, Robert C., 86
Porter, Dorothy, 57
Port Huron Statement, 108–9, 113; on love, 129; publication/distribution of, 106, 114; on uncertainty, 111–12
"Post-'68: Theory Is in the Streets" (Taylor), 117
postmodernism, 80, 116–20; academic issues and, 107; criticism/limits of, 100–104, 119–20, 127, 128, 187n51; *Crying of Lot 49* and, 179n3; deconstruction, 43, 122, 186nn42, 187n51, 188n74; history of, 116–17; New Criticism and, 118, 122, 182n59, 186n41, 186n43; radicalism and, 117–19
poststructuralism, 108. *See also* postmodernism
Potter, David M., 34, 109
power: canon wars and, 138; of definition, 141; diffusion of, 114, 118; facts and, 85; feminism and, 135; history and, 71; idealism and, 71; interpretation and, 130, 144; knowledge as, 157; language and, 34, 111; postmodernism on, 120; relation to, 127; of state, 70; of United States, 4. *See also* authority
Practical Classics (Smokler), 51
Prejudice and Your Child (Clark), 73
Presentation of Self in Everyday Life (Goffman), 35
Priceless Gift (Hirschberg), 25
protests, 96
Public Library—A People's University (Johnson), 24
publishing, 21, 27, 28, 36–37, 60, 134, 142, 156
pulp fiction, 28
Pynchon, Thomas, 84, 92. See also *Crying of Lot 49* (Pynchon)

Quan, Kit Yuen, 136

race/racism: access to education and, 24, 60–61, 175n29; canonicity and, 138–39, 141, 142; conservatism and, 136; facts and, 82; feminism and, 134–36; in founding ideas of U.S., 78; identity and, 143; postmodernism and, 120; postwar anxiety and, 12; publishing and, 138–39; segregation, 73–74; unlearning of, 136; white supremacy, 61, 62, 64, 65. *See also* literacy, African American
Raisin in the Sun (Hansberry), 54–55
Ransom, Crowe, 41, 119
reading, purpose of, 5–6, 157–58; citizenship, 54, 59, 75; democracy and, 1–2, 113, 158–59; ethics and, 114–15; gender and, 90–91; liberation, 136; peace, 3; race and, 54, 57, 65, 146; as resistance, 146; security, 165n26; self-transformation, 152; social status and, 54–55, 171n45; stability, 7, 156–57; values and, 40
Reading at Risk, 154–55
reading education: for adults, 161n1; gender and, 181n32; phonics and, 163n16; in reading, 8, 50–51, 59–60, 67–69, 81, 103, 134, 136, 140; segregated, 73–74; Soviet vs. American, 16–18. *See also* canonicity/canon wars; literacy
reading guides/lists, 3, 13–14, 25, 40–41, 77, 86–87; for adults, 51; criticism of, 115, 119; on ideal readers, 92; institutionalization of, 80–81; pluralism and, 77–78; post-9/11, 156; uncertainty/anxiety in, 141. *See also* canonicity/canon wars
reading initiatives, 4, 109, 154–56, 185n32. *See also* book clubs/literary societies; reading education; reading guides/lists
reading/interpretive methods, 1–2, 69–76; ambiguity and, 99–104; canon wars and, 140–41; character and, 37–38; as collaboration, 119, 149–50; for Communist literature, 83–84; cooperative, 136; dialogue, 42; either/or vs. both/and, 74–75, 77, 153; good vs. bad readers, 66, 91–92, 109, 148–49; identity and, 144, 146–47, 152; intertextuality, 119; liberation and, 144; marginalization and, 132–33; misreading, 66, 137–38; negative effects of, 95; participation/responsibility and, 107–8, 123–30, 131; reading aloud, 120; rereading, 41, 118, 130; revolutionary potential of, 89, 135–36; sanctioned vs. unsanctioned, 69–73; social structures and, 42–43; truth/facts and, 98, 99–100, 102, 148–49, 156; uncertainty and, 112–13. *See also* New Criticism; postmodernism

Reading I've Liked (Fadiman), 40
Reading Places (Pawley), 26
reading studies, 18–19
Reagan, Ronald, 95, 131, 141
Reconstructing American Literature (Lauter), 139
Redding, J. Saunders, 57
Red Plot against America (Stripling), 20
religion, 34, 56, 124, 136, 137, 138
Remembered Earth, The, 138
Responsibilities Program, 85
Revolution at Berkeley (Howe), 96
rhetoric, 5, 11; Communist, 83–84; of facts, 81–87, 179n16; of loyalty, 98; post-9/11, 154–55, 194n2; of Reagan, 131. See also language; narratives
Richmond Times-Dispatch, 63
Riesman, David, 34
Riggs Jr., Thomas, 86–87
Robbins, Louise S., 26
Roberts, Steven, 113–14
Robinson, Marilynne, 158
Rockefeller Foundation, 13, 120
Rogers, Bernice, 36, 89–90, 91
Roosevelt, Franklin D., 3, 21
Rosenberg, Bernard, 46
Rosenfeld, Seth, 85–86
Roth, Philip, 45
Rowe, John Carlos, 107, 117
Rubin, Joan Shelley, 29
Rudd, Mark, 117, 126
rural populations, 26–27
Rutgers University, 18–19

Saint John's College, 109–10
Salinger, J. D., 44, 169n24. See also Catcher in the Rye (Salinger)
Sane Society (Fromm), 34
San Francisco, 99
Saturday Review, 87
Savio, Mario, 117
Scherman, Henry, 28
Schloss, Carol, 122
Schrecker, Ellen, 85–86, 92, 94
Schueller, Malini, 150
Schultermandl, Silvia, 144
science, 86, 88
Scientific American, 89
SDS. See Students for a Democratic Society
Security Index, 85
Selective Service, 114
"Self-Reliance" (Emerson), 151

Senior Scholastic, 23
sex/sexuality: postmodernism and, 120; postwar anxiety and, 12; rape, 144; of Salinger, 169n24; sexual domination, 133–34
Sexual Politics (Millett), 133–34
Shatzkin, Leonard, 36–37
Sheils, Merrill, 140
Shils, Edward, 36
Simon, William, 137
Skelton, Ike, 155
Skolnik, Richard, 45–46
Skousen, W. Cleon, 20
Slater, Charles W., 1, 159
Slaughterhouse Five (Vonnegut), 7
slavery, 53, 55–56, 172n1, 173n10
Slow Learner (Pynchon), 92, 98
Smith Act, 19
Smokler, Kevin, 51
social status, 6, 30, 55–56, 133–34, 171n45
Solberg, Carl, 2, 10
Southern Christian Leadership Council, 64
Soviet Union, 5; criticisms of US by, 78; education in, 16–18; foreign policy of, 83–84; U.S. rhetoric about, 131. See also communism; United States
Spence, Larry D., 126
Sputnik, 16–18
stability. See certainty/uncertainty
State University of New York (Buffalo), 106–7, 183n2
Status Seekers (Packard), 34
Stein, Gertrude, 7
Steinle, Pamela, 34, 38
Stepto, Robert, 53
Strang, Ruth, 13
Stripling, Robert, 20
structuralism, 115–16, 120, 182n59, 183n61. See also postmodernism
"Structure, Sign and Play" (Derrida), 103–4, 116, 118–19
Stuckey, J. Elspeth, 62
student radicalism, 108–16; as anti-American, 110–11; as childish, 109–10; conservatism and, 136; gender and, 116, 133–34; postmodernism and, 116–20; repression of, 95, 117, 183n2, 184n14. See also Students for a Democratic Society (SDS)
Students for a Democratic Society (SDS), 97, 106, 184n9, 185n32; criticism of, 110, 115–16, 189n74; ideals of, 108–9, 111–15; on reading method, 114–15. See also Port Huron Statement
suburbs, 27, 80–81, 90–91, 109

SUNY-Bufflo. *See* State University of New York
Susman, Warren, 34–35
Switzer, Mary S., 91

Taylor, Astra, 117
Teacher in America (Barzun), 15
"Teddy" (Salinger), 44
terrorism, 154, 194n2
think tanks, 137
Third Woman, The, 138
Third World, 135
This Bridge Called My Back (Bambara), 136, 138
This Is Reading (Jennings), 87
Thompson, Chas. H., 59
"Thoughts on Soviet Foreign Policy" (Dulles), 83
Time, 120, 142
Time for Truth (Simon), 137
Time to Greez!, 138
Title IX, 134
Tololyan, Khachig, 122
To Reclaim a Legacy (Bennett), 140
Trace, Arthur S., 16
Travis, Trysh, 21
Trilling, Lionel, 90
Turmel, Wayne, 156
"Two Languages of Criticism" (Donato), 116

uncertainty. *See* certainty/uncertainty
Understanding the New Black Poetry (Henderson), 73
United Nations, 82
United States: foreign policy of, 83, 131; founding documents of, 59, 75, 78; immaturity of, 34, 36–37; international opinion of, 11–12, 14–16, 33, 36–37, 63–65, 78, 169n25; power of, 4; republican identity of, 3–4. *See also* Americanness; character, American; values, American
U.S. Department of Agriculture, 1, 161n1
U.S. Department of State, 15
U.S. Information Centers, 12, 15
U.S. Office of Education, 14, 59–60
U.S. Office of War Information, 22
universities: African Americans in, 60–61, 175n29; canon wars and, 138–39; conservatism and, 137, 182n51; G.I Bill and, 23–24; government monitoring of, 95–96, 106, 183n2; purpose of, 112; reading studies in, 18–19. *See also* student radicalism
University of California (Berkeley), 95–98

University of California (Davis), 109
University of Chicago, 36, 37
Uttal, Lynet, 152

values, American, 5; baseball and, 45; canon wars and, 139; character and, 34–35; conformity and, 77; culture, definition of, and, 141; culture war and, 137; distrust of, 95–96; education in, 155; as fixed, 143; idealist vs. pragmatist, 71; racism and, 59, 143; romanticization of, 40; social classification and, 44; student radicalism and, 111. *See also* Americanness; character, American
Varela, Mary, 116
Vietnam War, 106–7
Viguerie, Richard, 138
violence: of canon formation, 147; literature as cause of, 169n22; narratives and, 66, 73, 79; of social hierarchies, 133; against women, 144–45
Violence of Literacy (Stuckey), 62
Vonnegut, Kurt, 7

Waldenbooks, 27
Walker, Alice, 135, 138, 147
Walker, David, 56
Wallace, Viola, 25
Washington, D.C., 134
welfare, 137
Westervelt, Linda, 127–28
What Every American Needs to Know (Hirsch), 141
"What Good Are Poems?" (Riggs), 87
What Ivan Knows That Johnny Doesn't (Trace), 16
What Our Children Need to Know (Hirsch), 141
What We Must Know about Communism (Overstreet), 20
White Collar (Mill), 34
white supremacy, 61, 62, 64, 65
Whitman, Walt, 151
"Who Reads What Books and Why?" (Berelson), 91
Whose America? Culture Wars in the Public Schools (Zimmerman), 138
Why Johnny Can't Read (Flesch), 16–17
"Why Students Want Power" (Roberts), 113–14
Whyte, William, 34, 35, 36–37
Winfrey, Oprah, 156
Witness (Chambers), 19

Wolin, Sheldin S., 96
womanism, 135
Woman Warrior, The (Kingston), 8, 131–53; critical reception of, 142–43; identity in, 142–44; reading methods in, 144–47
women: authors, canonicity of, 138–39, 155; violence against, 144–45; women's studies, 139. *See also* feminism; gender
Women in Print Conference, 134
Women's Press, 134
women's studies, 139
Wonderful World of Books, 1–2, 86–87, 91, 157–58, 159
Wong, Sau-ling Cynthia, 142
Woodson, Carter G., 57, 73
Works Progress Administration, 58

"World and the Jug" (Ellison), 77–78
World Trade Center, 154
World War II: African Americans in, 57–59; book publishing during, 27; social instability/anxiety following, 10–12, 30–31, 35
Worthington, Marjorie, 128
Wright, Richard, 6

Yamada, Mitsuye, 134–35
"You, Citizen-Reader in a Democracy" (Solberg), 11
"Young Radicals and the Fear of Power" (Keniston), 114

Zimmerman, Jonathan, 138

www.ingramcontent.com/pod-product-compliance
Lightning Source LLC
Chambersburg PA
CBHW030651230426
43665CB00011B/1050